Essentials of MMPI-A™ Assessment

Essentials of Psychological Assessment Series

Series Editors, Alan S. Kaufman and Nadeen L. Kaufman

Essentials

of MMPI-A™ Assessment

Robert P. Archer

Radhika Krishnamurthy

 John Wiley & Sons, Inc.

BS

Library of Congress Cataloging-in-Publication Data:
Archer, Robert P.
    Essentials of MMPI-A assessment / Robert P. Archer and Radhika Krishnamurthy.
        p. cm. — (Essentials of psychological assessment series)
    Includes bibliographical references and index.
    ISBN 0-471-39815-2 (pbk. : alk. paper)
    1. Minnesota Multiphasic Personality Inventory for Adolescents.   2. Minnesota Multiphasic Personality Inventory.   I. Krishnamurthy, Radhika.   II. Title.   III. Series.

RJ503.7.M56 A729 2002
616.89′075′0835—dc21

                                                                                    2001026961

Printed in the United States of America.

10   9   8   7   6   5   4   3

8/29/06

*To my daughter, Elizabeth Meghan Archer, for generously spending
the past few years providing me with intensive post-doctoral training in
adolescent development.*

ROBERT P. ARCHER

*To my parents who are my "essential" guides in life;
And my siblings, Uma and Karthik, who are always close to my heart.*

RADHIKA KRISHNAMURTHY

CONTENTS

SERIES PREFACE

In the *Essentials of Psychological Assessment* series, we have attempted to provide the reader with books that will deliver key practical information in the most efficient and accessible style. The series features instruments in a variety of domains, such as cognition, personality, education, and neuropsychology. For the experienced clinician, books in the series will offer a concise, yet thorough way to master utilization of the continuously evolving supply of new and revised instruments, as well as a convenient method for keeping up to date on the tried-and-true measures. The novice will find here a prioritized assembly of all the information and techniques that must be at one's fingertips to begin the complicated process of individual psychological diagnosis.

Wherever feasible, visual shortcuts to highlight key points are utilized alongside systematic, step-by-step guidelines. Chapters are focused and succinct. Topics are targeted for an easy understanding of the essentials of administration, scoring, interpretation, and clinical application. Theory and research are continually woven into the fabric of each book, but always to enhance clinical inference, never to sidetrack or overwhelm. We have long been advocates of "intelligent" testing—the notion that a profile of test scores is meaningless unless it is brought to life by the clinical observations and astute detective work of knowledgeable examiners. Test profiles must be used to make a difference in the child's or adult's life, or why bother to test? We want this series to help our readers become the best intelligent testers they can be.

In *Essentials of MMPI-A™ Assessment,* the authors present a broad range of basic information intended for clinicians, researchers, and students who are seeking an introduction to the most widely used objective personality assessment instrument with adolescents. The text provides a summary of the development and available research on the MMPI-A and a step-by-step procedure for test interpretation. *Essentials of MMPI-A™ Assessment,* also provides a concise review of all the standardly used MMPI-A scales and subscales, including a section on single scale and two-point codetype approaches to basic scale profile interpretation. Additionally, this text introduces the MMPI-A Structural Summary approach developed by the coauthors. The Structural Summary approach simplifies the process of MMPI-A interpretation by emphasizing the basic underlying dimensions of psychopathology found in the scale and subscale structure of this instrument. Topics include applying the MMPI-A to special populations of adolescents including juvenile delinquents, substance abusers, sexually abused adolescents, and adolescents with eating disorders. Clinical interpretation principles are illustrated in a series of four clinical case examples to provide a better understanding of the application of interpretive principles with individual cases. The goal of the text is to enable the reader to approach the task of MMPI-A assessment in an organized and confident manner, while also ensuring that the test user has an appreciation of the complexity and limitations inherent in the use of this instrument.

Alan S. Kaufman, PhD, and Nadeen L. Kaufman, EdD, Series Editors
Yale University School of Medicine

Essentials of MMPI-A™ Assessment

One

INTRODUCTION

The Minnesota Multiphasic Personality Inventory (MMPI) has been described as the "psychometric success story of the 20th century" and has been the dominant objective personality assessment instrument in surveys of test usage since the early 1950s. This test has generated a massive research literature entailing thousands of articles, hundreds of book chapters, and dozens of books and has been a dominant commercial force in the psychological assessment market. Before presenting the adaptation of the MMPI that was released in 1992 specifically for use with adolescents, it is useful to briefly review the history of this singularly important personality assessment instrument.

HISTORY OF THE MMPI

The original form of the MMPI was developed in a collaborative effort between Stark Hathaway and John McKinley that began in the late 1930s. Hathaway, the driving force in the development of the MMPI, received his master's degree in psychology from Ohio State University in 1928 and his doctorate in Physiology with a minor in Anatomy from the University of Minnesota in 1932. Hathaway spent his early faculty years pursuing post-graduate studies in gross and microscopic anatomy and teaching courses in laboratory psychology and statistics. In 1937, in his role as a medical school psychologist, he began collaboration with McKinley on the MMPI project. John McKinley received his MD degree in 1919 and his PhD in 1921 from the University of Minnesota and subsequently trained as a neuropsychiatrist and neuropathologist. After psychiatric training at the New York City Psychiatric Institute, McKinley returned to the University of Minnesota and progressed through the faculty ranks until he became head of the Department of Medicine and Neuropsychiatry. Hathaway and McKinley initiated work on what was to become the MMPI with the goal of assisting physicians in screening medical patients for psychiatric problems at the University of Minnesota Hospitals.

The MMPI was not the first effort to develop an objective personality assessment instrument. Earlier self-report personality questionnaires can be traced back to the late 19th century. In particular, the need for psychiatric screening of military recruits during World War I supported the development and use of self-report measures of psychopathology. Test developers usually selected the items for these self-report measures based on a rational scale construction method in which items were included in a scale or test if such items appeared to be logically or rationally related to the measurement task based on the test developer's theory, clinical experience, or intuition. Unfortunately, many of these tests proved to be more interesting in theory than useful in actual practice.

The earliest versions of the MMPI were referred to as the "Medical and Psychiatric Inventory" and the "Multiphasic Personality Schedule," and the MMPI developed through a series of stages. In the initial stage, Hathaway and McKinley developed an item pool for test construction purposes by generating items from psychiatric examination forms, from various psychiatric text books, and from earlier published scales of social attitudes, temperament, and personality. This original list consisted of more than 1,000 items, which the researchers then reduced to an item pool of 504 by eliminating duplicate items and items that appeared to be less relevant to the purpose of a personality inventory. These original items were subsequently supplemented by additional items primarily related to masculinity and femininity.

Hathaway and McKinley then administered this preliminary item pool to participants from several normal control groups that predominantly included 724 visitors of patients receiving treatment at the University of Minnesota Hospitals. This group, referred to as the "Minnesota Normals," was also augmented by three smaller groups of normal individuals including high school graduates receiving precollege counseling at the University of Minnesota, skilled workers engaged in local projects funded through the Federal Work Progress Administration (WPA) Program, and a group of medical patients at the University of Minnesota Hospitals who did not have symptoms of psychiatric disorder. In addition to these normal groups, test data was also collected on a group of 221 patients receiving treatment for psychiatric disorders at the University of Minnesota Hospitals. These clinical patients were divided into subgroups based on discrete diagnostic categories such as hypochondriasis, depression, hysteria, psychopathic deviancy, schizophrenia and hypomania.

The existence of the normal and clinical samples allowed Hathaway and McKinley to group their items into scales using an empirical method in which item selection was based on the ability of items to discriminate effectively between psychiatric and normal patients. An item analysis was conducted separately for each of the clinical criterion groups (reflected in the labels of MMPI basic clinical scales) in order to identify those items that differentiated significantly between the specific clinical groups and the group of normal individuals. This methodology of scale construction has been referred to as "criterion keying" or "empirical scale construction," and the critics of this approach have referred to it as "dustbowl empiricism." In contrast to earlier test development approaches in which items were generally selected rationally based on face validity, or the extent to which the items appeared to be relevant to the domain being measured, the empirical keying procedure selected individual test items using statistical analyses that indicated the extent to which a test item could differentiate among the criterion groups. Variations of the empirical keying technique were used to construct the item pools for the *Hypochondriasis (Hs)*, *Depression (D)*, *Hysteria, (Hy)*, *Psychopathic Deviancy (Pd)*, *Paranoia (Pa)*, *Psychasthenia (Pt)*, *Schizophrenia (Sc)*, and *Mania (Ma)* scales. Following the construction of these clinical scales, two additional scales were added to the MMPI. As previously noted, the *Masculinity-Femininity (Mf)* scale was subsequently added to the MMPI through an item-selection process that initially included a comparison of homosexual and heterosexual men, but eventually also included items that were differentially endorsed by men and women in the normative sample. Finally, the *Social Introversion (Si)* scale was included as the final basic MMPI scale adopted from a previously existing scale developed by Drake (1946), and cross-validated by comparing the scores of female college students who scored on the higher or lower ranges of an introversion-extroversion scale. The *Si* scale is the only basic scale that was developed outside of the Hathaway and McKinley group and is the only basic scale for which a psychiatric criterion group was not obtained.

DEVELOPMENT OF THE VALIDITY SCALES

In addition to the 10 basic clinical scales on the MMPI, Hathaway and McKinley (1943) also developed several validity scales to detect problematic test-taking attitudes or response sets. These scales include the *Cannot Say* or (?) scale, which is not actually a scale in itself but rather reflects the total number of MMPI items that the participant either omitted or endorsed as both true and false. The *Lie* or *L* scale consists of 15 rationally derived items that represent a variety of common human failings or faults (e.g., "I do not like everyone I know," and "I gossip a little at times"). The *L* scale was developed to detect crude attempts to present oneself in an unrealistically favorable light. Although very few people endorse a majority of *L*-scale items, many individuals endorse several of these items in the scored (*False*) direction. The *Infrequency* or *F* scale was originally composed of 64 items that were selected because they were endorsed in the infrequent direction by 10% or fewer of the Minnesota Normative Sample. These items cover a broad array of content (e.g., "I have a cough most of the time," and "Evil spirits possess me at times"), but share a low frequency of endorsement among normals. Hathaway and McKinley (1946) suggested that elevations on the *F* scale might invalidate the interpretation of the clinical scale profile because the participant was careless or unable to comprehend the content of the items. The final validity scale added to the original MMPI was the *Correction* or *K* scale. When early experiences with the MMPI indicated that the *L* scale may be insensitive to certain less blatant types of test distortion, the *K* scale was developed as a more subtle indicator of attempts to deny psychopathology and to present oneself in the most favorable light. Typical *K* scale items are "I certainly feel useless at times," and "Criticism or scolding hurts me terribly." The original *K* scale included 30 items (all but one item scored in the false direction) that were empirically identified by contrasting item responses of clearly disturbed psychiatric patients who produced normal range scores on the clinical scales with the item responses of a group of normal individuals. The main function of the *K* scale was to improve the ability of the clinical scales to detect psychopathology accurately, and specific proportions of the *K*-scale raw score have traditionally been added to five of the MMPI basic scales when using the *K*-correction procedure with adult respondents. These basic clinical scales that receive different proportions of *K* are scales *Hs (1), Pd (4), Pt (7), Sc (8),* and *Ma (9)*. Although the *K*-scale correction procedure was carried over to the MMPI-2 (Butcher, Dahlstrom, Graham, Tellegen, & Kaemmer, 1989), K-correction is not used for the basic clinical scales on the MMPI-A because the research on this topic has not shown that such a procedure improves the interpretive accuracy derived from adolescents' profiles.

IMPORTANT FEATURES CONTRIBUTING TO THE POPULARITY OF THE MMPI

Hathaway and McKinley developed the MMPI to offer pragmatic assistance in assessing and diagnosing patients with mental disorders at the University of Minnesota Hospitals. However, its use quickly extended far beyond the University of Minnesota Hospitals into clinical settings across the United States for use with both adolescent and adult populations. As noted earlier, by the 1950s the MMPI was routinely appearing in lists of the most frequently used psychological assessment instruments. By the 1960s, MMPI use had extended into employment selection procedures and was particularly used to test individuals who were applying for highly responsible or sensitive positions such as police officer, nuclear power plant worker, airline pilot, or other positions in which psychological stability and resiliency were important to the public safety. Furthermore, the MMPI rapidly became an international instrument, with the first translations of the MMPI appearing in the late 1940s and early 1950s and with more than 50 foreign language translations of the MMPI available by 1976. Butcher and Williams (2000) report that by 1992 there were more than 140 translations of the MMPI into the languages of 46 countries. Finally, as previously noted, the MMPI has been the subject of a phenomenal amount of scholarship and research. Butcher and Owen (1978) report that 84% of all research in personality assessment instruments has focused on the MMPI, and Butcher (1987) estimates that over 10,000 books and articles have been published on this test instrument.

What factors are responsible for the remarkable success of the MMPI? In the mid-1960s, Stark Hathaway listed several aspects of the MMPI that he believed contributed to its popularity. These include "the provision for some control over undesirable response patterns, detection of invalid records such as those from non-readers, the use of simple language, the simplicity of administration and scoring, and, finally, the general clinical familiarity of the profile variables" (1965, p. 463). To underscore and expand on Hathaway's observations, the current authors would like to propose three factors that have been centrally important to the unique amount of success of the MMPI. These factors may be described as the atheoretical foundation of the test instrument, the extensive development of validity scales, and the advantages accrued by the massive research literature underlying the use of the instrument.

The MMPI, as previously noted, was based on an empirical scale development procedure that was atheoretical in terms of the actual selection of items for scale membership. Specifically, Hathaway and McKinley did not use a preconceived notion of which particular items should be included in scale membership, but rather empirically compared the responses of normal subjects with those of groups of well-defined clinical patients to determine which items were selected for a specific scale. This "atheoretical" approach allows clinicians from a wide variety of theoretical orientations to use the test instrument for personality assessment purposes. Psychoanalytically oriented psychotherapists from Boston, health psychologists from the Midwest, behaviorally oriented practitioners from Georgia, and neuropsychologists from California may all enthusiastically embrace the MMPI as an important tool in describing and diagnosing their patients. Thus, in contrast to instruments that are based on specific theoretical formulations and implicit or explicit views of personality structure, the MMPI is attractive to a wide variety of practitioners. Perhaps as importantly, this atheoretical foundation is also attractive to a wide variety of university graduate school and professional school instructors and professors who teach personality assessment courses to future generations of psychologists. From this standpoint, the MMPI is so popular today because its strong empirical base was widely popular 15 to 20 years ago among a wide variety of college professors responsible for teaching objective personality assessment.

The second factor, noted by Hathaway in 1965, relates to the remarkable usefulness of the validity scales in detecting and describing important test-taking approaches consciously or unconsciously employed by the individual responding to the MMPI item pool. The MMPI was among the first personality assessment instruments to strongly emphasize the use of validity scales in determining the interpretability of test findings. Furthermore, the use of validity scales on the MMPI has been developed far beyond that found in any other widely used psychological assessment instrument. The MMPI validity scales allow the interpreter to estimate both the degree of confidence he or she may place in test findings and the capacity and willingness of the respondent to provide an accurate and valid self-report. As we address in future chapters, both the MMPI-2 and MMPI-A bring additional validity scales (beyond the four provided on the original MMPI) to bear on issues related to the technical validity of an individual profile. The availability of these numerous validity scales have, in turn, allowed for the psychological screening of individuals in a variety of settings beyond the traditional clinical settings originally envisioned by Hathaway and McKinley. For example, the interpretation of validity scale data plays a central and crucial role in the assessment of individuals in personnel screening settings, and in forensic evaluations in which the accuracy and honesty of the individual's self-report may become the primary focus of the clinical psychologist's evaluation.

Finally, the massive research literature available for the MMPI has been salient in promoting the clinical success of this instrument. The large number of research studies documenting the MMPI's reliability and validity have allowed clinicians to confidently use the test instrument to describe individual client characteristics, behaviors, and problem areas. Because the MMPI has been so useful in describing various types of psychopathology, researchers have used it extensively in studies of special populations including alcoholics and drug abusers, chronic pain populations, brain-injured patients, medical patients, prisoners, military personnel, and delinquent adolescents, to name just a few of these groups. These studies, in turn, have frequently shed light not only on the population of interest but also on the characteristics of the test instrument. Additionally, much research has focused specifically on the functioning and characteristics of the MMPI as a psychometric instrument. Thus, numerous studies have dealt with the reliability and validity of various MMPI scales and subscales, the effectiveness of various combinations of validity scales in detecting particular response sets, and issues related to the operation of norms and normative samples with this test instrument. All of this information provides an empirical foundation which the clinician may use to provide a useful and practical assessment of the individual's psychological functioning and psychopathology. This foundation is unique among objective personality assessment instruments and rivaled only by the Rorschach Inkblot Technique among projective personality assessment measures. It is a foundation based on the efforts of hundreds of researchers involving hundreds of thousands of participants across a time frame spanning 6 decades. Although it is possible that other personality assessment instruments may be developed that rival the MMPI in terms of the array and usefulness of validity scales, and it is certainly likely that many instruments may surpass the MMPI in terms of overall psychometric elegance, it will take many years for any personality assessment instrument to amass the extent of empirical research base that is associated with the original MMPI instrument.

DEVELOPMENT OF THE MMPI-2

Perhaps because the original form of the MMPI worked so well for so many people for so long, serious efforts to revise the test instrument did not occur until the early 1980s. Specifically, the University of Minnesota Press appointed a committee in 1982 to undertake a restandardization revision of the MMPI. The committee's task was to revise and modernize the test booklet by deleting, modifying, or replacing outdated items, potentially developing new scales to address problem areas not covered in the original MMPI, and to collect a new adult normative sample representative of the population of the United States in terms of ethnic background, age, and geographic location. The MMPI-2 was released in 1989, 46 years after the original publication of the test instrument. In addition to modernizing the content and language of test items and eliminating objectionable items, the MMPI-2 presented new scales, including a series of 15 content scales. The development of the MMPI-2 also involved collecting a nationally representative normative data sample of 2,600 adult men and women throughout the United States. The MMPI-2 contains 567 items that heavily overlap with the content and item pool of the original test instrument. In addition to the MMPI-2 test manual, other comprehensive guides to the MMPI-2 are now available, including several texts that serve as interpretive guides for the instrument. In addition, a research base is gradually developing for the MMPI-2, including several large-scale studies that have used MMPI-2 data from psychiatric patients in inpatient and outpatient settings. It should be specifically noted, however, that the MMPI-2 was designed and normed for individuals who are 18 years of age or older. The MMPI-2 is not intended for the assessment of adolescents ages 17 or younger, and adolescent norms were not developed for the MMPI-2.

In summary, the MMPI-2 is a revised version of the original MMPI, intended for evaluating adults, in which the MMPI basic validity and clinical scales have remained virtually intact. However, a number of new scales have also been developed for the MMPI-2 that expand the clinical applications available for the test instrument. New norms based on a large representative sample of 2,600 men and women provide a contemporary point of comparison for the interpretation of test scores. In addition to the standard four validity scales contained within the original test instrument, a series of new validity scales was developed for the MMPI-2 that were also carried over in the development of the MMPI-A; these scales are addressed under the description of this latter instrument.

USE OF THE MMPI WITH ADOLESCENTS

The application of the original MMPI to adolescent populations began in the early 1940s, around the time of the original publication of the MMPI. Several of these early studies examined the usefulness of the MMPI scale *4* in accurately discriminating adolescents who did and did not have histories of juvenile delinquency. In the largest MMPI data sample ever gathered on adolescents, for example, Hathaway and Monachesi (1953, 1963) conducted a longitudinal examination of the relationships between MMPI test scores and delinquent behavior in samples involving approximately 15,000 Minnesota adolescents, using data collected in the late 1940s and early '50s. Their study provided very valuable information on the MMPI correlates of delinquency, but it also generated important data on differences in item endorsement patterns between boys and girls, and between adults and adolescents.

The most frequently used adolescent norms available for the original MMPI were developed by Phil Marks and Peter Briggs in the late 1960s and published in a variety of guides and textbooks on the MMPI. The adolescent norms developed by Marks and Briggs (1972) were based on the responses of approximately 1,800 normal adolescents and were reported separately for boys and girls at age groupings of 17, 16, 15, and "14 and below." Unfortunately, there was also a substantial amount of norm-related confusion in using the MMPI with adolescents, and many clinicians mistakenly continued to use adult norms when interpreting adolescent profiles. This practice often resulted in grossly elevated profiles that were not accurate in terms of describing adolescent characteristics or predicting important behaviors. In 1974, Marks, Seeman, and Haller published a textbook that contained actuarial-based personality descriptors for a series of 29 MMPI high-point codetypes. A high-point codetype refers to the configural pattern produced by the MMPI basic scales, with codetypes classified by the most elevated scales present in the basic scale profile. For example, a *2-4* high-point codetype refers to an MMPI basic scale pattern in which the highest elevations occur for MMPI basic scale *Depression (2)* and *Psychopathic Deviancy (4)*. Marks and his colleagues derived their codetype descriptors for 29 high-point pairs based on a study of 834 adolescents evaluated between 1965 and 1970, ages 12 through 18, who had received at least 10 hours of psychotherapy and an additional sample of 419 adolescents who received psychiatric services during 1970 to 1973. The Marks et al. clinical correlate data, which included therapists' ratings, were crucial in providing clinicians with the first correlate information available to interpret adolescents' MMPI codetype patterns. Based on a survey conducted with clinicians working with adolescents, Archer, Maruish, Imhof, and Piotrowski (1991) report that the MMPI was the most widely used objective personality assessment instrument with this age group and the third most frequently mentioned assessment instrument with adolescents overall.

DEVELOPMENT OF THE MMPI-A

Despite the relative popularity of the MMPI for assessing adolescents in clinical settings, both researchers and clinicians had concerns regarding the use of the original test instrument with teenagers. Many clinicians felt that the 566-item original form of the MMPI was too long to use with teenagers. Many were also aware that the original adult norms were not applicable to adolescents and that the available adolescent norms (based on data collected between the late 1940s to mid-1960s) were substantially outdated in assessing contemporary adolescents. Additionally, many researchers and clinicians had concerns regarding the reading level presented by some of the original MMPI items and the inappropriate or outdated language used in others. For example, two of the original items in the MMPI that were eliminated or modified in the test revisions were, "In school my marks in deportment were quite regularly bad," and "I used to like drop-the-handkerchief." Finally, the original MMPI item pool, although extensive, also lacked items in certain specific areas relevant to adolescent experience, including issues related to drug use, peer relationships, and school-related problems.

In response to these and other concerns, the University of Minnesota Press initiated an adolescent-specific revision of the MMPI in 1989. One important goal of the revision was to maintain as much continuity with the original MMPI as possible, including preserving the basic structure of the MMPI validity and clinical scales. Therefore, the test revisors made an effort to minimize the amount of changes that occurred in the MMPI basic scales, while also recognizing that more extensive changes might be needed for MMPI scales *F*, *Mf*, and *Si*. In developing a form suitable for assessing adolescents, it was also deemed desirable to include items and scales directly relevant to adolescent development and to the expression of psychopathology during adolescence. Finally, it was anticipated that releasing an adolescent form of the MMPI would help to standardize assessment practices with adolescents, particularly in terms of appropriate administration criterion, selection of useful special scales, and elimination of confusion regarding the appropriate norms to employ with adolescents. Rapid Reference 1.1 provides a summary of the basic reasons for developing the MMPI-A.

The Experimental Form

The process of developing the MMPI-A began with the creation of an experimental test booklet that contained 704 items, identified as MMPI Form TX. The 704-item Form TX was administered to 815 girls and 805 boys in the MMPI-A normative sample and was also used in the collection of various clinical samples. The first section of the test booklet contained 550 items from the original MMPI form, followed by 154 experimental items that covered a variety of potentially relevant

≡ Rapid Reference 1.1

Reasons for Developing the MMPI-A

- To obtain contemporary norms based on a nationally representative adolescent sample
- To modify and improve MMPI items, including improving grammar and wording, and to eliminate inappropriate or objectionable items
- To develop new scales relevant to adolescent problem areas
- To standardize approaches for evaluating adolescents using the MMPI

content areas, including problems in peer group and family relationships, alcohol and drug abuse, eating disorders, and identity problems. Of the original 550 items in Form TX, approximately 13% had been reworded to increase content clarity for adolescent respondents. For example, items related to childhood and adolescent experiences that were worded in the past tense in the original booklet (primarily designed for adults) were changed to the present tense in the experimental form. In this process, MMPI validity scale F was revised extensively in order to increase its effectiveness as a measure of infrequent item endorsement for adolescents, and the item pools for the nonclinical basic scales Mf (5) and Si (0) were somewhat shortened. Finally, the item pools for the remaining eight basic clinical scales were essentially held intact with only minor revisions to some items to improve clarity.

The MMPI-A Normative Sample

Normative data on MMPI Form TX was collected in eight states and involved a total of approximately 2,500 adolescents. After implementing a series of exclusion criteria to eliminate unreliable or incomplete data, the resulting adolescent norms were based on 805 boys and 815 girls between the ages of 14 and 18, inclusive. The ethnic distribution of the MMPI-A normative sample was reasonably consistent with the relative distribution of ethnicity as revealed in the 1980 U.S. Census, and certainly more diverse than both the adult norms for the MMPI collected in the late 1930s and early 1940s and the MMPI adolescent norms developed by Marks and Briggs.

Structure of the MMPI-A

After examining the preliminary data, the MMPI Adolescent Project Committee created a final form of the MMPI for adolescents, the Minnesota Multiphasic Personality Inventory–Adolescent (MMPI-A). Most of the items on the MMPI-A appeared on the original form of the MMPI. However, a number of new items were also added to the test booklet to address a variety of problems areas that occur during adolescence. Rapid Reference 1.2 provides some basic facts about the MMPI-A.

The final form of the MMPI-A includes the original 13 standard scales combined with four new validity scales (see Rapid Reference 1.3), 15 content

≡Rapid Reference 1.2

Basic Facts about the MMPI-A

Test Authors: Butcher, J. N., Williams, C. L., Graham, J. R., Archer, R. P., Tellegen, A., Ben-Porath, Y. S., & Kaemmer, B.

Publication Date: 1992

Measures: Personality and psychopathology in adolescents

Age Range: 14–18 years

Reading Level: 7th grade

Administration Time: 60–90 minutes

User Qualification: Graduate training in testing, adolescent development, personality, psychopathology, and psychodiagnostics

Publisher: University of Minnesota Press
111 Third Avenue South, Suite 290
Minneapolis, MN 55401-2520

Distributor: National Computer Systems, Inc.
P.O. Box 1416
Minneapolis, MN 55440

≡Rapid Reference 1.3

MMPI-A Basic Scales

Validity Scales		Clinical Scales	
VRIN	Variable Response Inconsistency	1	(Hs: Hypochondriasis)
TRIN	True Response Inconsistency	2	(D: Depression)
F_1	(subscale of F)	3	(Hy: Hysteria)
F_2	(subscale of F)	4	(Pd: Psychopathic Deviate)
F	Infrequency	5	(Mf: Masculinity-Femininity)
L	Lie	6	(Pa: Paranoia)
K	Correction	7	(Pt: Psychasthenia)
		8	(Sc: Schizophrenia)
		9	(Ma: Hypomania)
		0	(Si: Social Introversion)

≡Rapid Reference 1.4

MMPI-A Content and Supplementary Scales

Content Scales		Supplementary Scales	
A-anx	Anxiety	MAC-R	MacAndrew Alcoholism–Revised
A-obs	Obsessiveness		
A-dep	Depression	ACK	Alcohol/Drug Problem Acknowledgment
A-hea	Health Concerns		
A-aln	Alienation	PRO	Alcohol/Drug Problem Proneness
A-biz	Bizarre Mentation		
A-ang	Anger	IMM	Immaturity
A-cyn	Cynicism	A	Anxiety
A-con	Conduct Problems	R	Repression
A-lse	Low Self-Esteem		
A-las	Low Aspirations		
A-sod	Social Discomfort		
A-fam	Family Problems		
A-sch	School Problems		
A-trt	Negative Treatment Indicators		

scales, 6 supplementary scales (see Rapid Reference 1.4), and 28 Harris-Lingoes and 3 *Si* subscales (see Rapid Reference 1.5). These scales are presented in more detail in subsequent chapters.

From a broad perspective, it may be stated that the MMPI-A is a new instrument that is based substantially on the original form of the MMPI, but that it also incorporates several of the innovative features of the MMPI-2. Nevertheless, the MMPI-A also contains some distinctive features that are found only in this adaptation of the MMPI for adolescents. Because a considerable emphasis was placed on maintaining continuity between the original form of the MMPI and the MMPI-A, much of the research done using the original form of the MMPI with adolescents may be validly generalized to the MMPI-A.

≡*Rapid Reference 1.5*

MMPI-A Harris-Lingoes and *Si* Subscales

Harris-Lingoes Subscales

- Scale 2 Subscales

    D_1 Subjective Depression

    D_2 Psychomotor Retardation

    D_3 Physical Malfunctioning

    D_4 Mental Dullness

    D_5 Brooding

- Scale 3 Subscales

    Hy_1 Denial of Social Anxiety

    Hy_2 Need for Affection

    Hy_3 Lassitude-Malaise

    Hy_4 Somatic Complaints

    Hy_5 Inhibition of Aggression

- Scale 4 Subscales

    Pd_1 Familial Discord

    Pd_2 Authority Problems

    Pd_3 Social Imperturbability

    Pd_4 Social Alienation

    Pd_5 Self-Alienation

- Scale 6 Subscales

    Pa_1 Persecutory Ideas

    Pa_2 Poignancy

    Pa_3 Naivete

- Scale 8 Subscales

    Sc_1 Social Alienation

    Sc_2 Emotional Alienation

    Sc_3 Lack of Ego Mastery, Cognitive

    Sc_4 Lack of Ego Mastery, Conative

    Sc_5 Lack of Ego Mastery, Defective Inhibition

    Sc_5 Bizarre Sensory, Experiences

- Scale 9 Subscales

    Ma_1 Amorality

    Ma_2 Psychomotor Acceleration

    Ma_3 Imperturbability

    Ma_4 Ego Inflation

- **Si Subscales**

    Si_1 Shyness/Self-Consciousness

    Si_2 Social Avoidance

    Si_3 Alienation—Self and Others

RELIABILITY AND VALIDITY OF THE MMPI-A

Reliability

The MMPI-A manual provides extensive information concerning the reliability of this instrument. For example, 154 adolescents in the normative sample volunteered to return 1 week later to provide important test-retest information on the test instrument. The range of test-retest correlations for the basic clinical scales was .65 to .84, which is comparable to the test-retest correlations reported in the MMPI-2 manual for the adult revision of the test. Furthermore, based on these reliability data, the typical standard error of measurement for the MMPI-A basic scales is 4 to 6 T-score points. Thus, we are able to state that if an adolescent retakes the MMPI-A within a relatively short time interval, and without significant change in his or her psychological functioning, his or her basic scale scores will fall in a range of roughly ±4 to 6 T-score points approximately 50% of the time. The standard error of measurement data are very important in evaluating any changes obtained from readministering the MMPI-A to adolescents in order to measure changes over time, such as those associated with treatment effects. Changes of 5 T-score points or less are more likely to reflect measurement error than reliable change. Beyond the test-retest reliability on the basic scales, test-retest data are also available in the MMPI-A manual for the content and supplementary scales.

In addition to test-retest data as an index of reliability, evidence of internal consistency based on coefficient alpha is also presented in the test manual for the MMPI-A basic scales, content scales, and supplementary scales. The coefficient alpha statistic developed by Cronbach in 1951 is a measure of the extent to which the items comprising scale membership tend to be intercorrelated, a desirable feature in scales attempting to measure a unitary or homogeneous construct. Contemporary scale development procedures often use coefficient alpha results to select or eliminate items (this was part of the method used in the construction of the MMPI-A content scales, for example), thereby creating scales with relatively high internal consistency values. In contrast, scales derived through empirical item selection, such as the MMPI-A basic scales, often tend to produce lower internal consistency findings because these scales are typically more heterogeneous in terms of content areas. In general, these trends are clearly reflected in the coefficient alpha findings for the MMPI-A scales; that is, basic scales have widely fluctuating alpha coefficient levels, ranging from relatively low values on scales such as Mf and Pa (.40 to .60) to much higher values on other MMPI-A scales such as Hs and Sc (ranging from .78 to .89). In contrast, the MMPI-A content scales tend to yield somewhat higher internal consistency values of .55 to .89 on the psychometric equivalency between the original and revised forms of items modified on the MMPI-A.

In addition to test-retest and internal consistency measures of reliability, the MMPI-A manual also provides information concerning the intercorrelation of

MMPI-A scales, the factor structure of the MMPI-A, and information concerning the item endorsement frequencies and reading levels related to each MMPI-A item.

Validity

During the half-century of use of the original MMPI, an extensive literature had developed on the use of this instrument with adolescents. Because of the substantial continuity between the original form of the MMPI and MMPI-A, much of this basic literature may be generalized to the MMPI-A. In support of this point, the MMPI-A manual provides data on the rate of agreement between adolescents' profiles generated from the original test instrument on adolescent norms and the same response pattern produced for the MMPI-A. Although the two forms are clearly not identical, there is ample evidence of substantial compatibility or congruency. Eventually, however, the MMPI-A (like all revised tests) must develop a research literature based on this specific form in order to have full confidence in the revised test instrument. Fortunately, there is evidence that this research literature has been developing on the MMPI-A. Archer's (1997) text on the MMPI-A, for example, provides more than 400 references, although many of these are related to either the original test instrument or to the MMPI-2. A recent survey of the literature reveals more than 50 studies that have been published in the 8 years following the 1992 publication of the MMPI-A and focus on various aspects of this instrument. These research studies include investigations of the effectiveness of the MMPI-A validity scales in detecting response sets such as random responding and underreporting or overreporting of symptoms. This literature also examines the usefulness of the MMPI-A basic clinical and content scales in detecting disabilities such as Attention-deficit Disorder and learning disabilities, and psychopathology including delinquency, eating disorders, suicidal ideation, depression, Conduct Disorder, substance abuse, and fire-setting tendencies.

A number of MMPI-A studies have focused on the factor structure of the MMPI-A, including the characteristics and effectiveness of the MMPI-A Structural Summary, which is based on the MMPI-A factor structure. Additionally, a number of studies have also looked at responses to the MMPI-A as a function of age, ethnicity, socioeconomic status, and gender. Studies of the MMPI-A have also been undertaken among Mexican-American adolescents and with Hong Kong residents using a Chinese translation of the MMPI-A. It should also be noted that the MMPI-A manual provides extensive validity data, including scale correlates for normative and clinical samples for the MMPI-A basic scales, provided separately by gender. Finally, the MMPI-A text by Archer (1997) provides extensive validity and correlate data for the MMPI-A, and the text by Archer, Krishnamurthy, and Jacobson (1994) provides correlate data in support of the validity of the Structural Summary approach to MMPI-A organization and interpretation.

Information concerning the correlates of the original MMPI basic scales for adolescents was reported by several researchers, including Hathaway and Monachesi (1963). These studies are also relevant and applicable to the interpretation of the MMPI-A because of the high degree of similarity between the MMPI and MMPI-A basic scales. In addition, however, the MMPI-A manual provides substantial MMPI-A basic scale correlate information based on analyses conducted with both normal adolescents and adolescents in treatment settings. For the normative sample, MMPI-A correlates were based on biographical and life events information provided by each adolescent. A wider array of correlates was reported for the clinical sample based on biographical and life events information, and parental ratings and treatment staff ratings, as well as information obtained through review of the adolescents' residential or inpatient treatment records. Furthermore, basic clinical scale correlate information has also been provided by Archer (1997) for a sample of 222 adolescents receiving psychiatric inpatient treatment. Thus, our understanding of the correlates or descriptors of the MMPI-A basic clinical scales rests on research on the meaning of these scales with the original form of the test instrument, as well as new data generated through independent studies of the clinical correlate patterns for the MMPI-A. In general, the clinical correlates found for the basic clinical scales of the MMPI, MMPI-2, and MMPI-A show a high degree of consistency. Furthermore, correlate patterns are typically better documented and better understood for elevated scores in contrast to lower-range scores, and, hence, there is greater confidence in interpreting high-point elevations.

COMPREHENSIVE REFERENCES ON THE MMPI-A

The *MMPI-A (Minnesota Multiphasic Personality Inventory–Adolescent): Manual for Administration, Scoring, and Interpretation* (Butcher, et al., 1992) provides detailed information about the development of the test, such as descriptions of scales and subscales, standardization, reliability, and validity. The second edition of *Essentials of MMPI-2 and MMPI-A Interpretation* (Butcher & Williams, 2000) presents an overview and interpretive guidelines for both instruments, and *MMPI-A Content Scales: Assessing Psychopathology in Adolescents* (Williams, Butcher, Ben-Porath, & Graham, 1992) details the development and interpretation of these latter scales using illustrations with clinical cases. The *MMPI-A Casebook* (Archer, Krishnamurthy, & Jacobson 1994) provides an introduction to the use of the MMPI-A Structural Summary developed by Archer and Krishnamurthy (1994) for the interpretation of this test instrument, and highlights profile interpretation strategies through the presentation of several clinical case examples. The *MMPI-A: Assessing Adolescent Psychopathology (2nd Edition)* (Archer, 1997) provides a comprehensive overview of the MMPI-A and coverage of the literature relevant to this test instrument. This text offers practical information to clinicians regarding the use of the MMPI-A and also furnishes sufficient technical information to stimulate future research efforts with the instrument. Interpretive strategies are addressed and illustrated in depth, and extensive appendices provide normative information, scale composition, and *T*-score conversions.

 TEST YOURSELF

1. **The MMPI-A has substantial continuity with the original MMPI.** True or False?

2. **Hathaway and Monachesi's longitudinal study found that selected MMPI scales**
   (a) were associated with adolescent depression.
   (b) were effective predictors of adolescent Post-Traumatic Stress Disorder.
   (c) were effective predictors of adolescent delinquency.
   (d) were never elevated for adolescents.

3. **Which of the following were adolescent norm sets for the original MMPI?**
   (a) Marks and Briggs' norms
   (b) Hathaway and Dahlstrom's norms
   (c) a and b
   (d) none of the above

(continued)

4. **Which of the following test construction methods was used for developing the MMPI-A basic scales?**

   (a) rational/intuitive

   (b) criterion keying

   (c) factor analysis

   (d) all of the above.

5. **How many items appear on the MMPI-A?**

   (a) 478

   (b) 550

   (c) 566

   (d) 350

Answers: 1. True; 2. c; 3. a; 4. b; 5. a

Two

HOW TO ADMINISTER THE MMPI-A

Administering the MMPI-A is relatively straightforward and involves procedures similar to those used with other self-report inventories. Brief instructions are printed on the test booklet, which can be easily brought to the attention of the test taker. However, the test administrator should be sure to set the stage for the testing with care and skill and to deliver clear instructions; these are crucial for obtaining valid and interpretable results. Finn (1996) has discussed the merits of engaging the client in the testing process, taking the time to address his or her doubts and concerns, and maintaining a collaborative stance when testing adults with the MMPI-2. All these issues acquire greater significance when testing adolescents who (a) generally do not seek the testing voluntarily but are referred by a parent or teacher, (b) are more likely than adults to view the examiner as an authority figure and, therefore, react accordingly, and (c) are less likely to be motivated to produce accurate results. In essence, then, the goal of the examiner should be to establish good rapport and to obtain the cooperation of the adolescent *before* the formal testing begins, followed by careful observation of the adolescent's test-taking attitude during the ensuing testing session.

APPROPRIATE TESTING CONDITIONS

Testing Environment and Supervision Requirements

Providing a comfortable testing environment that is free of noise and other distractions is an essential condition for successful MMPI-A administration. Ideally, there should be a well-lit testing room containing a desk and comfortable chair, which provides a private, noise-free space for the test taker. In most settings, the examiner could ensure that the adolescent has the testing room to him- or herself by reserving the room for the projected testing duration. Improvised variations such as using the couch and coffee table of a therapy room or using a propped-up position in a hospital bed are sometimes inevitable, but the examiner should be mindful that they may create discomfort, which interferes with the adolescent's attention and concentration.

Another crucial requirement of MMPI-A administration is ensuring that the testing setting is appropriately supervised. In individual clinical assessments, this is best achieved by the examiner remaining in the room for an initial period to ensure that the client is following test-taking procedures and particularly to check that the adolescent marks the correct response number corresponding to the test item number. Subsequently leaving the room but checking back periodically during the testing period enables the examiner to maintain a watchful presence without being intrusive. The adolescent's parent or legal guardian should be encouraged to wait in a waiting room instead of the testing room itself. The MMPI-A should *never* be sent home with the client, nor should any alternative to the standard administration procedure (e.g., completing it over lunch in a restaurant) be offered. Such concessions have the dual impact of compromising both the obtained results and the protected test materials.

MMPI-A testing should also be completed within one testing session whenever possible. Although some adolescents may find it difficult to complete the testing in one continuous session due to problems of inattention, hyperactivity, marked restlessness, impulsiveness, or physical limitations, their needs can be addressed by providing breaks as needed, thus subdividing the testing session into several shorter segments. In all cases, the examiner should be alert for signs of fatigue or distractibility and promptly offer rest periods to the adolescent. This is especially necessary when the MMPI-A is administered as part of a comprehensive battery of tests. Administering the MMPI-A over a period of several days or weeks is not advisable because it creates the possibility that the results would be affected by different state characteristics. For example, the adolescent may be in a different frame of mind in the two test sessions if significant intervening experiences, such as conflict with parents or friends, suspension from school, or breakup of a relationship, occur. A pronounced variation in response style sufficient to render the results invalid is likely in these circumstances, ultimately causing a waste of time and effort.

Finally, MMPI-A testing is best accomplished when the adolescent's physical and mental state is equal to the demands of testing. The examiner should consider the fatigue effects of testing a teenager at the end of the school day or when he or she is ill, and the motivational effects of testing during school holidays.

Establishing Rapport with the Adolescent

As mentioned earlier, the examiner needs to get the adolescent involved and invested in the MMPI-A testing, which can be achieved partly by efforts to establish a good sense of rapport. This is particularly important because the teenager has before him or her the task of completing a rather lengthy questionnaire, which is presented in the format suggestive of academic examinations and which may hold little personal interest. The examiner could begin with some neutral and nonthreatening social talk, proceed to inquire about the adolescent's understanding of the reason or reasons for the referral, expand on or correct the teenager's impressions with honest and clear explanation of the purpose of testing, and discuss how the results will be used. It is important to inform the teenager that he or she will receive testing feedback and to follow through with it, so that the teenager is respected and kept involved in the entire process. It should be noted that developing a working alliance with the adolescent examinee does not mean the examiner should align with him or her against parental or other authority figures. The examiner should also refrain from making promises that cannot be kept. Specifically, the examiner cannot offer assurances of complete confidentiality when the test taker is a minor. On the other hand, assuming an authoritarian stance or getting into a power struggle will likely only create rebellion, resistance, or refusal, and will result in an unproductive testing session. Overall, a sincere and empathic approach that is also adequately firm and task-oriented will likely produce appropriate participation. MMPI-A testing should be deferred when the adolescent displays marked oppositionality, negativity, or poor motivation, so that the examiner can make efforts to achieve examinee cooperation.

The age of the adolescent and status as a minor does not prohibit using a collaborative approach to the assessment process. A useful method for engaging the examinee as a participant in a joint venture, as articulated by Finn (1996), consists of using a portion of the pre-testing interview to determine what the adolescent would like to discover from the testing. By encouraging or tapping into the adolescent's curiosity, the examiner could gently draw the teenager into the testing process and enable him or her to view it as having personal relevance. The examiner would need to actively assist the teenager in constructing questions that can be answered from the test profiles, anticipating that some questions may be too broad ("Am I a misfit?") or too narrow ("Why do I keep thinking about my ex-girlfriend?"). Moreover, some types of questions, particularly those that are externally directed (e.g., "What is wrong with my parents?"), cannot be answered by the MMPI-A and warrant redirection. The end goal would be to arrive at a manageable number of practical, appropriately devised questions or issues that can be systematically addressed in the test feedback session. The following section illustrates a typical discussion.

Examiner: I understand that you are not sure about how this testing may be useful to you. Often, this type of testing helps teenagers to learn things about themselves that they hadn't fully been aware of, or actively thought about.

Adolescent: What kinds of things?

Examiner: For example, most people don't really think about how they come across to other people, or whether their ways of thinking and feeling are very different from those of others. The MMPI-A can shed light on these issues. Does that make sense?

Adolescent: I guess.

Examiner: The testing can also help to better understand things that adolescents might already suspect about themselves. For example, a teenager may be aware that she often feels unhappy and grouchy but not have a clear idea of what is going on. The MMPI-A results may help her to realize that she is in a depressed state, which may include being very sensitive to others' reactions, having negative thoughts about herself, and feeling that no one understands her. Does this give you an idea of how this works?

Adolescent: Yes.

Examiner: OK. Now all of this can be best done if you take a few moments to think about some questions you have about yourself that you would like answered by the testing.

Adolescent: Uh. . . . about feeling depressed?

Examiner: The type of question varies from person to person and is up to you. What are some things that you have wondered about regarding yourself?

Adolescent: I don't know. . . . Sometimes I feel that everyone in my class, and all my friends, are so sure of themselves and know what they want better than I do.

Examiner: That is a good place to start. It sounds like you feel uncertain about yourself and your goals, and don't feel like you have as much confidence as other teenagers. Is that correct?

Adolescent: Yes. Seems like I'm the only one who doesn't have a clue.

Examiner: The question for testing, then, can be, "Am I low in self-confidence and self-esteem compared to other teenagers?" How does that sound?

Adolescent: That sounds right.

Examiner: Good. The MMPI-A can certainly give us an answer to this question and help us see what kinds of things contribute to this feeling. Let's make a note of that question and then try another one.

Adolescent: Well, I also get mad at people who show off or are in my face. My parents make me mad too. I can really pitch a fit and it comes out of nowhere. I guess I wonder why I blow up so easily.

Examiner: That is an excellent issue for which we should get useful information from the MMPI-A. It sounds like there are two related questions here, one being, "Do I get angry more quickly than other people?" and the other one being, "Why do I get easily angered?"

Adolescent: That's exactly it.

It should be noted how the examiner would guide the teenager in identifying the issues of concern and in phrasing them in terms that the testing can address. The dialog would continue at an unhurried pace that permits modifications and refinements of questions as needed until a satisfactory list of queries is compiled. The examiner could also use a modified procedure that includes both the adolescent and his or her parent/legal guardian in this process, which enables both parties to be involved and to have their queries addressed in the feedback session. Alternatively, another professional (e.g., case worker, psychotherapist) who is the referring agent or otherwise involved in the adolescent's care could take the place of the adult party.

The adolescent will be able to cooperate and follow directions best when he or she is given clear instructions. Hastily provided instructions may result in a level of confusion that renders the resulting profiles invalid or may create an impression of examiner disinterest. The simplest approach is for the examiner to read aloud the instructions written in the MMPI-A test booklet while positioning the booklet in front of the adolescent so that he or she can follow along. It is also worth the time to review the answer sheet with the examinee to ensure that he or she knows where and how to mark responses, and to answer any questions that may arise. For example, the typical adolescent would want to know how long the testing would take. An honest and direct response would be that it takes approximately 1 to 1.5 hours, depending on the examinee's reading speed and concentration ability. Another common question concerns the True/False response format; some adolescents may consider this format unsuitable for test items that they would prefer to answer as "maybe" or "sometimes." In these instances, the teenager should be encouraged to respond based on whether the item is mostly true or mostly untrue of him or her.

Examiners can also facilitate rapport by thoughtful measures such as indicating the locations of the water fountain, snack machine, and restroom prior to testing, offering encouragement and praise for the adolescent's efforts during testing, and inquiring if a rest period is needed. In summary, establishing a working alliance with the adolescent has wide-reaching benefits such as reducing the likelihood of random responding, increasing honest and open responding, and achieving meaningful testing and feedback processes.

Testing Materials

The basic materials for a typical MMPI-A administration consist of a test booklet containing the instructions and test items, a separate answer sheet, and a soft black lead pencil for marking the responses. Additional pencils with erasers should also be at hand. The test booklet is available in softcover and hardcover formats, each having a corresponding answer sheet. The examiner should ensure that the correct form of the answer sheet is used (i.e., the answer sheet should match the form of the test booklet). A handscoring answer sheet cannot be scored by mail-in or optical scanning procedures and would create a problem for the examiner who does not have hand-scoring templates.

Some alternative methods of test administration are also available. An audiotape version of the MMPI-A can be purchased from National Computer Systems, Inc. (NCS), the distributor of MMPI products, for use with individuals who have difficulty with the written formats, including individuals with vi-

---

CAUTION

Common Pitfalls in Administration

- Failing to establish rapport with the adolescent before testing
- Failing to provide an appropriate, noise-free testing environment
- Forgetting to determine the test-taker's reading capacity
- Forgetting to review test instructions with the adolescent
- Leaving the adolescent unsupervised during the testing session
- Sending the test booklet home with the adolescent for him/her to complete the testing on his or her own
- Using the incorrect answer sheet (e.g., handscoring sheet for mail-in scoring)
- Assisting the adolescent too much by offering examples to explain test items
- Forgetting to offer feedback on test results

---

sual impairments or reading difficulties. This method of administration only requires the additional component of an audiocassette player and takes a standard administration time of 1 hour and 40 minutes. A computerized administration is also possible, with purchase of the NCS Microtest Q software, whereby test items are presented on the computer monitor and the adolescent can enter *True* or *False* responses using the keyboard. Different scoring methods associated with the selected administration method are described in Chapter 3. Examiners can find details about these products and services in the NCS Assessments catalog, or view them online at the NCS Website (*http://assessments.ncspearson.com,* at the time of this writing). A review of common pitfalls in test administration is provided in the Caution callout box.

Abbreviated and Short Forms

The standard administration of the MMPI-A involves completion of all 478 items of the test. This enables scoring and interpretation of the full range of validity scales, basic scales, Harris-Lingoes and *Si* subscales, and the content and supplementary scales. One alternative to a complete administration involves limiting the test administration to the first 350 items, which will yield validity scales F_1, L, and K, and the basic scales 1 through 0. This option of an abbreviated administration may be used in extenuating circumstances, such as (a) with a markedly uncooperative adolescent client or with a teenager who has significant problems of inattention or hyperactivity; and (b) when the clinician feels that partial test data is preferable to the absence of MMPI-A test information in the given case. However, using an abbreviated form of the test should be considered a last resort and not be used routinely because valuable test data is unavailable in this method. Specifically, validity scales $VRIN$, $TRIN$, F, and F_2, which are critical for determining random response sets that would render the test profiles uninterpretable, are not scorable. Moreover, the content and supplementary scales, which furnish useful information about several adolescent problem areas, are also unavailable in an abbreviated form of the MMPI-A.

There is an important distinction between an abbreviated MMPI-A and a *short form* of the test. A short form, by definition, involves achieving brevity by reducing the length of scales. Several short forms were developed for the original MMPI, the most well-known ones being the 71-item Mini-Mult and the MMPI-168. Recently, a 150-item short form of the MMPI-A was developed by Archer, Tirrell, and Elkins (2001). The limitation of all short forms is that the obtained scales are generally less reliable than their full-length counterparts as a function of their loss of items. Furthermore, the high-point codetypes produced by short forms often differ significantly from those produced by a full-length administration. Consequently, the profiles obtained from a short form are of questionable interpretive accuracy when codetype analysis is the central approach to interpretation. For these reasons, a short form of the MMPI-A is not recommended for standard use, nor is it a desirable shortcut for obtaining a useful MMPI-A profile. The short form may, however, have some limited utility in determining whether an adolescent reveals clinical levels of psychopathology and may be considered for use in rare instances when testing with the full-length instrument or its abbreviated version is not possible. Rapid Reference 2.1 summarizes key issues concerning MMPI short forms and abbreviated assessments.

Testing of Adolescents with Reading Disabilities

The MMPI-A is most suited for adolescents who have sufficient reading ability and comprehension of the words and issues presented in the test questions. In

≡Rapid Reference 2.1

Short Forms and Abbreviated Administrations

- An abbreviated assessment can be done by administering the first 350 items of the MMPI-A. Note, however, that validity scales F, F_2, VRIN, and TRIN, and the content and supplementary scales cannot be scored by this method.
- A short form (150-item MMPI-A) has fewer items and shorter scales, and produces codetypes that are less reliable or accurate than codetypes from a full-length administration.
- Neither abbreviated nor short form administrations are recommended for routine use.

clinical settings, however, a substantial number of adolescent clients have histories of academic underachievement and below-grade-level reading capacity. A significant number of them are actually diagnosed with a Reading Disorder, Receptive Language Disorder, or other forms of learning disability. The competent clinician would have to determine whether the teenager can meaningfully respond to the booklet version of the MMPI-A, noting that use of the test does not have to be automatically ruled out. If reading achievement scores are available, they can be used to determine if the adolescent has the requisite reading ability. The clinician can also do an informal assessment of reading capacity and reading comprehension by asking the adolescent to read selected items and explain their meaning. Using the audiocassette version of the MMPI-A can circumvent problems of reading ability and produce valid results. The repeated presentation of the test items in the audiotape version makes it well suited to this population. The examiner is cautioned not to read the items aloud to the adolescent as a substitute for using the standard audiotape version because of the potential adverse effects on the test-taker's level of openness and disclosure.

Foreign Language Translations

The original form of the MMPI received widespread international application within a few decades after its release, and considerable efforts were made to develop foreign language translations, collect culturally appropriate norms for test interpretation, and conduct research studies on the psychometric and applied aspects of the translated test instruments. The same trend continues with the MMPI-2 for adults and the MMPI-A for adolescents. For example, the MMPI-2 has already been translated into several languages (including Dutch/Flemish, French, French Canadian, Hebrew, Hmong, and Italian), and there are three Spanish language translations for use in the United States, Mexico, and Spain. Several other foreign language adaptations are underway (see Butcher, 1996), including the Japanese, Korean, Chinese, Thai, Vietnamese, Chilean, Norwegian, Icelandic, Russian, Greek, Arabic, and Farsi MMPI-2 adaptations. The MMPI-A follows in the same path and currently has a Spanish version available for use in the United States and French, Dutch/Flemish, and Italian translations with several other translation projects in progress.

ADMINISTRATION CONSIDERATIONS

Examiner Qualifications

Although administering a self-report instrument such as the MMPI-A is ostensibly easy, the MMPI-A examiner is expected to meet certain basic qualifications, as he or she is entrusted with the responsibilities of accurate test scoring, interpretation of results, and delineation of the examinee's personality profile in a professional report. First and foremost, the examiner should have adequate knowledge of test theory, test construction methods, and psychometric concepts, including an understanding of norms and their use, conversion of raw scores to standard scores, and issues of measurement error, base rates, and cutting scores. In addition, the personality evaluation of adolescents requires knowledge of adolescent development, personality theories and concepts, psychopathology, and psychodiagnosis. Graduate courses in developmental psychology, theories of personality, personality assessment, and psychopathology would represent the typical method of acquiring the requisite background for MMPI-A testing. These guidelines are also described in the MMPI-A manual (Butcher et al., 1992) and Archer's (1997) text. The examiner may also want to consult the user qualifications specified by NCS for purchase of MMPI-A materials, which, in essence, require a minimum of graduate-level training in tests and measurements. As a final step, the MMPI-A user could examine the guidelines for training in personality assessment provided by the Society for Personality Assessment (SPA), which can be seen at its Web site (currently *http://www.personality.org*), or obtained by contacting its central office.

In some cases, the professional psychologist may delegate the mechanics of MMPI-A administration and scoring to a psychometrist or student-in-training. It is essential, however, that the psychologist retains responsibility for careful supervision of these procedures to ensure that controllable sources of error and invalidity have not been present and that ethical/professional standards have not been compromised. The examiner is ultimately accountable for the accuracy of results.

Age Criteria

The MMPI-A is designed to evaluate adolescents in the age range of 14 through 18 years. Test items represent a broad spectrum of experiences, behaviors, and emotional responses common to teenagers in this age range and may have less applicability for those in preteen and young adult stages of development. At the lower end of the age continuum, however, the MMPI-A could be selectively used with 12- and 13-year-olds if they are developmentally advanced, that is, demonstrate the level of cognitive and interpersonal maturity seen in adolescents and have had life experiences that render MMPI-A items relevant to them. A separate set of norms for 12- to 13-year-olds is provided by Archer (1992, 1997) and is described in the subsequent chapters.

The overlap in age range between the MMPI-A and MMPI-2 presents the examiner with the choice of testing 18-year-olds with either instrument. The standard guideline for making this decision involves considering whether the individual is more like an adolescent (for example, living at home as a dependent child and attending high school) or more adult-like in terms of living away from home, attending college, and having gainful employment. It should be noted, however, that the choice of MMPI-A versus MMPI-2 norms has significant practical implications. A recent study by Shaevel and Archer (1996) indicates that sizable differences in T-score elevations can occur depending on which test is used with 18-year-olds, with MMPI-2 norms typically producing lower validity scale values and higher clinical scale values than MMPI-A norms. The discrepancy, which is more likely for higher-range scores, can reach as high as 15 T-score points and results in different profile classifications. As a related point, the MMPI-2 is more likely to overestimate psychopathology and the MMPI-A is more likely to underestimate the individual's actual level of disturbance. These issues have to be weighed when selecting the appropriate instrument in a given case.

Assessment of individuals ages 19 and older should be conducted with the MMPI-2, which is normed for the adult age groups, even with young adults in this age range who may appear developmentally delayed or immature. Similarly, adolescents ages 17 and younger should always be tested with the MMPI-A, regardless of how mature they may appear.

Reading Level

Examiners need to consider reading and reading-comprehension capacities for MMPI-A testing because low skills in these areas are likely to result in random or inconsistent responding, which would invalidate the testing. MMPI-A test items vary in level of reading difficulty and complexity, ranging from the 1st grade level up to the 15th and 16th grade level for a couple of items. The MMPI-A test manual reports an analysis of the reading difficulty level of each item based on indices of reading ease, reading difficulty, and sentence structure, and it indicates that the majority of test items are at a fifth- to seventh-grade reading level. Using a conservative estimate, the seventh-grade level is the recommended reading level for the MMPI-A.

When the adolescent's reading level is in question, it would be useful to administer a standardized reading test to determine if the client is capable of adequately reading and comprehending MMPI-A items. The reading subtest(s) of standard achievement tests, such as the Wide Range Achievement Test–Revised (WRAT-3), Woodcock-Johnson Psycho-Educational Battery, Tests of Achievement–Revised (WJ-R), Wechsler Individual Achievement Test (WIAT), Kaufman Test of Educational Achievement (K-TEA), or the Peabody Individual Achievement Test–Revised (PIAT-R), are appropriate for this purpose. As mentioned earlier, the examiner can also perform an informal assessment by asking the adolescent to read and explain selected MMPI-A items. Archer (1992, 1997) has suggested that items at an eighth-grade reading level are most useful for this kind of assessment. Examples include:

Item 5: *I am easily awakened by noise.*
Item 17: *I am troubled by attacks of nausea and vomiting.*
Item 18: *I am very seldom troubled by constipation.*

Item 25: *I am bothered by an upset stomach several times a week.*
Item 29: *I have had very peculiar and strange experiences.*

Some MMPI-A items may contain words that are unfamiliar even to the adolescent who has the requisite reading capacity. A dictionary definition of these words may be provided if the adolescent asks for their meaning. For example, "misfortunes" could be defined in terms of "bad luck," and "hotheaded" as "becoming easily angered or excited." The term "brood," which appears in MMPI-A Item 203 "I brood a great deal," is frequently not comprehended by current generations of adolescents, and the examiner should be prepared to explain it as "to unhappily think about something over and over again." However, clinicians should avoid further explanations of words and phrases with examples as they may bias or skew the adolescent's responses to those items. The examiner should *not* define words such as "often," "overly," "regularly," and "sometimes" in terms of their estimated frequency as this introduces the examiner's subjective judgments into the testing process. Finally, clinicians need to examine the applicability of the English language version of the MMPI-A in cases when English is not the client's dominant language. In many regions of the United States, it may be necessary to regularly use the Spanish version of the test.

Mental Status Considerations

Adolescents evaluated in clinical settings, particularly acute inpatient facilities, may present for testing in states of functioning that are not conducive to MMPI-A testing. Acute states of confusion and disorientation that are associated with psychotic conditions and seizure disorders are prime examples of when the testing should be delayed until the adolescent has been stabilized. In both inpatient and outpatient settings, the examiner should be vigilant for signs of substance-related altered states and severe behavioral problems that may prevent compliance with testing.

SUMMARY

After administering the MMPI-A, the examiner's concluding task is to review the MMPI-A answer sheet for possible item omissions and to ask the adoles-

DON'T FORGET

Keys to Competent Administration

- Engage the adolescent as a joint participant in the testing process.
- Check that the examinee can read and understand test items.
- Rule out the presence of detrimental factors such as intoxication, disorientation, or confusional states that would prevent appropriate responding.
- Provide a testing environment that is comfortable and free of noise and other distractions.
- Supervise the testing session.
- Provide breaks as needed to prevent fatigue or distractibility, which may interfere with test validity.
- Use an audiotape version for adolescents who have visual impairments or reading problems.
- Review item omissions before the adolescent leaves the testing setting.

cent to complete the omitted items prior to leaving. A large number of item omissions interferes with profile accuracy and may render the results uninterpretable. The examiner needs to consider if the client omitted responses to certain items due to difficulty understanding key words (in which case the examiner could provide a limited amount of guidance), or because the adolescent was uncomfortable answering them. The examiner could address discomfort with item content by pointing out that responses to individual items are not the primary focus of interpretation and reminding the adolescent of the purposes of testing.

In summary, the first critical step in MMPI-A assessment involves proper administration of the test. A well-conducted administration gives the examiner confidence that the results are likely to be useful and permits the clinician to progress to the subsequent phases of test scoring and interpretation.

TEST YOURSELF

1. When an adolescent has reading difficulties, the test examiner

(a) cannot administer the MMPI-A.

(b) can consider using an audiotape version of the test.

(c) can consider using an online administration procedure.

(d) can consider using a short form of the test.

2. Establishing good rapport prior to testing

(a) can reduce the chances of inconsistent responding.

(b) can improve the chances of honest responding.

(c) can facilitate meaningful testing and feedback processes.

(d) all of the above.

3. The MMPI-A examiner should provide a testing environment that

(a) minimizes distractions and facilitates concentration.

(b) is supervised.

(c) both a and b.

(d) does not require any special considerations.

4. Using an abbreviated administration permits scoring of

(a) measures of inconsistent, but not inaccurate, responding.

(b) validity scales L, F_1, and K, and basic clinical scales.

(c) content component scales but not content scales.

(d) $VRIN$ and $TRIN$ but not F and F_2.

5. The MMPI-A examiner should

(a) have knowledge of adolescent development, psychopathology, and psychometrics.

(b) be certified by an assessment board.

(c) have experience with the MMPI-2.

(d) all of the above.

Answers: 1. b; 2. d; 3. c; 4. b; 5. a

Three

HOW TO SCORE THE MMPI-A

The initial step of scoring the MMPI-A is to obtain the raw score values for the desired scales. The full range of scales that can be scored by either handscoring or computer-scoring methods includes the validity scales, basic clinical scales, Harris-Lingoes and Si subscales, content scales, and supplementary scales. The second step in scoring is to obtain the T-score values, separately for boys and girls, corresponding to raw scores for each of these scales. Once the clinician has derived a profile based on the T scores, he or she can also summarize the resulting patterns of the basic scale profile using the Welsh code. A final step is to obtain scores for the factor-based groupings of the MMPI-A Structural Summary. Some additional indices can also be obtained from computer scoring (which we address in the next section).

Accuracy of MMPI-A scoring is crucial because relatively minor errors can occasionally, depending on the scale in question, have a large impact on the obtained profiles in the course of converting raw scores to T scores. For example, on a relatively short scale such as *ACK,* a raw score of 4 converts to a T score of 51 for girls, which is well within the average range. However, misscoring by 2 points produces a raw score of 6 and would raise the T-score value to 60, placing it in the marginal range of clinical elevation. This error might lead the clinician to conclude that the adolescent has some problems with substance use when, in fact, correct scoring of this scale would indicate otherwise. Another type of error that could occur involves using the incorrect gender norms, which could affect the elevation of a given scale. For example, a raw score of 25 on scale *4* converts to a marginally elevated T score of 60 for boys but a normal-range T score of 57 for girls. The clinician should therefore exert reasonable effort to minimize errors in MMPI-A scoring, particularly during the various processes involved in handscoring.

SCORING THE MMPI-A

Materials for Handscoring

The materials needed for handscoring the MMPI-A include the scoring templates or answer keys for each scale, a *VRIN/TRIN* grid, and profile forms. These scoring materials can be purchased from NCS. Clinicians also need the MMPI-A Structural Summary form to obtain the factor-based groupings; this form can be purchased from Psychological Assessment Resources, Inc. (PAR). Clinicians should note that the answer keys for use with softcover test booklets are different from those for hardcover test booklets, so they should be sure to obtain the appropriate set. The examiner should also note that the profile sheets are two-sided, with one side presenting the norms for females and the other side for males. The profile must always be plotted on the appropriate gender norms.

Handscoring Procedures

For all scales with the exception of *VRIN* and *TRIN*, the procedure for obtaining raw scores is as follows. First, as mentioned in Chapter 2, the clinician should examine the answer sheet and identify omitted and double-marked items. The examiner could draw a red line through the *True* and *False* circles for these items which can be easily viewed through the answer keys to avoid including them in the scoring. The examiner then counts the number of omitted and double-marked responses and transfers this numerical value to the space indicated for the *(?)* Raw Score at the bottom left corner of the MMPI-A Profile for Basic Scales sheet. The examiner would proceed to use the scoring templates for scoring each scale. The scoring template, which is a translucent plastic overlay, is placed over the answer sheet and lined up by placing the black bars appearing on the upper and lower right corners of the template over the corresponding bars on the answer sheet. It is important to align the scoring template correctly in order to get an accurate count of responses answered in the critical direction. The examiner then counts the number of blackened responses that are visible through the clear circles on the scoring template. This count, which represents the raw score for the scale, should be recorded as the raw score for the given scale at the bottom of the appropriate profile sheet.

There are several points worth attending to in the course of handscoring. First, the examiner should note that there is a separate scoring template for each scale.

The examiner would minimize errors by ensuring that the templates are organized in the correct order and proceeding sequentially across each set of scales. In handscoring the basic scales, it should be noted that there are two templates for scale 5, one for males and one for females, and only one of them would be used based on the sex of the adolescent examinee.

Handscoring templates are not currently available for the recently developed MMPI-A content component scales. The examiner who wishes to obtain these scales to refine content scale interpretation can manually score them by referring to the directions given in the monograph by Sherwood, Ben-Porath, and Williams (1997).

Handscoring *VRIN* and *TRIN* scales

Scoring the *VRIN* and *TRIN* validity scales requires an additional beginning step. The examiner needs to transfer the item responses for these scale items from the answer sheet to the *VRIN* and *TRIN* recording grids that present pairs of 42 and 21 items, respectively, in two adjacent columns. The examiner places the scoring templates over the recording grid—not over the answer sheet as was done with the other scales. It should be noted that there are two templates for *VRIN* (*VRIN-1* and *VRIN-2*) and two for *TRIN*, and the directions for scoring are printed on the recording grids. The examiner places the *VRIN-1* scoring template over the *VRIN* recording grid, once again lining the bars on the two sheets, and counts the number of blackened responses showing through the clear circles on the template. For each positive count, a "+" sign is recorded in the space to the right of the item columns. The same procedure is followed using the *VRIN-2* template. The examiner adds the total number of "+" signs to obtain the *VRIN* raw score, which is then transferred to the bottom of the Profile for Basic Scales. A slight variation of this procedure is needed for scoring *TRIN*. Similar to the method for *VRIN*, the examiner records "+" signs based on the *TRIN-1* template and then enters this total in the space provided at the bottom of the grid for *TRIN-1*. For *TRIN-2*, however, "−" signs are marked when the client endorses a pair of items in the critical direction. The sum of these "−" signs represent the *TRIN-2* total. The sum total of *TRIN-2* is subsequently deducted from the *TRIN-1* total and a constant of 9 is added to get the final *TRIN* score. This obtained *TRIN* raw score is then transferred to the bottom of the Profile for Basic Scales. Figure 3.1 presents a sample of the *TRIN* Scale recording grid.

In summary, the full range of standard MMPI-A scales can be handscored.

Minnesota Multiphasic
Personality Inventory— ADOLESCENT™

James N. Butcher, Carolyn L. Williams, John R. Graham, Robert P. Archer,
Auke Tellegen, Yossef S. Ben-Porath, and Beverly Kaemmer
S. R. Hathaway and J. C. McKinley

14 ⓉⒻ	424 ⓉⒻ	_____
37 ⓉⒻ	168 ⓉⒻ	_____
46 ⓉⒻ	475 ⓉⒻ	_____
53 ⓉⒻ	91 ⓉⒻ	_____
60 ⓉⒻ	121 ⓉⒻ	_____
62 ⓉⒻ	360 ⓉⒻ	_____
63 ⓉⒻ	120 ⓉⒻ	_____
70 ⓉⒻ	223 ⓉⒻ	_____
71 ⓉⒻ	283 ⓉⒻ	_____
82 ⓉⒻ	316 ⓉⒻ	_____
95 ⓉⒻ	294 ⓉⒻ	_____
119 ⓉⒻ	184 ⓉⒻ	_____
128 ⓉⒻ	465 ⓉⒻ	_____
146 ⓉⒻ	167 ⓉⒻ	_____
158 ⓉⒻ	288 ⓉⒻ	_____
242 ⓉⒻ	260 ⓉⒻ	_____
245 ⓉⒻ	257 ⓉⒻ	_____
264 ⓉⒻ	331 ⓉⒻ	_____
304 ⓉⒻ	335 ⓉⒻ	_____
355 ⓉⒻ	367 ⓉⒻ	_____
463 ⓉⒻ	476 ⓉⒻ	_____

RECORDING GRID
TRIN Scale
(True Response Inconsistency)

The TRIN scale is made up of 21 items that are opposite in
content. If a subject responds inconsistently by answering True to both
items of certain pairs, one point is added to the TRIN score; if the
subject responds inconsistently by answering False to certain item pairs,
one point is subtracted. (Refer to the *MMPI-A Manual for Administration,
Scoring, and Interpretation* for directions on interpreting scores.)

Directions for scoring:

1. Transfer responses to the item pairs from the answer
   sheet to the recording grid on the right by blackening in the
   appropriate circle:
   Example: If response to item 14 was False: 14 Ⓣ●

2. Place the scoring template TRIN-1 over the grid; in the blank
   provided in the third column, enter a "+" (plus sign) for each item
   pair in which both template boxes show a blackened response.
   Example: the response   14 ●Ⓕ   424 ●Ⓕ   would receive a "+"
   because both template boxes show a blackened response.

3. Count the number of "+"s and enter the TRIN-1 total.

4. Place the TRIN-2 scoring template over the grid; in the blank
   provided in the third column, enter a "-" (minus sign) for each item
   pair in which both template boxes show a blackened response.

5. Count the number of "-"s and enter the TRIN-2 total.

6. Subtract the TRIN-2 total from the TRIN-1 total and enter the result.

7. Add 9 points to obtain the TRIN total.
   Example: TRIN-1 total   2
            TRIN-2 total   −1
                          ────
                            1
                          +9
                          ────
            TRIN Total   10

TRIN-1 _____

− TRIN-2 _____

= _____

+9

TRIN TOTAL _____

Figure 3.1   TRIN Scale Recording Grid

DON'T FORGET

Points to Remember for Handscoring the MMPI-A

- Score the validity scales ($VRIN, TRIN, F, F_1, F_2, L$ and K) first to determine whether the profile is valid for interpretation.
- Score the MMPI-A item responses from the answer sheet for
  (1) basic scales,
  (2) Harris-Lingoes and Si subscales, and
  (3) content and supplementary scales.
- For scoring $VRIN$ and $TRIN$ scales, remember to first transfer the relevant item responses to the recording grid. Place the templates over the recording grid and follow the instructions on the grid.
- Use the gender-appropriate scoring template for all scales and pay particular attention to the gender-appropriate template for scale 5 (Mf).

The clinician who uses a handscoring method would be advised to score validity scales $VRIN, TRIN, F, F_1, F_2, L$, and K and determine whether the profile is valid for interpretation before scoring the other scales, in order to avoid the wasteful effort of scoring 62 more scales that ultimately would not be interpreted.

Computerized Scoring Procedures

There are different computer-scoring methods available to the test user depending on whether he or she uses the Microtest Q Assessment System software or the Mail-in Scoring option. One commonly used format based on the Microtest Q software is for the examiner to manually enter the adolescent's *True* or *False* responses for each item into a personal computer (PC) unit using a keyboard. Alternatively, the client could directly enter his or her responses on the computer instead of using the paper-and-pencil format. Both of these methods of item-response entry allow the item responses to be processed immediately into raw score and *T*-score results. Using the Microtest Q system does require certain hardware features such as having an IBM-compatible PC, a CD-ROM drive for software installation, current or recent versions of a Pentium processor and Microsoft Windows, and minimum requirements of RAM and available MB space. Specifics may be found in the NCS catalog or website (mentioned in Chapter 2). Another option, in place of key entry, involves scanning the item responses marked on the answer sheet using the NCS Opscan® scanner. The examiner who opts for mail-in scoring mails or faxes the mail-in answer sheet to NCS Assessments for processing; the results are mailed back by regular mail or by overnight delivery if the next-day delivery option is selected.

Computer scoring yields either a Basic Scale Profile Report or an Extended Score Report, depending on the amount of information sought by the examiner. The Basic Scale Profile Report provides a single-page profile of the validity and clinical scales and also lists the raw and T scores for each scale as well as the Welsh code (to be described shortly) to summarize the overall profile. This report also gives some additional information, such as the Response % for each scale, and the Percent True and Percent False response rates, which are auxiliary indices to detect whether the adolescent has responded with a style that disregards item content. In addition to the Basic Scales Profile, the Extended Score Report offers a separate Content Scale Profile followed by a Supplementary Score Report, which lists the raw and T scores for the supplementary scales and the Harris-Lingoes and Si subscales. It also provides a printout of the item responses paralleling the answer sheet. If the clinician opts to use the computer-scoring option, it is recommended that he or she routinely obtain the Extended Score Report because the content, supplementary, and Harris-Lingoes subscale data are essential to the interpretation process. Those using a computer-scoring method should be aware that the profiles will not print if the age of the adolescent entered in the demographic section is outside the 14 to 18 range.

THE MMPI-A NORMS

Standard Adolescent Norms

As noted in Chapter 1, the MMPI-A norms are based on the 1,620 adolescents (805 boys and 815 girls) in the standardization sample who fall in the age range of 14 through 18 years. In contrast to the Marks and Briggs (1972) adolescent norms provided for the original MMPI that were subdivided into four separate sets by age

---

CAUTION

Avoiding Common Errors in Scoring the MMPI-A

When Handscoring:
- align the scoring template with the answer sheet.
- exclude the double-marked items from the raw-score count.
- recheck your raw-score count.

When computer scoring:
- ensure that the correct (T or F) response is key-entered for each item, and recheck as needed.

When using mail-in scoring:
- use the optically scannable answer sheet that is specific to this method.

groupings, the MMPI-A norms consist of a single norm set for the entire age range. This is because research conducted during the test's development revealed that there were no significant differences in mean scale scores as a function of age within this age span. However, similar to the original MMPI and the MMPI-2, separate norms are provided for males and females due to the fact that numerous studies have indicated different item response patterns by males and females. In the MMPI-A standardization and clinical samples, item endorsement frequencies were substantially different for boys and girls on many items. For example, a review of Table E-2 in the MMPI-A manual (Butcher et al., 1992) reveals that:

- 63.8% of girls but only 30.2% of boys in the normative sample endorsed Item 21, "At times I have fits of laughing and crying that I cannot control."
- Normal boys were more likely than girls to endorse Item 60, "My feelings are not easily hurt" at a rate of 49.6%, compared to 23.4% for girls.

In the clinical sample of 420 boys and 293 girls that was collected during the test development process:

- Only 48.8% of girls compared to 62.9% of boys endorsed Item 146, "I do not tire quickly."

Scale 5 of the MMPI-A, which is directly related to masculine and feminine interests and contains items such as "I enjoy reading love stories," "I very much like hunting," "I keep a diary," and "I think I would like the work of a building contractor," predictably produces different response patterns by boys and girls. Thus, the MMPI-A norms are gender-based norms in that *T*-score conversions were developed separately for males and females.

It should also be noted that the MMPI-A norms described here are the national norms, based on representative sampling of adolescents in terms of geographic region, ethnicity, and selected socioeconomic indicators. Specifically, the standardization sample was collected in eight states across all four geographic regions of the United States. The sample represented White, Black, Asian, American Indian, Hispanic, and "Other" ethnic groups. The adolescent samples' parental education ranged from grade school to graduate school, and nine categories of parental occupational status, ranging from high-level professional to unemployed, were represented. The MMPI-A norms replace the multiple adolescent norms sets that existed for the original MMPI and present a common yardstick for the evaluation of adolescents in North America. Adult (MMPI-2) norms should *not* be used with adolescents under the age of 18. Several studies (e.g., Archer, 1984; Ehrenworth & Archer, 1985) have clearly demonstrated that the use of adult norms erroneously makes adolescents appear much more disturbed than they appear on age-appropriate norms.

The development of the national norms involved transforming the raw scores into *T*-score values, which are standard scores with a mean of 50 and standard deviation of 10. In contrast to the linear *T*-score transformation procedure used for the original MMPI, the *T* scores for the MMPI-A basic scales (excluding the validity scales and the nonclinical scales *5* and *0*) and content scales were developed using a uniform *T*-score transformation method. This change was based on the observation that MMPI clinical and content scales tend to have positively skewed distributions rather than a normal distribution, and each scale is also somewhat differently skewed. A linear *T*-score transformation retains the skew and results in different percentile values for a given *T*-score value across these scales. The uniform *T*-score transformation provides an adjustment that permits percentile equivalence across the scales, which enables the test interpreter to compare the scale scores directly with each other, without altering the underlying skewness of the scale distributions. Linear *T*-score transformations were, however, retained for the MMPI-A supplementary scales and the Harris-Lingoes and *Si* subscales.

Norms for 12- and 13-Year-Olds

The age criteria for the MMPI-A described in Chapter 2 indicate that the test can be used judiciously with 12- and 13-year-olds who are bright and developmentally comparable to adolescents 14 and older. The key issues are that the test items are relevant to their life experiences and that they are able to understand the test items and respond to them in a valid manner. Archer (1992) collected a separate set of norms for 13-year-old adolescents (81 boys and 144 girls), which is provided in the appendixes to his 1992 and 1997 texts. These norms are based on linear *T*-score transformations of raw scores. The test user is cautioned that these norms are not intended for routine use, but they may be used in certain cases when the clinician seeks to evaluate a younger adolescent and compare his or her functioning to that of other younger teenagers as well as adolescents in general. Archer (1992, 1997) and Archer and Krishnamurthy (1996) further state that the norms for 13-year-olds are not a substitute for the standard MMPI-A norms. Rather, the examiner is advised to derive a set of profiles based on standard norms (entering the adolescent's age as 14 for the purpose of computer scoring) and superimpose the profile based on the norms for 13-year-olds. This procedure enables the clinician to examine points of divergence and refine profile interpretation.

CONSTRUCTING THE MMPI-A PROFILE

The Basic Scale Profile

The MMPI-A Profile for Basic Scales is the starting point for profile development. Information concerning the examinee (name, address, grade level, age) and testing-related information (date of testing, setting, referral source, scorer identification) are entered in the upper right section of the profile sheet. Figure 3.2 presents an MMPI-A Basic Scale Profile Sheet for females. Again, examiners should note that the Basic Scale Profile Sheet is two-sided, with one side presenting female norms and the other side presenting male norms. In the earlier stages of handscoring the MMPI-A, the examiner would have already obtained the raw scores for the validity and basic clinical scales and recorded the raw scores in the bottom row of the profile sheet. Next, the examiner locates the raw score value for each scale on the ascending column of raw scores printed on the profile sheet for each scale, and marks an "X" or a dot at that point. This identifies the T-score value for the scale along the vertical T-score scale presented at the right and left corners of the profile sheet. The examiner should note that for the *TRIN* validity scale there are two adjacent columns of raw scores pertaining to response biases in the *True* and *False* directions, respectively. The examiner is advised to write a *T* or an *F* beside the raw score point to indicate clearly whether there was an acquiescent or nay-saying direction to the response style.

One important point to remember concerns scale *5* on the profile form for females where the raw score values are in descending, rather than ascending, order. This occurs because scale *5* is developed as a bipolar scale with lower scores representing a feminine orientation using female norms and a masculine orientation based on the male norms. The examiner who overlooks the direction of the raw scores could, for example, incorrectly locate a raw score of 27 for females at the $T = 64$ point (≥ 1 SD from the mean) instead of the $T = 53$ point (within the normal range), which would influence the interpretation of the scale score. Profiling the basic scales is completed by connecting the data points separately for validity and clinical scales.

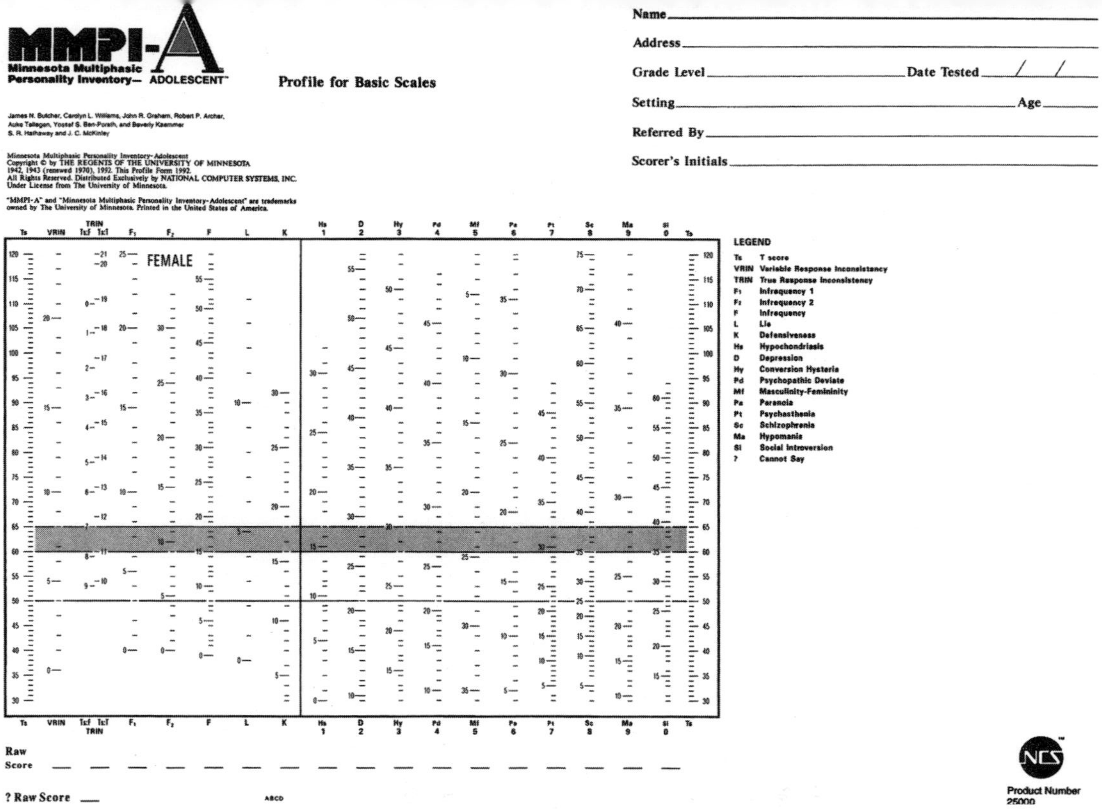

Figure 3.2 Profile for Basic Scales

Minnesota Multiphasic Personality Inventory–Adolescent (MMPI-A). Copyright © the Regents of the University of Minnesota 1942, 1943 (renewed 1970), 1992. Reproduced by permission of the publisher: "Minnesota Multiphasic Personality Inventory–Adolescent" and "MMPI-A" are trademarks owned by the University of Minnesota.

Examiners who have used the MMPI-2 to evaluate their adult clients would be familiar with a *K*-correction procedure that involves adding the *K*-scale raw score value, or a fraction of it, to the raw scores for scales *1, 4, 7, 8,* and *9* before deriving the final raw- and *T*-score values for those scales. The MMPI-A, however, does not use a *K*-correction procedure. This follows the approach used on the original MMPI for adolescents where *K* correction was not attempted because research indicated that it does not produce an improvement to adolescents' profile accuracy. More recent research with the MMPI-A also found that *K* correction did not improve profile accuracy (Alperin, Archer, & Coates, 1996).

The MMPI-A Basic Scale Profile Sheet (as well as the Content and Supplementary Scale Profile Sheet) contains a horizontal line at the *T* = 50 level, which denotes the average score for scales as found for the MMPI-A normative sample. Another line at the *T* = 60 level represents 1 standard deviation (SD) above the mean and marks the beginning of the marginal range of elevation. The gray or shaded zone between *T* scores of 60 and 65 is a new feature on the MMPI-A that reflects the marginal elevation range. The *T* = 65 line represents the level at which a scale is considered clinically elevated. Chapter 4 describes what these elevations mean and provides a strategy for interpreting marginally and clinically elevated scores.

The Content and Supplementary Scale Profile

The MMPI-A Profile for Content and Supplementary Scales is organized in a similar manner to the Basic Scale Profile, with the identifying information section at the upper right corner, a row of spaces for raw score values at the bottom of the profile sheet, raw score ranges in ascending order for each scale, and corresponding *T* scores at the right and left ends of the profile. The examiner marks the raw score data points for each scale and connects them separately for content and supplementary scales. Figure 3.3 shows a sample of the profile form, which is plotted on male norms.

The Harris-Lingoes and *Si* Subscale Profile

The MMPI-A has a third profile sheet devoted to the various subscales that identify the content domains of several of the basic scales. This profile presents the Harris-Lingoes subscales developed for the original MMPI and the more recently developed *Si* subscales. The legend on the profile sheet provides the complete scale name for each of the subscale acronyms and should help the test pro-

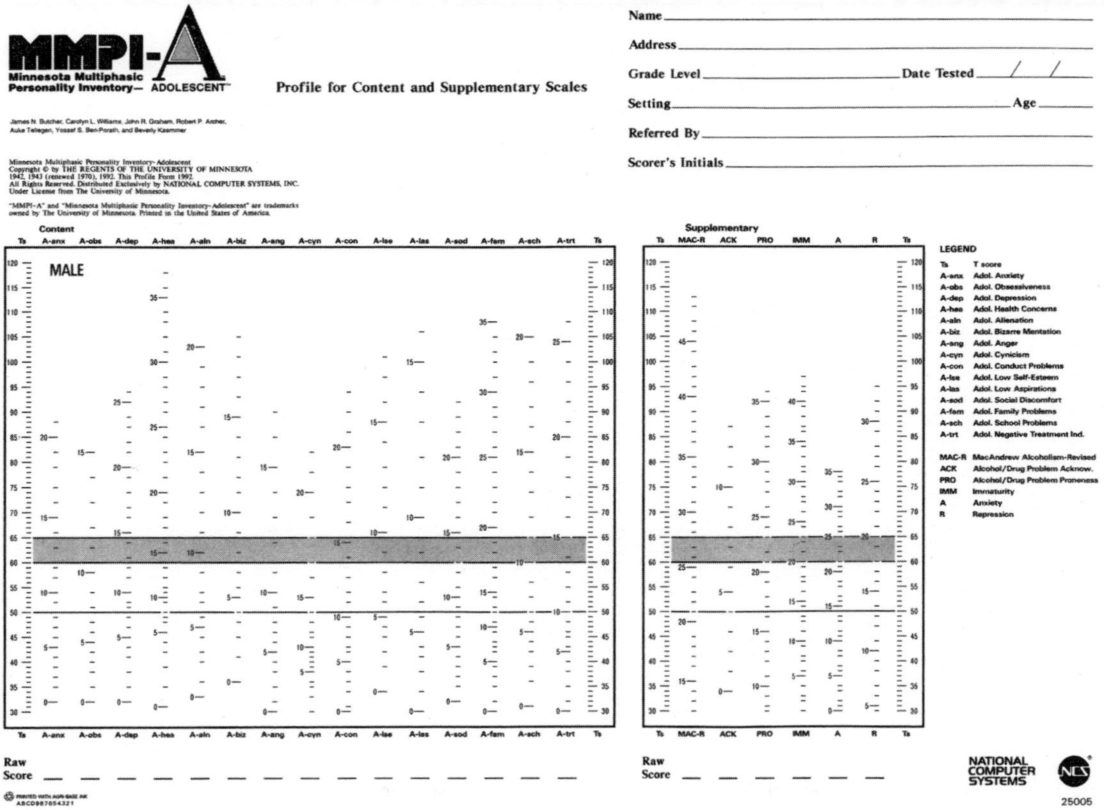

Figure 3.3 Profile for Content and Supplementary Scales

Minnesota Multiphasic Personality Inventory–Adolescent (MMPI-A). Copyright © the Regents of the University of Minnesota 1942, 1943 (renewed 1970), 1992. Reproduced by permission of the publisher: "Minnesota Multiphasic Personality Inventory–Adolescent" and "MMPI-A" are trademarks owned by the University of Minnesota.

DON'T FORGET

Points to Remember in Developing the MMPI-A Profile

- Make sure you fill in the *(?)* raw score on the bottom left of the Profile for Basic Scales.
- Use the gender-appropriate norms (i.e., profile sheet for males versus females).
- On the Basic Scale Profile Sheet, remember that the raw scores are in *descending* order for scale 5 for females, whereas all other raw scores for males and females are in ascending order.
- On the validity scale section of the Basic Scale Profile Sheet, write *T* or *F* beside the appropriate raw score point for *TRIN*.
- Remember that a K-correction procedure is *not* used for the MMPI-A.
- Provide the Welsh code for the basic scales.

filer avoid confusion when plotting the profile. Figure 3.4 presents a sample of this profile form using norms for females.

The Profile for Harris-Lingoes and *Si* Subscales differs from the Basic Scale and the Content and Supplementary Scale Profile Sheets in that a shaded zone between the $T = 60$ and $T = 65$ range does not appear for the subscales. This alerts the clinician to interpret only scales at elevations of T score ≥ 65, an issue that is addressed in the next chapter.

CODING THE MMPI-A BASIC SCALE PROFILE

Application of the Welsh Coding Procedure

The original MMPI had a profile coding procedure (initially developed by Hathaway, 1947, and later modified by Welsh, 1948) to summarize the profile elevation features of the basic scales. The Welsh code became the standard approach to delineate the patterns evident across the validity scales *L, F,* and *K* and the clinical scales *1* through *0,* and particularly to identify the high-point scales or codetypes of the profile. Until a couple of decades ago, it was routine practice for psychologists to report the Welsh code in their psychological test reports, thus enabling the reader to reproduce the Basic Scale Profile in the absence of access to the Basic Scale Profile form. Although the Welsh code is less commonly employed today, examiners continue to use it for the MMPI-A and MMPI-2, and it has been slightly revised for these tests to improve its use. Specifically, the Welsh code traditionally

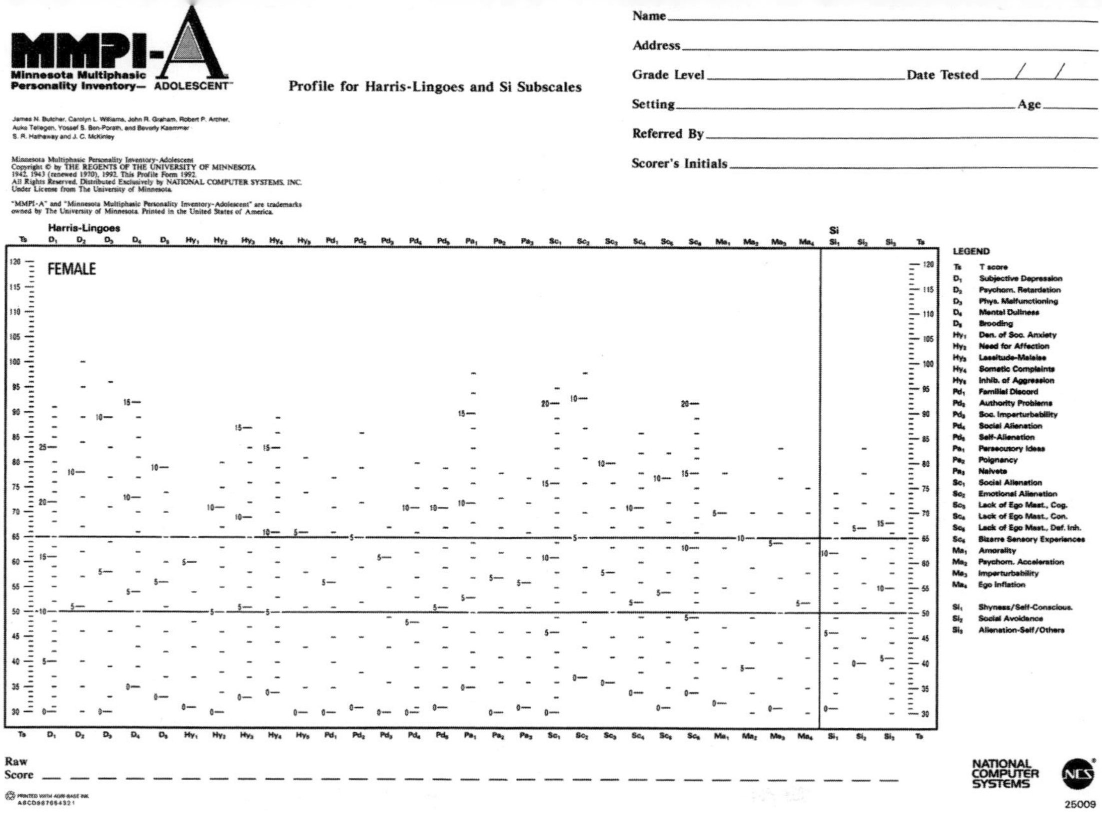

Figure 3.4 Profile for Harris-Lingoes and Si Subscales

Minnesota Multiphasic Personality Inventory–Adolescent (MMPI-A). Copyright © the Regents of the University of Minnesota 1942, 1943 (renewed 1970), 1992. Reproduced by permission of the publisher: "Minnesota Multiphasic Personality Inventory-Adolescent" and "MMPI-A" are trademarks owned by the University of Minnesota.

consists of symbols designating intervals of 10 T-score points. However, given the importance of the T = 65 level in determining clinical elevations, separate symbols are now provided for the 5-point T-score ranges of 60 to 64 and 65 to 69, respectively. The validity scales represented in the Welsh code continue to be limited to scales F, L, and K, despite the development of several newer validity scales.

Developing the Welsh code requires the examiner to initially arrange the basic clinical scales, designated by their numerical labels, in descending order from the highest to the lowest in terms of T-score elevation. An example would be as follows:

Highest ← 4   9   6   8   3   1   2   5   7   0   → Lowest

The validity scales are similarly organized from highest to lowest and are placed after the clinical scales. In the case of two or more scales that are at an identical T-score level, the convention is for the scale with the lower number to be listed first. Thus, if scales *3* and *1* are identical in elevation, scale *1* is listed before scale *3*. The symbols presented in Rapid Reference 3.1 are then inserted to the immediate right of a scale or scales that fall within the T-score range represented by the symbol. For example, if scale *4* in the preceding example had a T score of 75 and scale *9* was elevated at a T score of 66, the initial part of the Welsh code would be 4'9+. If both scales *4* and *9* fell in the 70 to 79 T-score range and the next highest scale, scale *6*, achieved a T score of 68, the code would begin as 49'6+. Some additional rules also apply. Scales that are identical in elevation or separated by only 1 T-score point are grouped by a shared underline. If no scales fall within a given T-score range, the symbol for that range is nonetheless recorded after the preceding symbol, such that no in-between symbols are omitted. The symbols at the upper and lower end of the entire range can, however, be omitted if they are considered superfluous.

A complete Welsh code can be illustrated based on the same ordering of scales as in the previous example, with the addition of the validity scales and provision of the T-score values for all basic scales, as shown in Figure 3.5.

Scale:	4	9	6	8	3	1	2	5	7	0	*K*	*L*	*F*
T score:	85	75	69	67	66	60	60	54	51	46	63	46	42

The above listing shows that the clinical and validity scales seen in the profile have been ordered from highest to lowest T scores. The resulting Welsh code would be: 4"9'*683*+*12*–57/0: *K*–/*LF*:

═Rapid Reference 3.1

Symbols for Welsh Coding

Symbol	T-Score Range
**	100 and above
*	90–99
"	80–89
'	70–79
+	65–69
–	60–64
/	50–59
:	40–49
#	30–39

Note: No symbol for T scores of 29 and below; write the scale number to the right of #.

New Optional Symbols for Higher-Range Scores

Symbol	T-Score Range
!	110–119
!!	120 and above

THE MMPI-A STRUCTURAL SUMMARY

Scores from the MMPI-A profiles can be further organized by using the MMPI-A Structural Summary form, developed by Archer and Krishnamurthy (1994) and presented in Figure 3.6. The upper section of the form provides a relatively quick and easy mechanism for identifying deviant test-taking attitudes that would affect profile interpretation, while the main component of the Structural Summary form provides a means for determining which of the eight factor-based MMPI-A scale groupings are most important in describing the adolescent's functioning.

The test-taking attitudes section of the MMPI-A Structural Summary concerns validity-related issues of response omissions, consistency of response, and accuracy of response reflected in the absence of overreporting and underreporting response sets. This segment precedes the core section of the Structural Summary because the examiner has to ascertain the validity of the MMPI-A profile

Figure 3.5 Profile for Basic Scales: Welsh Coding

Minnesota Multiphasic Personality Inventory–Adolescent (MMPI-A). Copyright © the Regents of the University of Minnesota 1942, 1943 (renewed 1970), 1992. Reproduced by permission of the publisher: "Minnesota Multiphasic Personality Inventory–Adolescent" and "MMPI-A" are trademarks owned by the University of Minnesota.

MMPI-A Structural Summary
Robert P. Archer and Radhika Krishnamurthy

Name: _____   Date: _____

Age: _____   Grade: _____

Gender: _____   School: _____

Test-Taking Attitudes

1. Omissions (raw score total)

_____ ? (Cannot Say scale)

2. Consistency (T-score values)

_____ VRIN

_____ TRIN

_____ F_1 vs. _____ F_2

3. Accuracy (check if condition present)

Overreport

_____ F scale T score ≥ 90

_____ All clinical scales except 5 and 0 ≥ 60

Underreport

_____ High L (T ≥ 65)

_____ High K (T ≥ 65)

_____ All clinical scales except 5 and 0 < 60

Factor Groupings
(enter T-score data)

1. General Maladjustment

_____ Welsh's A

_____ Scale 7

_____ Scale 8

_____ Scale 2

_____ Scale 4

_____ D_1 (Subjective Depression)

_____ D_4 (Mental Dullness)

_____ D_5 (Brooding)

_____ Hy_3 (Lassitude-Malaise)

_____ Sc_1 (Social Alienation)

_____ Sc_2 (Emotional Alienation)

_____ Sc_3 (Lack of Ego Mastery – Cognitive)

_____ Sc_4 (Lack of Ego Mastery – Conative)

_____ Si_3 (Alienation)

_____ Pd_4 (Social Alienation)

_____ Pd_5 (Self-Alienation)

_____ Pa_2 (Poignancy)

_____ A-dep

_____ A-anx

_____ A-lse

_____ A-aln

_____ A-obs

_____ A-trt

__/23 Number of scales with T ≥ 60

2. Immaturity

_____ IMM

_____ Scale F

_____ Scale 8

_____ Scale 6

_____ ACK

_____ MAC-R

_____ Pa_1 (Persecutory Ideas)

_____ Sc_2 (Emotional Alienation)

_____ Sc_6 (Bizarre Sensory Experiences)

_____ A-sch

_____ A-biz

_____ A-aln

_____ A-con

_____ A-fam

_____ A-trt

__/15 Number of scales with T ≥ 60

Figure 3.6 MMPI-A Structural Summary

3. Disinhibition/Excitatory Potential

_____ Scale 9
_____ Ma_2 (Psychomotor Acceleration)
_____ Ma_4 (Ego Inflation)
_____ Sc_5 (Lack of Ego Mastery, Defective Inhibition)
_____ D_2 (Psychomotor Retardation) (low score)*
_____ Welsh's R (low score)*
_____ Scale K (low score)*
_____ Scale L (low score)*
_____ A-ang
_____ A-cyn
_____ A-con
_____ MAC-R

_____/12 Number of scales with $T \geq 60$ or ≤ 40 for scales with asterisk

4. Social Discomfort

_____ Scale 0
_____ Si_1 (Shyness/Self-Consciousness)
_____ Hy_1 (Denial of Social Anxiety) (low score)*
_____ Pd_3 (Social Imperturbability) (low score)*
_____ Ma_3 (Imperturbability) (low scores)*
_____ A-sod
_____ A-lse
_____ Scale 7

_____/8 Number of scales with $T \geq 60$ or $T \leq 40$ for scales with asterisk

5. Health Concerns

_____ Scale 1
_____ Scale 3
_____ A-hea
_____ Hy_4 (Somatic Complaints)
_____ Hy_3 (Lassitude-Malaise)
_____ D_3 (Physical Malfunctioning)

_____/6 Number of scales with $T \geq 60$

6. Naivete

_____ A-cyn (low score)*
_____ Pa_3 (Naivete)
_____ Hy_2 (Need for Affection)
_____ Si_3 (Alienation–Self and Others) (low score)*
_____ Scale K

_____/5 Number of scales with $T \geq 60$ or $T \leq 40$ for scales with asterisk

7. Familial Alienation

_____ Pd_1 (Familial Discord)
_____ A-fam
_____ Scale 4
_____ PRO

_____/4 Number of scales with $T \geq 60$

8. Psychoticism

_____ Pa_1 (Persecutory Ideas)
_____ Scale 6
_____ A-biz
_____ Sc_6 (Bizarre Sensory Experiences)

_____/4 Number of scales with $T \geq 60$

Note. The presentation of scales under each factor label is generally organized in a descending order from the best to the least effective marker. Within this overall approach, scales are grouped logically in terms of basic clinical scales, Harris-Lingoes and _Si_ subscales, and content scales. The majority of scales included in this summary sheet were correlated $\geq .60$ or $\leq -.60$ with the relevant factor for the MMPI-A normative sample.

PAR **Psychological Assessment Resources, Inc.**
P.O. Box 998/Odessa, Florida 33556/Toll-Free 1-800-331-TEST

Figure 3.6 Continued

before attempting to interpret the factor patterns. Each of these validity issues is addressed in more detail in Chapter 4 and our presentation here is limited to how these data are encoded on the Structural Summary form. The user fills in the number of item omissions that were previously recorded on the Profile for Basic Scales, and transfers the T scores from the Basic Scale Profile for scales $VRIN$, $TRIN$, F_1 and F_2. He or she would also note if any of the conditions listed under the Accuracy section were present. This completes the information needed for subsequent interpretation of profile validity.

The main section of the Structural Summary form presents groupings of MMPI-A scales and subscales that are organized into eight factor groupings. Within each grouping, scales are listed in descending order from those having the highest to lowest (but still substantial) correlation with the particular factor. For example, the First Factor, General Maladjustment, contains 23 scales ranging from Welsh's A scale, which is the strongest marker of the factor, to the A-trt content scale, which has a relatively weaker association with the factor. The user of this form could place checkmarks against those scales that are elevated at a T-score level ≥ 60 (in lieu of the directions presented on the form to record all T-score values for the scales). This procedure was supported by Krishnamurthy and Archer's recent (1999) research findings demonstrating that the results of a simple count of the number of scales and subscales elevated within a particular dimension are comparable to the results of computing the mean T-score value for each dimension. As addressed in Chapter 4, these checkmarks are used as a quick method of determining if the majority of scales or subscales within a given factor produce critical-range T scores, which would render that factor salient in the psychological description of the adolescent. The user should note that in certain instances, such as for Welsh's R, scale K, and scale L listed under the Disinhibition/Excitatory Potential dimension, he or she places a checkmark when the scale's T score is at ≤ 40, which is the critical direction for these scales. This exception only occurs for three factors—Disinhibition/Excitatory Potential, Social Discomfort, and Naivete—and requires some additional attention.

In summary, MMPI-A scoring involves a variety of steps and procedures that may appear somewhat complicated, particularly when a handscoring method is used. Computer-scoring methods are easier and more time-efficient but also require some attention to details and are generally more expensive than handscoring. Both methods become relatively effortless with experience. Scoring and obtaining the MMPI-A profiles provide the data needed for the crucial step of test interpretation.

TEST YOURSELF

I. **The standard MMPI-A norms are provided separately for**

   (a) ages 14, 15, 16, 17, and 18.

   (b) boys and girls.

   (c) inpatients and outpatients.

   (d) ethnic minority groups.

2. **A unique feature of the MMPI-A profile sheet compared to the original MMPI is**

   (a) the conversion of the item-omissions raw score to a scale score.

   (b) the development of a new K-correction procedure.

   (c) the presence of a shaded zone denoting marginal-range elevation.

   (d) the use of a *T* score of 70 and above to denote clinical elevation.

3. **Raw scores are transformed to uniform *T* scores for**

   (a) MMPI-A clinical scales except scales *5* and *0*.

   (b) MMPI-A content scales.

   (c) MMPI-A supplementary scales.

   (d) a and b.

4. **A new weighted scoring procedure is used for MMPI-A Harris-Lingoes subscales.** True or False?

5. **In selected instances, 19-year-old adolescents can be tested with the MMPI-A using the separate set of norms available for this age group.** True or False?

Answers: 1. b; 2. c; 3. d; 4. False; 5. False

Four

HOW TO INTERPRET THE MMPI-A

INTRODUCTION

The MMPI-A is a complex instrument and several guides have been developed to facilitate the interpretation of this test, including the MMPI-A manual (Butcher et al., 1992), and textbooks on this topic by Archer (1997) and by Butcher and Williams (2000). The purpose of this chapter is to provide a concise review of basic interpretation approaches to the MMPI-A, and to summarize the extensive correlate literature available for many of the MMPI-A scales and subscales. It is important to stress at the onset, however, that the MMPI-A should always be interpreted within the context of information about the adolescent's history, background information, clinical interview findings, and the results of other psychological test instruments. While it is possible to interpret the MMPI-A in a "blind" fashion without such background data concerning the adolescent, such an approach is never desirable and inherently yields less accurate MMPI-A test information. For example, consideration of the adolescent's level of cooperation and intellectual ability often provides crucial information in understanding and interpreting the MMPI-A validity scales. Knowledge of the adolescent's academic history also provides a much richer context within which to interpret findings from MMPI-A scales related to academic performance issues, while knowledge of the adolescent's medical history may help to interpret scores on measures of physical health and functioning. To give additional examples, knowledge of an adolescent's neuropsychological history or drug and alcohol use may dramatically effect interpretation of scales containing infrequently endorsed items, while understanding of the adolescent's family and interpersonal history may provide crucial clues in interpreting scales related to these important domains. In short, the MMPI-A should always be interpreted within a much broader context that includes information and data from multiple sources.

In the following sections we review the descriptions and interpretations of MMPI-A scales and subscales based on natural or logical groupings. We begin by reviewing the validity scales, present a model of validity assessment, and discuss how each of the validity indices are used in application of this model. We then turn to a review of the MMPI basic scales and subscales and present individual scale and configural interpretation guidelines. The use of content and supplementary scales in refining interpretive output from the MMPI-A is also presented. Next, we discuss the development, description, and application of the MMPI-A Structural Summary. Finally, under the heading of "Putting it All Together," we summarize these interpretation steps or stages and provide a brief overview of the uses and limitations of computerized interpretive reports.

EVALUATING PROFILE VALIDITY

The Validity Scales

The interpretation of the MMPI-A begins with an evaluation of the validity of the MMPI-A profile. There are several primary measures on the MMPI-A designed to assess the extent to which the adolescent has provided consistent and accurate responses to test items, which would help determine if a meaningful interpretation of clinical scales is possible. The following sections present each of these validity scales and subscales.

Cannot Say (?) Indicator

The *Cannot Say* (?) Indicator consists of the total number of items that an adolescent fails to answer, or answers in both the *True* and *False* directions. Thus, the *Cannot Say* measure is not a formal MMPI-A scale because it does not have a fixed or a consistent item pool. Adolescents may omit MMPI-A items for a variety of reasons, including limitations in intellectual functioning or reading ability, carelessness in responding to test items, or as an expression of oppositional tendencies. Research on the content of items more frequently omitted on the MMPI and MMPI-A indicate that adolescents tend to omit items in more sensitive categories such as drug and alcohol use or sexuality, as well as items that are more complex and difficult to read.

In general, greater item omissions produce lower scores on MMPI-A scales.

Most adolescents leave 10 or fewer items unanswered in the test booklet. This level of item omission does not have serious consequences in terms of profile distortion and does not create interpretation problems. Item omissions ranging from 11 through 30 items are higher than would typically be expected and may indicate that the adolescent has significant reading problems or is indecisive or careless. However, this level of item omission is still consistent with a valid interpretation of the MMPI-A protocol. *Cannot Say* scores of 31 or more are quite rare and render the overall profile invalid and uninterpretable. Under these circumstances, an effort may be made to request that the adolescent complete unanswered items *if* the clinician is able to rule out the presence of a significant reading disability or intellectual limitation that would contraindicate valid completion of the test items.

Response Consistency Scales

The *Variable Response Inconsistency* (*VRIN*) and *True Response Inconsistency* (*TRIN*) scales are innovative validity scales designed to measure the extent to which the adolescent has responded to the MMPI-A booklet in a consistent manner. The *VRIN* and *TRIN* scales consist of specifically selected pairs of items. The members of each *VRIN* item pair are either similar or opposite in content, and each pair is scored for the occurrence of a logical inconsistency in the response to the two items. For example, responding *True* to Item 70 ("I am certainly lacking in self-confidence") and *True* to Item 223 ("I am entirely self-confident") results in a point being added to the *VRIN* scale. The raw score on the *VRIN* scale is simply the total number of item pairs answered inconsistently. A markedly elevated *VRIN* score ($T \geq 80$) indicates that the adolescent may have answered the items in an indiscriminate manner and that the MMPI-A protocol is invalid and uninterpretable.

The *TRIN* scale, unlike the *VRIN* scale, is based solely on item pairs that are opposite in content. Thus, if a client responds inconsistently by answering *True* to two items that are opposite in meaning or content, one point is added to the *TRIN* score; if a client responds inconsistently by answering *False* to opposite item pairs, one point is subtracted from the total. Based on this scoring approach, a high *TRIN* score indicates a tendency for the test participant to indiscriminately answer *True* to the items, and thus reflects an acquiescence response set. In contrast, a very low *TRIN* raw score indicates a tendency on the part of the adolescent to answer *False* indiscriminately and reflects a "nay-saying" or nonacquiescence response set. *TRIN T* scores, however, are scaled in such a way that they increase as they deviate from the mean in either direction, so that both the acquiescence and the nonacquiescence (or nay-saying) response patterns result in elevated *T* scores. As in the case of the *T*-score cutoff for the *VRIN* score, *TRIN T* scores ≥ 80 indicate acquiescence or nay-saying responding to an extent that invalidates the MMPI-A protocol.

Frequency Measures

The original MMPI *F* scale consisted of 64 items that were selected based on the criterion that no more than 10% of the Minnesota normative adult sample answered those items in a deviant direction. As a result of this development process, the *F* scale has often been referred to as the *Frequency* or *Infrequency* scale. The *F* scale includes a variety of items related to strange and unusual experiences, paranoid or psychotic symptoms, and antisocial or asocial attitudes and behaviors.

Prior to the development of the MMPI-A, it was apparent that adolescents produced marked elevations on the original *F* scale because many of the *F*-scale items did not function effectively for this age group. Stated differently, adolescents often had an endorsement rate on the original MMPI that greatly exceeded 10% for several of the original *F*-scale items. Thus, the *F* scale underwent a major revision in the development of the MMPI-A, leading to the creation of a 66-item *F* scale. The scale was determined by selecting items endorsed in a deviant direction by no more than 20% of the 1,620 boys and girls in the MMPI-A normative sample. The first 33 of these items, which extend to roughly the midpoint of the test booklet, form the F_1 subscale, and the last 33 items to appear on the *F* scale (corresponding to the second half of the item pool) comprise the F_2 subscale.

Elevated scores on *F* or its subscales indicate that the adolescent is endorsing a high number of unusual or infrequently endorsed symptoms. Adolescents who produce marked or extreme elevations on the MMPI *F* scale may be attempting to "fake bad" or "overreport" symptomatology, may be engaging in a random response pattern, may be unable to adequately read and understand the item pool, or may be suffering from very severe psychiatric illness. In many cases, the use of other validity scales may help to clarify the reasons for an elevated *F* scale. For example, an elevated *F* scale combined with an elevated *VRIN* scale score might indicate an invalid response pattern caused by inadequate reading ability or random responding. In contrast, a normal range

VRIN score combined with a markedly elevated *F* scale suggests a tendency to overreport symptomatology in an adolescent who responded in a consistent but exaggerated manner. MMPI-A profiles with *F* scale *T* scores ≥ 90 are typically declared invalid and clinical interpretation of these protocols is unwarranted. The F_1 and F_2 subscales for the MMPI-A may be used in an interpretive strategy that takes advantage of the fact that these scales occupy the first half and second half of the item pool, respectively. For example, a normal range F_1 scale combined with an elevated F_2 value suggests an adolescent who has changed his or her test-taking approach in the latter stages of the test session in a manner that might reflect carelessness or random responding. Archer (1997) recommends that there should be a minimum difference between F_1 and F_2 of at least 20 *T*-score points before these subscales are viewed as substantially different in elevation level.

Measures of Defensiveness or Underreporting of Symptomatology: The *L* and *K* Scales

The MMPI-A *Lie* (*L*) scale consists of 14 items that were selected to identify adolescents who display unsophisticated or naïve attempts to present themselves in a favorable light and to deny common human foibles or failings. Adolescents who produce elevated *Lie* scores are responding to the MMPI-A item pool (either consciously or unconsciously) in a manner that denies relatively minor flaws or weaknesses and claims excessive virtue. The MMPI-A *Lie* scale covers a variety of content areas, including the denial of hostile or aggressive impulses, nonadmission of minor flaws or weaknesses, and the claim of an excessively high standard of virtuous or ethical behavior. Moderate elevations on the *L* scale (*T*-score values of 60–65) are related to an adolescent's need for conformity and denial, and marked elevations ($T \geq 65$) raise significant questions concerning the validity of the response protocol, particularly when they are combined with similar range elevations on the *Defensiveness* (*K*) scale. Because all of the 14 items on the *L* scale are keyed in the *False* direction, scores on this measure also serve as a valuable index (in conjunction with the *TRIN* scale) in detecting All-True and All-False response patterns.

The *K* scale consists of 30 items that were empirically selected to identify individuals who overtly displayed significant degrees of psychopathology but produce profiles that were within normal limits on the original MMPI. Elevated scores on the *K* scale indicate more subtle efforts to deny psychopathology and to present oneself in a guarded manner. All but one of these items are scored in the *True* direction; thus this scale also provides useful information (in conjunction with *TRIN*) concerning the presence of All-True or All-False response patterns. The item content of the *K* scale is quite diverse and covers issues ranging from interpersonal and family relationships to self-control. In addition to its role as a validity scale related to defensiveness, the use of a *K*-correction procedure for five of the basic scales has become standard practice with adult respondents. As noted in Chapter 3, this *K*-correction procedure is not used with adolescent profiles, either on the original MMPI or with the MMPI-A.

Elevations on the MMPI-A *K* scale are often produced by adolescents who are defensive and who are consciously or unconsciously underreporting psychological symptoms or problems. Furthermore, adolescents who produce elevated *K* scales often fail to perceive a need for psychological treatment and hide behind a façade of adequate adjustment and coping. In both the adolescent and adult MMPI literatures, *T*-score elevations ≥ 65 on the *K* scale reflect poorer prognoses for change and longer treatment durations.

A Conceptual Model for Validity Assessment

Greene (2000) has presented a conceptual model or approach for understanding validity assessment issues that emphasizes the use of sequential steps or stages in the validity assessment process. The first stage involves determining the number of items omitted, reflected in the *Cannot Say* value. Omitting more than 30 items requires test readministration. The next step in evaluating the validity of an adolescent's responses involves assessing the consistency of item endorsement, or the extent to which the adolescent describes his or her functioning in a logically consistent manner. Response inconsistency, evident in *VRIN* or *TRIN* scale elevations or markedly discrepant F_1 and F_2 scale scores, may be the result of a variety of processes including carelessness, marked indecisiveness, or impaired reading ability. Regardless of the cause, however, substantial inconsistency renders the MMPI-A profile invalid and prevents meaningful profile interpretation.

The final step in Greene's model of validity assessment involves assessing the extent to which the MMPI-A reflects accurate item endorsement. In this context, accuracy refers to the extent to which the item endorsement pattern produced by the adolescent reflects an undistorted and meaningful report of his or her level of symptomatology and psychological functioning. In this model, overreporting and underreporting of symptomatology represent points on a continuum, and any particular respondent may be placed at some point along this dimension of response accuracy. The most useful method for determining response accuracy involves investigating the configural pattern produced by the adolescent on MMPI-A validity scales F, L, and K. As we show in the following section, several important response sets are reflected in the relative evaluation of F in contrast to the T-score elevations found for L and K.

Effects of Response Sets on Validity Scales

Adolescents may consciously or unconsciously distort their responses to the MMPI-A to an extent that invalidates the meaningful interpretation of the resulting clinical profile. Some of these response sets are relatively easy to identify based upon the occurrence of certain salient characteristics or features, while others are more difficult to detect through the use of MMPI-A validity scales. The following section provides a brief summary of the effects of a variety of response sets on the MMPI-A.

All-True

The All-True response set is indicated by extremely low scores on scales L and K and markedly elevated scores on F, F_1, and F_2. The All-True Basic Scale Profile, plotted using the norms for adolescent females, is presented in Figure 4.1. The extreme elevation on the $TRIN$ scale indicates clearly an inconsistent response set in the acquiescence or "yea-saying" direction, combined with T-score values much above 90 on F, F_1, and F_2. There is a very noticeable positive or psychotic slope to the profile, with marked clinical range elevations on basic scales measuring *Paranoia (6)*, *Psychasthenia (7)*, *Schizophrenia (8)*, and *Hypomania (9)*.

All-False

The profile shown in Figure 4.2 results if an adolescent responds *False* to all of the MMPI-A items. Although Figure 4.2 exemplifies the All-False profile based on norms for adolescent males, the same general configuration would occur for females. The $TRIN$ scale is again markedly elevated, this time as a result of the extreme nay-saying response direction. In addition, MMPI-A validity scales L and K are both extremely elevated because these scales are composed primarily of items keyed in the *False* direction. In this case, the left-hand side of the basic clinical scale profile is elevated, particularly on the basic clinical scales *1, 2,* and *3*. Like the All-True profile, the All-False profile is relatively easy to detect based on its dramatically elevated characteristics.

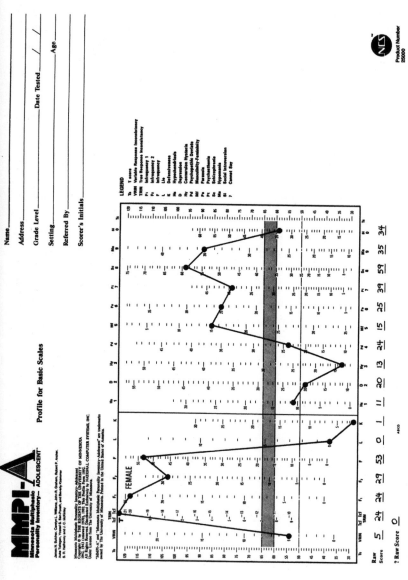

Figure 4.1 All-True Response Set

Minnesota Multiphasic PersonalityInventory–Adolescent (MMPI-A). Copyright © the Regents of the University of Minnesota 1942, 1943 (renewed 1970), 1992. Reproduced by permission of the publisher: "Minnesota Multiphasic Personality Inventory–Adolescent" and "MMPI-A" are trademarks owned by the University of Minnesota.

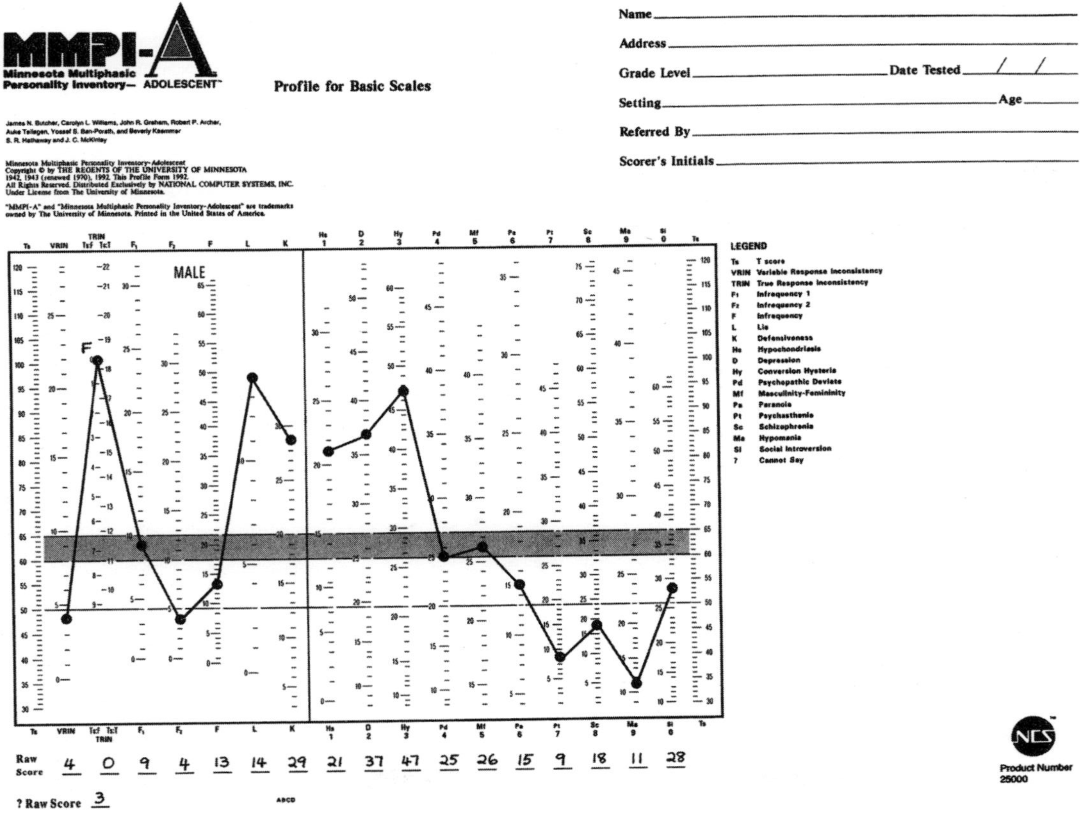

Figure 4.2 All-False Response Set

Minnesota Multiphasic Personality Inventory–Adolescent (MMPI-A). Copyright © the Regents of the University of Minnesota 1942, 1943 (renewed 1970). 1992. Reproduced by permission of the publisher: "Minnesota Multiphasic Personality Inventory–Adolescent" and "MMPI-A" are trademarks owned by the University of Minnesota.

Random Response Sets

Because an adolescent may respond randomly to the MMPI-A in a variety of ways or patterns, it is difficult to characterize a prototypic random response pattern. Nevertheless, the mean value produced by a large number of random profiles should closely parallel that presented in Figure 4.3. The most useful detector of a random response pattern is an elevation on the MMPI-A $VRIN$ scale, although it may be noted that the mean value for both boys and girls is only moderately elevated in the T-score range of 70 to 80. In addition, the random profile is characterized by a highly unusual validity scale configuration in which clinical range elevations occur on F, F_1, and F_2 as well as on the MMPI-A L scale. Again, the actual profile characteristics produced by a specific random response set vary substantially, depending on the particular approach used to randomize the response pattern. The clinician should always consider a random response pattern when an adolescent completes the MMPI-A in less than the expected 60 to 90 minutes, particularly when the response time is less than 45 minutes.

Underreporting and Overreporting Response Styles

Another response set found on the MMPI-A involves a distortion in the accuracy of responses by adolescents who consciously or unconsciously underreport or overreport problems on the MMPI-A. In addition to the terms "underreporting" and "overreporting," other authors have described these distortions in the accuracy of a participant's self-report as "positive self-presentation" versus "negative self-presentation." In general, the available literature with both adolescents and adults strongly suggests that it is often easier to detect an attempt to overreport symptomatology than an attempt to underreport symptoms. This is because most individuals who are attempting to overreport do so in a relatively general and unsophisticated manner, resulting in marked elevations on the F scale, and any protocols with F T-score values ≥ 90 generally indicate overreporting response sets. The classic overreporting response set pattern involves an extremely elevated F scale combined with low-range scores on validity scales L and K, as illustrated in the clinical case example from a 16-year-old boy in a residential treatment center (see Figure 4.4).

In contrast, detecting underreporting response styles appears more problematic. An underreporting response style typically involves marked elevations on L and K combined with relatively low scores on F, as illustrated in the clinical case example of a 15-year-old girl evaluated in an inpatient treatment setting (see Figure 4.5).

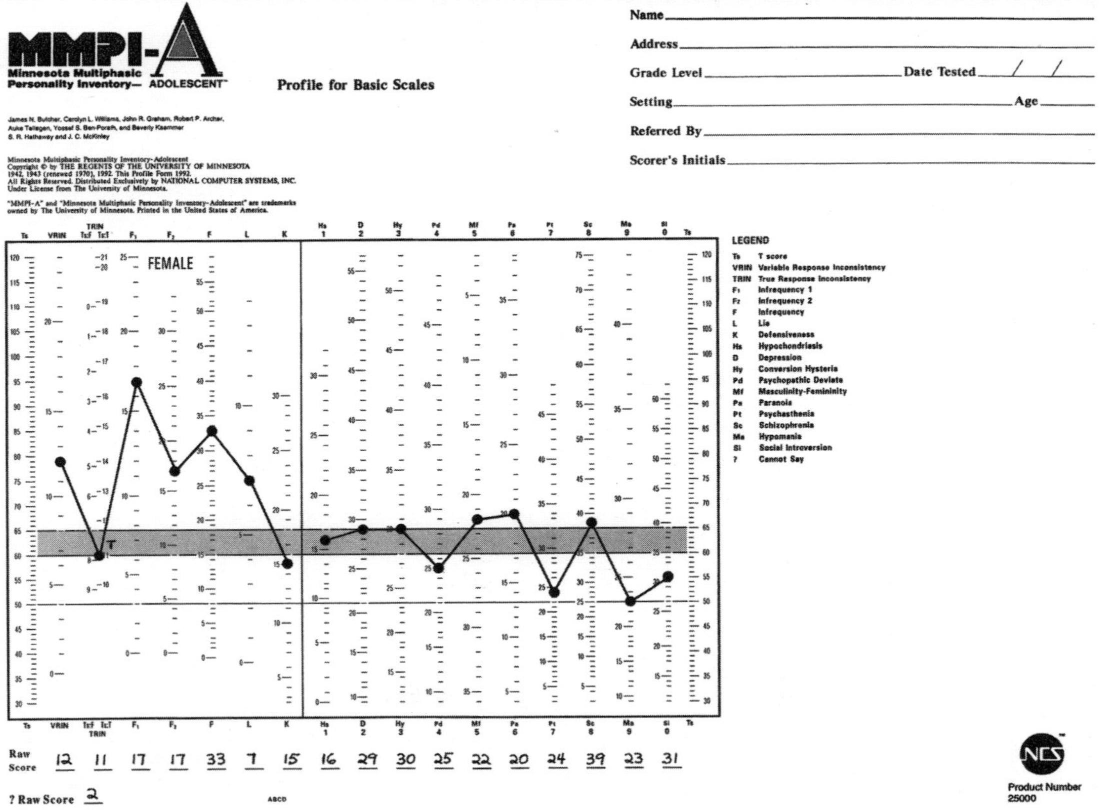

Figure 4.3 Random Response Set

Minnesota Multiphasic Personality Inventory–Adolescent (MMPI-A). Copyright © the Regents of the University of Minnesota 1942, 1943 (renewed 1970). 1992. Reproduced by permission of the publisher: "Minnesota Multiphasic Personality Inventory–Adolescent" and "MMPI-A" are trademarks owned by the University of Minnesota.

MMPI-A
Minnesota Multiphasic
Personality Inventory— ADOLESCENT™

Profile for Basic Scales

James N. Butcher, Carolyn L. Williams, John R. Graham, Robert P. Archer,
Auke Tellegen, Yossef S. Ben-Porath, and Beverly Kaemmer

Minnesota Multiphasic Personality Inventory–Adolescent
Copyright © THE REGENTS OF THE UNIVERSITY OF MINNESOTA.
1942, 1943 (renewed 1970), 1992. This Profile Form 1992.
All rights reserved. Distributed Exclusively by NATIONAL COMPUTER SYSTEMS, INC.
Under License from The University of Minnesota.

"MMPI-A" and "Minnesota Multiphasic Personality Inventory–Adolescent" are trademarks
owned by The University of Minnesota. Printed in the United States of America.

Name R. C.
Address
Grade Level
Date Tested / /
Setting
Age 16
Referred By
Scorer's Initials

NCS
Product Number
25000

LEGEND
Ts   T score
VRIN   Variable Response Inconsistency
TRIN   True Response Inconsistency
F₁   Infrequency 1
F₂   Infrequency 2
F   Infrequency
L   Lie
K   Defensiveness
Hs   Hypochondriasis
D   Depression
Hy   Conversion Hysteria
Pd   Psychopathic Deviate
Mf   Masculinity-Femininity
Pa   Paranoia
Pt   Psychasthenia
Sc   Schizophrenia
Ma   Hypomania
Si   Social Introversion
?   Cannot Say

MALE

	Ts	VRIN	Tcf	Tcf	F₁	F₂	F	L	K	Hs 1	D 2	Hy 3	Pd 4	Mf 5	Pa 6	Pt 7	Sc 8	Ma 9	Si 0	Ts
Raw Score		4	11		24	33	55	4	10	20	31	33	34	26	27	34	53	30	30	

? Raw Score   1

Figure 4.4 Overreporting Profile

Minnesota Multiphasic Personality Inventory–Adolescent (MMPI-A). Copyright © the Regents of the University of Minnesota 1942, 1943 (renewed 1970), 1992. Reproduced by permission of the publisher: "Minnesota Multiphasic Personality Inventory–Adolescent" and "MMPI-A" are trademarks owned by the University of Minnesota.

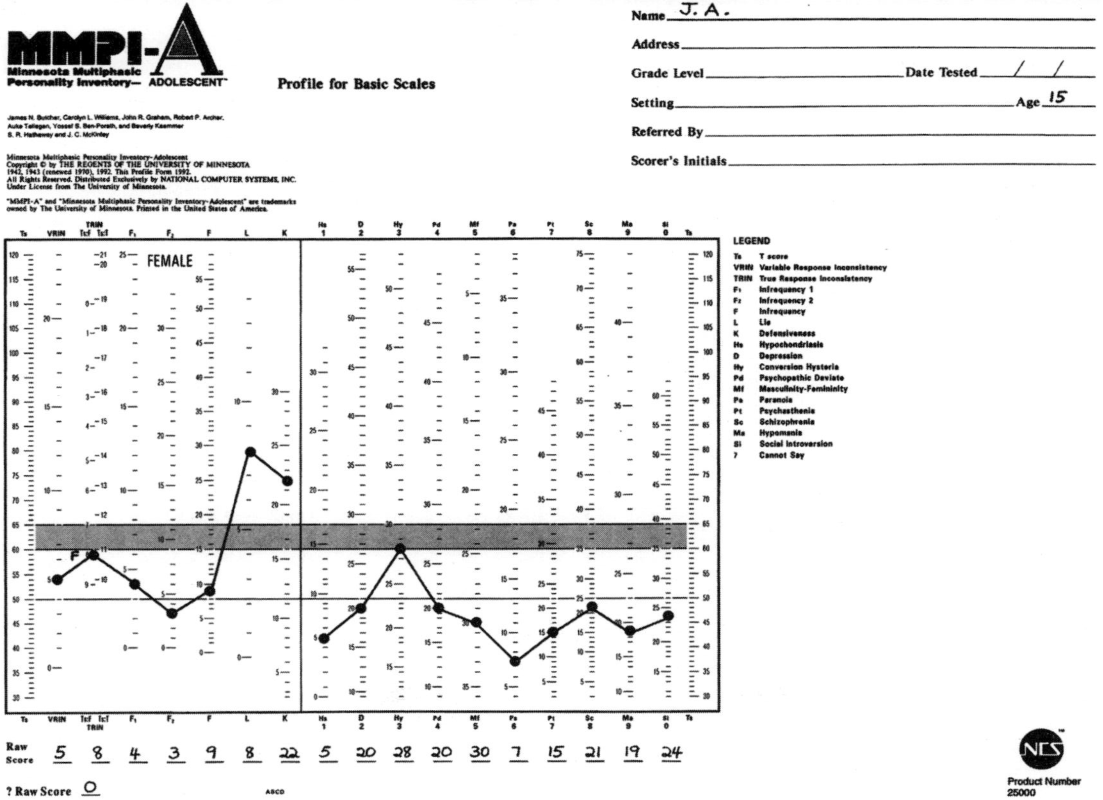

Figure 4.5 Underreporting Profile

Minnesota Multiphasic Personality Inventory–Adolescent (MMPI-A). Copyright © the Regents of the University of Minnesota 1942, 1943 (renewed 1970), 1992. Reproduced by permission of the publisher: "Minnesota Multiphasic Personality Inventory–Adolescent" and "MMPI-A" are trademarks owned by the University of Minnesota.

≡ Rapid Reference 4.1

Validity Assessment Guidelines

Consider a profile suspect or not valid for interpretation when
- the *Cannot Say (?)* raw score is > 30.
- *VRIN* or *TRIN* scales are elevated at *T* score ≥ 80.
- scale *F* is elevated at *T* score ≥ 90.
- scales *L* and *K* are elevated at *T* scores > 65.
- an All-True response set is evident by marked elevation on *F* with extremely low scores on *L* and *K*, and *TRIN* is elevated in the *True* direction.
- an All-False response set is evident by extreme elevation on *L* and *K* with normal-range *F*, and *TRIN* is elevated in the *False* direction.
- a Random response set is evident by elevations on *F, L,* and *VRIN.*
- an underreporting bias is evident by elevation on *L* and *K* relative to a nonelevated *F,* and all clinical scales are at *T* score ≤ 60.
- an overreporting bias is evident by *F*-scale elevation > 90 and normal-range or lower *L* and *K,* and a clinical scale floating profile.

Many individuals attempting to underreport symptomatology, however, appear to be able to do so without necessarily producing the elevated values on *L* and *K* that are shown in Figure 4.5. Thus, it is often difficult to distinguish responses of a somewhat guarded and defensive normal adolescent without significant psychiatric problems from those of a significantly disturbed adolescent consciously or unconsciously attempting to appear normal in his or her responses to MMPI-A items. Until more sensitive indicators are developed, the best approach to detecting underreporting response style remains examining elevations on validity scales *L* and *K.* Rapid Reference 4.1 provides guidelines for determining MMPI-A profile validity.

MAKING SENSE OF THE BASIC CLINICAL SCALES

After determining whether an MMPI-A profile is valid, the next step in interpretation is to evaluate the adolescent's scores on the Basic Clinical Scale Profile. This step involves evaluating the degree to which a particular adolescent's scores on the basic scales are elevated in comparison to those of the normative group by examining the *T*-score elevation for each scale and applying the appropriate descriptors or correlates for scales that produce clinically elevated *T* scores. The reader is reminded that for each of the MMPI-A basic clinical scales, the mean *T*-score value is 50 with a standard deviation value of 10. If the MMPI-A scale has a *T*-score value of 41 through 59, inclusive, these values are similar to those produced by the normative sample and are considered to be within normal limits. Interpretations can, however, be made for *T*-score values found in the shaded zone spanning *T* scores 60 through 64, inclusive, although less confidence should be placed in these interpretations, and scores in these ranges are likely to reflect less extreme descriptors. A *T* score of 65 or greater is critical for determining clinically elevated scores, and several research studies (e.g. Fontaine, Archer, Elkins, & Johansen, 2001) have supported the view that a *T*-score value ≥ 65 is necessary for the application of the full range of clinical descriptors to the adolescent respondent.

The next section briefly describes each of the 10 MMPI-A basic clinical scales.

Scale 1 (Hs): Hypochondriasis

Scale *1* (*Hypochondriasis*) originally consisted of 33 items developed to identify individuals who showed symptoms associated with hypochondriasis. These symptoms typically included vague physical complaints and ailments and a marked preoccupation with bodily functioning and disease. In the creation of the MMPI-A, one item was dropped from the original scale due to objectionable content, resulting in an MMPI-A *Hs* scale of 32 items.

Scale *1* is among the most homogeneous and unidimensional of the MMPI-A basic clinical scales, with an item composition and content primarily focused on somatic complaints and concerns. The research on this scale using adult samples has established that individuals who produce elevations on the *Hs* scale typically report exaggerated complaints regarding physical functioning and numerous somatic symptoms. Additionally, the research literature supports the view that these individuals typically have little psychological insight or "psychological mindedness." Research studies with both adolescents and adults have found that scale *1* scores are influenced, to a limited degree, by the presence of actual physical disorders, and marginal *T*-score elevations of 60 to 64 may be expected for adolescents with chronic physical illnesses. Based on these findings, clinicians should be aware of the actual presence of any significant physical disorders when they are interpreting elevations on this MMPI-A basic clinical scale.

Several researchers have reported that it is unusual for adolescents to produce elevations on scale *1*. Boys in clinical settings who elevate this scale are likely to display a variety of internalizing problems such as fearfulness, guilt, worry, and social withdrawal, as well as numerous physical complaints, while there is some evidence that girls in clinical settings who produce elevations on this scale may have a higher incidence of physical problems and complaints, including eating disorders.

The following is a summary of descriptors for high scale *1* scores ($T \geq 65$):

- Excessive bodily and somatic concerns that are often vague in nature
- Greater likelihood of internalizing problems such as guilt, fears, social withdrawal, perfectionism, dependency, and anxiety
- Greater likelihood of reporting school problems including academic and adjustment difficulties
- Lesser likelihood of displaying delinquent behaviors
- Clinging and dependent interpersonal relationships

In addition, lower scores on scale *1* have been associated with the following characteristics ($T \leq 40$):

- Fewer physical complaints or symptoms
- Greater psychological sophistication and insight

Scale 2 (D): Depression

Scale *2* (*Depression*) originally consisted of 60 items, and 57 of these were retained in the MMPI-A. Hathaway and McKinley (1943) originally described this scale as a measure of general dissatisfaction. The essential characteristics of this dimension include poor morale, social withdrawal and excessive social sensitivity, lack of hope for the future, a variety of physical problems and complaints, discouragement, and pervasive dissatisfaction with one's life. In general, numerous research studies in both adolescent and adult samples have established that elevations on scale *2* are produced by self-critical and introspective individuals who are prone to feelings of guilt, depression, and shame. Interestingly, for adolescents receiving psychiatric treatment services, there are some positive features associated with elevations on this scale. In particular, adolescents with higher scale *2* scores have been rated by clinicians and psychiatric staff as more motivated to engage in psychotherapy and more willing to discuss their feelings and problems. In general, their depression appears to be a powerful stimulus for these adolescents to actively participate in psychotherapy efforts. Additionally, clinicians also saw these boys and girls as less likely than other adolescents to engage in rebellious or conduct-disordered behaviors.

The psychiatric records of both boys and girls in treatment settings who produce elevations on scale *2* show a higher rate of depressive symptoms, including histories of suicidal ideation or gestures. In addition, adolescent girls with elevated scale *2* scores who are in treatment settings are more likely to show social withdrawal, eating problems, lower levels of self-esteem, greater social isolation, and more frequent somatic complaints. Interestingly, girls who produce elevations on scale *2* are less likely to have histories of truancy or school avoidance, delinquency, and externalizing or acting-out behaviors. Because of the multidimensional heterogeneous nature of scale *2,* the Harris-Lingoes subscales (addressed in the next section) are often useful in clarifying scale *2* elevations in adolescents and adults.

The following is a summary of descriptors associated with elevations on scale *2* ($T \geq 65$):

- Feelings of unhappiness, dissatisfaction, and hopelessness
- Apathy and lack of interest in activities
- Feelings of guilt, shame, and despondency
- Social isolation and withdrawal
- Feelings of inadequacy, pessimism, and low self-esteem

In addition, the following characteristics may be associated with lower scores on scale *2* ($T \leq 40$):

- Relative freedom from depression, guilt, and anxiety
- Self-confidence and high levels of self-esteem
- Emotional stability and increased stress tolerance

Scale 3 (Hy): Hysteria

The MMPI-A basic clinical scale *3* (*Hysteria*) consists of 60 items originally selected to identify individuals who respond to stressful situations with hysterical reactions. The hysterical syndrome, as reflected in the scale's items, includes physical or sensory disorders that do not have an organic basis and the strong need for social acceptance and social approval. In the adult literature on scale *3*, marked elevations on this scale have been typically associated with the more classic features of hysterical disorder involving physical symptoms and somatic complaints, while more moderate elevations have often been associated with a personality style marked by social extroversion, exhibitionistic behavior, superficial relationships, and self-centeredness. A number of MMPI authors and researchers have noted that adolescents who produce elevations on scale *3* appear to be achievement-oriented and driven to meet social expectations and demands. High scores have also been related to higher levels of both intelligence and socioeconomic status. Scale *3* elevations appear to be more frequent among girls than boys, and female adolescents with elevations on this scale report various physical complaints and somatic concerns.

The following is a summary of characteristics associated with elevations on scale *3* ($T \geq 65$):

- Somatic preoccupations and concerns
- Social involvement and achievement orientation
- Pattern of overreaction to stress that involves the development of physical symptoms
- Self-centered, egocentric, and immature actions
- Strong needs for attention, affection, and social approval

In addition, lower scores on scale *3* have been related to the following characteristics ($T \leq 40$):

- Unfriendly, tough-minded, and realistic orientation
- Limited social involvement and avoidance of leadership roles
- Freedom from physical complaints or discomfort

Scale 4 (Pd): Psychopathic Deviate

The MMPI-A scale *4* (*Psychopathic Deviate*) consists of 49 items developed based on a clinical sample that was court-referred for psychiatric evaluations because of delinquent behaviors that included lying, stealing, truancy, alcohol abuse, forgery, and sexual promiscuity. Scale *4* items cover a wide range of content areas, including problems with authority figures, family conflicts, social isolation, delinquency, and dissatisfaction with everyday life. The severity of delinquent behavior has been associated with increased T scores on scale 4, and elevations on this scale have also been associated with problems in school adjustment and school conduct as well as a higher frequency of conduct disorder diagnoses.

Adolescents who produce elevations on scale 4 have been described as rebellious, hostile, more difficult to treat in psychotherapy, and more likely to be involved in alcohol and drug abuse. Scale 4 is a frequent basic scale high-point for adolescents in clinical treatment settings, and nearly half of all adolescent psychiatric patients produce an MMPI-A Basic Scale Profile with scale 4 as either the most elevated or second most elevated scale among the 10 basic clinical scales. For both boys and girls in the MMPI-A normative sample, elevations on scale 4 reflect a higher incidence of school problems involving course failures, disciplinary actions, and suspensions. In addition, these adolescents had a higher rate of disagreements or arguments with parents and were more likely to use drugs or alcohol. In the MMPI-A clinical sample reported in the test manual, high scale 4 scores for both boys and girls were related to both higher levels of delinquency and externalizing and aggressive behaviors. In addition, higher scale 4 scores among boys are related to higher incidences of acting out behavior, a greater frequency of running away, and increased occurrences of physical abuse. Other researchers have shown that elevated scale 4 scores among adolescents are associated with a higher frequency of lying, cheating, stealing, aggression, and temper outbursts.

The following is a summary of characteristics associated with high scale 4 scores ($T \geq 65$):

- Increased probability of delinquency, oppositional and aggressive behaviors, and overall externalizing behavioral problems
- Hostility and rebelliousness toward authority figures
- History of poor school adjustment
- Greater likelihood of conduct disorder diagnoses
- Poor planning ability, low frustration tolerance, and impulsivity
- Use of acting out as a primary defense mechanism
- Higher incidence of risk-taking and sensation-seeking behavior
- Higher incidence of use and abuse of drugs and alcohol
- Relative absence of guilt and remorse concerning wrong-doing

In addition, lower scores on scale *4* ($T \leq 40$) have been associated with the following characteristics:

- Conventionality, compliance, and conformity
- Lower probability of delinquency and conduct disorder diagnoses
- Concerns involving security and status rather than dominance and competition

Scale 5 (Mf): Masculinity/Femininity

Scale *5* (*Masculinity/Femininity*) was originally developed based on a sample of adult males, and it underwent substantial revision in the development of the MMPI-A. Specifically, 16 of the items in the original scale were eliminated in the creation of the 44-item MMPI-A *Mf* scale. The content areas of scale *5* are heterogeneous and include such issues as family relationships, preferences concerning work and recreational activities, and willingness to report physical and psychological symptoms. Of the 44 items in the scale, 41 are keyed in the same direction for both genders, with the three remaining items (dealing with overt sexual material) keyed in opposite directions for boys and girls. *T*-score conversions are reversed for males and females so that a high raw-score value for boys results in a high *T*-score value, whereas a high raw-score value for girls converts to a lower *T*-score value. Thus, scale *5* represents a bipolar measure of gender role identification, with elevations in boys indicating interests that are more feminine than those of the average boy and elevations in girls indicating more masculine interests.

Substantial controversy has surrounded the interpretation and meaning of scale *5* scores, and it is probably best to think of this scale as measuring stereotypic gender characteristics, with normal range elevations on the scale typically indicating a relative balance between masculine and feminine characteristics. Markedly low scores on scale *5* for girls indicates identification with traditional feminine roles, including passivity and a lower likelihood of delinquent or aggressive behaviors. Among boys, low scale *5* scores are associated with traditional masculine identification, including an emphasis on strength and activity and a higher frequency of behavioral and school conduct problems. In contrast, boys with higher scores are likely to be more intelligent and to have better histories of school adjustment and school grades. Some recent research has also associated boys' higher scores with fearfulness, and girls' higher scores with aggressiveness. In general, it is also important to remember that scale *5* represents 1 of 2 "nonclinical" dimensions (the other being scale *0*) among the 10 basic clinical scales in which high or low scores are not necessarily associated with psychopathology.

High scores on scale *5* have been associated with the following characteristics for boys ($T \geq 65$):

- Intelligence with aesthetic interests
- Higher levels of academic achievement
- Passivity and submissiveness in interpersonal relationships
- Lower likelihood of delinquent or antisocial behaviors

The following is a summary of high Scale *5* characteristics for girls ($T \geq 65$):

- Assertiveness and competitiveness
- Aggressiveness with a greater likelihood of school conduct problems
- Possibility of masculine interests in academic areas and sports

Low scale *5* characteristics for boys include the following ($T \leq 40$):

- Presentation of self with stereotypic or extreme masculine emphasis
- Higher frequency of school conduct problems and delinquency
- Relatively narrow range of interests defined by traditional masculine stereotypes

The following is a summary of low scale *5* characteristics for girls ($T \leq 40$):

- Passivity and submissiveness in interpersonal relationships
- Presentation of self in stereotypic feminine manner
- Higher levels of academic achievement and lower levels of behavior problems

Scale 6 (Pa): Paranoia

The MMPI-A basic clinical scale *6* (*Paranoia*) consists of 40 items that were created to assess paranoid symptomatology including suspiciousness, ideas of reference, feelings of persecution, moral self-righteousness, and rigidity in beliefs and perceptions.

Extreme elevations on scale *6* are typically associated with a psychotic level of paranoid symptomatology such as that found for paranoid schizophrenics or individuals manifesting paranoid states. More moderate elevations in the *T*-score range of 60 to 70 are often produced by individuals who are not psychotic, but do have excessive sensitivity to the opinions and actions of others, and are guarded and suspicious in interpersonal interactions. Adolescents have traditionally endorsed more scale *6* items than adults have, particularly those items related to the belief that one is misunderstood or unjustly punished or blamed by others. In general, there appears to be an association between elevations on scale *6* and aggressive acting out and argumentative behaviors, particularly for teenage boys. For both boys and girls, elevations on scale *6* have been associated with higher incidence of school problems and lower grades in school. Among girls, elevations on this scale appear to be associated with increased parental conflicts and disagreements.

The following is a summary of characteristics for adolescents who produced marked elevations on scale *6* ($T \geq 70$):

- Use of projection as a primary defense mechanism
- Hostility, anger, and resentment
- Possible disturbances in reality testing
- Delusions of persecution or grandeur
- Ideas of reference

The following are features usually associated with moderate elevations on scale *6* (*T* ranging from 60 to 69, inclusive):

- Excessive interpersonal sensitivity
- Distrust and suspiciousness in interpersonal relationships
- Tendencies toward argumentativeness
- Increased disagreements/conflicts with parents
- Difficulty in establishing a trust relationship with therapist

The following are associated with lower range scores on scale *6* ($T \leq 40$):

- Cautious, conventional, and cheerful attitude
- Lack of awareness of the feelings and motives of others

Scale 7 (Pt): Psychasthenia

The MMPI-A basic scale 7 (*Psychasthenia*) consists of 48 items designed to measure symptoms related to psychasthenia, which was later conceptualized as obsessive-compulsive neurosis, and more recently described as Obsessive-Compulsive Disorder. The content of scale 7 covers a wide variety of areas including problems in concentration, obsessive thoughts, feelings of anxiety and tension, unhappiness and general emotional distress, and physical complaints. Scale 7 has a relatively high degree of internal consistency and is homogeneous in terms of content areas.

Adolescents who score high on scale 7 have been described as anxious, indecisive, and tense individuals who are perfectionistic and self-critical. At extreme elevations, adolescents may show more disabling symptomatology, including obsession and intense ruminations. High scores on scale 7 have also been related to increased frequency of nightmares among both boys and girls, as well as higher levels of depression and parental arguments for teenage girls and histories of sexual abuse for teenage boys.

The following is a summary of characteristics associated with high scores on scale 7 ($T \geq 65$):

- Perfectionistic and self-critical tendencies
- Tension, apprehension, and anxiety
- Feelings of inadequacy, inferiority, and insecurity
- Tendency to be introspective, ruminative, and lacking in self-confidence
- At marked elevations ($T \geq 70$), obsessive and ruminative thought patterns

The following are features associated with lower scale 7 scores ($T \leq 40$):

- Freedom from emotional distress and anxiety
- Capable and self-confident stance
- Flexibility, efficiency, and adaptability

Scale 8 (Sc): Schizophrenia

MMPI-A scale 8 (*Schizophrenia*) consists of 77 items and is the longest of the basic clinical scales. Scale 8 was originally developed to identify adult patients with schizophrenia and has been shown to be useful in identifying adolescents with this disorder. The scale deals with a variety of content areas involving peculiar thoughts, bizarre thought processes, social withdrawal and isolation, difficulties in concentration, impulse control deficits, and disturbances in mood and behavior. Early research on scale 8 among adolescents found that elevations on this scale were associated with a number of negative features including lower intelligence, histories of academic problems, and a greater likelihood of dropping out of high school. Other researchers have found elevated scale *8* scores for adolescent inpatients who were described as mistrustful, withdrawn, interpersonally isolated, and very vulnerable to stress. Additionally, these inpatient adolescents often had presenting problems involving impaired reality testing and were more likely to receive diagnoses related to schizophrenia. Other factors that appear to result in elevations in scale *8* involve adolescent's drug abuse or experimentation with hallucinogens. For that reason, the clinician's awareness of an adolescent's drug use history often benefits him or her when interpreting scale *8* elevations. Among both boys and girls, scale *8* elevations are related to a greater number of school problems and lower academic performance. In clinical settings, scale *8* elevations among boys appear to be associated with higher rates of somatic complaints, internalizing problems, low self-esteem, and increased incidence of schizoid and psychotic behaviors.

The following are characteristics associated with elevated scale *8* scores (*T* ≥ 65):

- Confused or disorganized thinking
- Withdrawn and seclusive behavior
- Feelings of inferiority, low self-esteem, and incompetence
- Feelings of unhappiness and frustration
- Social rejection and history of teasing by peers
- Vulnerability to stress and tendency to get easily upset
- Possible impairment in reality testing
- Perception by peers as being odd, unconventional, and socially deviant

The following are characteristics of lower range scores on scale *8* (*T* ≤ 40):

- Conventional, conforming, and conservative demeanor
- Practical, logical, and achievement oriented approach
- Cooperative and compliant behavior

Scale 9 (Ma): Hypomania

MMPI-A scale *9* (*Hypomania*) consists of 46 items covering content areas including grandiosity, flight of ideas, irritability, egocentricity, elevated mood, and cognitive and behavioral overactivity. Normal adolescents typically endorse more items on scale *9* than do well-functioning adults, particularly those related to a preference for action and a need to engage in activity. Among adolescent psychiatric patients, elevations on scale *9* have been related to the occurrence of temper tantrums, hostile or argumentative behaviors, and rapid mood shifts. Other researchers have described adolescents who produce elevated scale *9* scores as impulsive, unrealistic, and insensitive to criticism. Recent research on the MMPI-A basic scale *9* revealed that adolescent boys in psychiatric treatment settings who elevate this scale are more likely to abuse amphetamines, and girls with scale *9* elevations are more likely to have a history of school suspensions. Both boys and girls in clinical settings with elevated scale *9* scores are more likely to be described as delinquent, to have histories of externalizing behavior problems, and to be seen as aggressive. Boys with elevated scale *9* scores are more likely to have histories of running away and of being physically abused, while girls are more likely to have histories of being sexually abused and sexually active. For both genders, elevations on scale *9* are likely to be associated with disciplinary problems in school and histories of increased disagreements and conflicts with parents.

The following features are associated with elevations on scale *9* ($T \geq 65$):

- Talkative, energetic, and outgoing manner
- Rapid personal tempo and tendency to engage in excessive activity
- Preference for action rather than thought and reflection
- Restlessness, distractibility, and impulsiveness
- Grandiosity and unrealistic goal-setting
- Egocentric, self-centered, and self-indulgent actions
- Possibility of flight of ideas, grandiosity, and euphoric mood

The following are characteristics associated with low scores on scale *9* ($T \leq 40$):

- Lower energy levels
- Seclusive, withdrawn, depressed, and quiet appearance
- Inhibition and overcontrolled behavior
- Lower probability of delinquent behaviors or acting out
- Lethargic, apathetic, and depressed presentation

Scale *0 (Si): Social Introversion*

The MMPI-A scale *0* (*Social Introversion*) consists of 62 items. The original scale *0* was developed in the 1940s based upon the responses of introverted and ex-

CAUTION

Points to Remember in Interpretation of the Basic Clinical Scales

• The relationship between scale elevation and diagnosis is not simple (e.g., an elevation on scale 8 does not necessarily indicate a diagnosis of schizophrenia).

• Interpretation of low-point scores is less reliable for many scales than interpretation of elevated or high-point scores.

• The Mf and Si basic clinical scales (scales 5 and 0) are "nonclinical" and essentially measure non-pathological features or characteristics.

troverted college students. Higher-range T scores on this scale reflect greater degrees of social introversion. Like scale 5, scale 0 essentially measures a "nonclinical" or "non-pathological" dimension that may not necessarily be associated with psychopathology or pathological symptoms or characteristics. Three Si subscales, discussed later in this chapter, were created for scale 0 on the MMPI-2 and the MMPI-A by Ben-Porath, Hostetler, Butcher, and Graham (1989).

Elevated scale 0 scores for boys and girls are related to social introversion, insecurity, and discomfort in social situations. These adolescents tend to be timid, shy, submissive, and lacking in self-confidence. To some degree, elevations on scale 0 indicate decreased or inhibited potential for impulsive behavior and acting out. In contrast, adolescents who produce low scores on this scale are socially extroverted, gregarious, confident, friendly, and outgoing. These adolescents tend to have strong affiliation needs and appear to be more active and impulsive than their high scale 0 counterparts. Among adolescent boys in clinical settings, higher scores are related to greater social withdrawal and lower levels of self-esteem. Among girls in treatment settings, higher elevated scale 0 scores are related to a greater incidence of social withdrawal and depression, eating problems, suicidal ideation and gestures, and excessive weight gain. In addition, female adolescents who produce elevated scale 0 scores have lower rates of delinquency, acting out, and drug abuse.

The following are features that are associated with adolescents who produce higher scores on scale 0 ($T \geq 65$):

• Social introversion and social discomfort
• Low self-esteem

- Timid, withdrawn, and reserved presentation
- Decreased probability of delinquency or acting out
- Submissive, passive, and compliant demeanor
- Low self-confidence and high levels of insecurity

The following are features or characteristics associated with adolescents who score low on scale *0* (*T* ≤ 40):

- Extroversion, gregariousness, and sociability
- Energetic, talkative, and active mode
- Confident, competent, and socially sensitive stance

HARRIS-LINGOES AND *Si* SUBSCALES

Harris-Lingoes Subscales

Hathaway and McKinley (1943) used the "contrasting groups" or "empirical keying" approach in constructing the MMPI basic clinical scales. Preliminary test items were administered to a criterion group of patients presenting a particular diagnosis (e.g., schizophrenia) and a normal comparison group that did not share symptoms of the diagnostic group. Items that were endorsed differently by the two groups were retained in the scale, while items that produce similar responses were excluded from scale membership. Hathaway and McKinley's empirical keying method resulted in the creation of basic scales that contained a variety of content areas and were heterogeneous in nature. For example, the content of scale *4* includes items related to the individual's perception of the warmth and supportiveness of his or her home environment, items related to problems with authority figures, items related to comfort and confidence in social situations, and a variety of items related to feeling alienation and estrangement from self and others. Marginal elevations on scale *4* may result from the endorsement of some, but not all, of these content areas, rendering it more difficult and problematic to draw correlate inferences from marginally elevated scores.

In order to help clinicians determine the content endorsement associated with basic scale elevations, Harris and Lingoes (1955) constructed subscales for six of the basic scales, including *2, 3, 4, 6, 8,* and *9*. Harris and Lingoes did not attempt to develop subscales for basic scales *1* and *7* because these measures were viewed as homogeneous in terms of item composition; they also did not create subscales for scales *5* and *0* because these were viewed as substantively different from the other basic scales in that these latter scales include nonclinical dimensions. The Harris-Lingoes subscales developed for the original MMPI were carried over into the testing material and scoring programs for both the MMPI-2 and MMPI-A. The Harris-Lingoes subscales are used to refine interpretations for elevated basic clinical scales and are most useful when the basic clinical scale is elevated in moderate ranges corresponding to *T*-score values greater than or equal to 60 but below 80 or 90. For example, a *T*-score elevation of 70 on the *Pd (4)* scale could reflect an adolescent's sense of alienation, perception of substantial conflict with family members, or tendency to be rebellious and in conflict with authority figures. The relative pattern of elevation on the Harris-Lingoes subscales for this basic scale, for example, *Social Alienation (Pd₄)*, *Familial Discord (Pd₁)*, and *Authority Problems (Pd₂)*, would typically help to illuminate the content areas responsible for this *Pd* scale elevation. The Harris-Lingoes subscales should not be used to interpret any basic clinical scale with *T*-score elevations of < 60, and are generally less useful in interpreting basic scales that show extreme elevations because all content areas tend to be heavily endorsed when the basic clinical scales are markedly elevated. Moreover, the subscales need to be elevated at a *T*-score level of 65 or higher to be considered interpretable. While the MMPI-A and MMPI-2 Harris-Lingoes subscales are generally identical in item content, it is very important to use the appropriate adolescent norms in interpreting the MMPI-A Harris-Lingoes subscales because there are rather large and well-established differences in the tendencies of adults versus adolescents to endorse items in specific content areas. It should also be remembered that many of the Harris-Lingoes subscales are quite short, some containing as few as six items. The reliabilities for many of the Harris-Lingoes subscales are generally low, and these subscales should never be used as an independent source of information concerning the adolescent, but always restricted to refining or understanding an adolescent derived through interpretation of the basic clinical scales.

The following section lists suggested interpretations for the MMPI-A Harris-Lingoes subscales (grouped by basic scale membership) for *T*-score values ≥ 65.

Scale 2 (Depression) Subscales

Subjective Depression (D_1)

High scores on the D_1 subscale may be associated with the following characteristics:

- Feelings of guilt, unhappiness, and depression
- Apathy and lethargy
- Problems in concentration and attention
- Self-critical tendencies and poor self-confidence

Psychomotor Retardation (D_2)

High scores on the D_2 subscale may be associated with the following characteristics:

- Lack of energy and inability to mobilize resources
- Social withdrawal and avoidance
- Denial of aggressive or hostile feelings and impulses

Physical Malfunctioning (D_3)

High scores on the D_3 subscale may be associated with the following characteristics:

- Preoccupation with physical functioning and health
- A wide variety of physical complaints including nausea, constipation, convulsions, weight loss or gain, fatigue and weakness, and asthma

Mental Dullness (D_4)

High scores on the D_4 subscale may be associated with the following:

- Problems in concentration and attention
- Apathy and lack of energy
- Poor self-concept and little self-confidence
- Difficulties in making decisions

Brooding (D_5)

High scores on the D_5 subscale may be associated with the following:

- Brooding and rumination
- Lack of energy

- Excessive sensitivity to criticism
- Feelings of despondency, sadness, and uselessness

Scale 3 (Hysteria) Subscales

Denial of Social Anxiety (Hy_1)

High scores on the Hy_1 subscale are quite rare because it requires the endorsement of all of the six items in the scorable or critical direction on this subscale in order to produce a T-score value ≥ 65. With this caution in mind, higher scores on the Hy_1 scale may indicate the following:

- Social extroversion
- Ease and comfort in dealing with others

Need for Affection (Hy_2)

High scores on the Hy_2 subscale may be associated with the following:

- Strong needs for affection and attention
- Trust and optimism in interpersonal relationships
- Denial of hostile or negative feelings towards others

Lassitude-Malaise (Hy_3)

High scores on the Hy_3 subscale may be associated with the following:

- Tiredness, weakness, and fatigue
- Poor appetite and sleep disturbance
- Sadness and despondency
- Unhappiness and physical discomfort

Somatic Complaints (Hy_4)

High scores on the Hy_4 subscale may be associated with the following:

- Multiple somatic complaints and problems
- Nausea, vomiting, and gastrointestinal problems
- Fainting, dizziness, and problems with balance

Inhibition of Aggression (Hy_5)

High scores on the Hy_5 subscale may be associated with the following:

- Denial of aggressive or hostile impulses
- View of self as decisive and socially sensitive

Scale 4 (Psychopathic Deviate) Subscales
Familial Discord (Pd₁)

High scores on the Pd_1 subscale may be associated with the following:

- Hostile, rejecting, and unpleasant family life
- View of family as critical and controlling
- Frequent quarrels and conflict with family members

Authority Problems (Pd₂)

High scores on the Pd_2 subscale may be associated with the following:

- Resentment of authority
- Opinionated and defiant stance
- History of conflicts with societal standards, norms, or expectations

Social Imperturbability (Pd₃)

Pd_3 consists of six items, and all six must be endorsed in the deviant direction in order for T-score values to reach a ≥ 65 level. With this caution in mind, higher scores on the Pd_3 subscale may be associated with the following:

- Social extroversion, comfort, and confidence
- Opinionated and exhibitionistic tendencies

Social Alienation (Pd₄)

High scores on the Pd_4 subscale may be associated with the following:

- Feelings of loneliness, alienation, and social isolation
- Feelings of unhappiness
- Tendency to blame others for conflicts or problems

Self-Alienation (Pd₅)

High scores on the Pd_5 subscale may be associated with the following:

- Emotional discomfort and unhappiness
- Problems in attention and concentration
- Feelings of remorse, guilt, and regret
- View of daily life as uninteresting or unrewarding

Scale 6 (Paranoia) Subscales
Persecutory Ideas (Pa₁)

High scores on the Pa_1 subscale may be associated with the following:

- Perception of the world as threatening or hostile
- Externalization of blame for frustrations and problems
- Feelings of being misunderstood and unfairly punished by others
- Possibility of paranoid or persecutory delusions or ideas

Poignancy (Pa_2)

High scores on the Pa_2 subscale may be associated with the following:

- View of self as sensitive, high strung, and intense
- Sense of loneliness, sadness, and distance from others
- Belief that one feels emotions more intensely than others

Naivete (Pa_3)

High scores on the Pa_3 subscale may be associated with the following:

- Naive and optimistic attitudes
- Denial of cynical or hostile feelings
- Report of high moral or ethical standards

Scale 8 (Schizophrenia) Subscales

Social Alienation (Sc_1)

High scores on the Sc_1 subscale may be associated with the following:

- Feelings of being misunderstood and unfairly criticized or punished
- Perception of family life as lacking in love and support
- Feelings of loneliness and emptiness
- Hostility and anger towards family members

Emotional Alienation (Sc_2)

High scores on the Sc_2 subscale may be associated with the following:

- Feelings of hopelessness, depression, and despair
- Feelings of self-criticism
- Apathy, pessimism, and anxiety
- Possible suicidal ideation

Lack of Ego Mastery–Cognitive (Sc_3)

High scores on the Sc_3 subscale may be associated with the following:

- Feelings of unreality and fears of losing sanity
- Presence of strange or unusual thought processes
- Problems in attention and concentration

Lack of Ego Mastery–Conative (Sc_4)

High scores on the Sc_4 subscale may be associated with the following:

- Feelings of vulnerability and being overwhelmed
- Problems in attention and concentration
- Apathy and lethargy
- Guilt, despondency, and depression

Lack of Ego Mastery–Defective Inhibition (Sc_5)

High scores on the Sc_5 subscale may be associated with the following:

- Impulsivity, restlessness, and irritability
- Loss of control over emotions with episodes of laughing or crying
- Possible disassociative experiences or symptoms

Bizarre Sensory Experiences (Sc_6)

High scores on the Sc_6 subscale may be associated with the following:

- Strange or unusual thoughts with possible hallucinations
- Unusual physical sensations, including sensory and motor disturbances

Scale 9 (Hypomania) Subscales

Amorality (Ma_1)

High scores on the Ma_1 subscale may be associated with the following:

- Antisocial or asocial beliefs, behaviors and attitudes
- Tendency to view others as selfish, dishonest, and motivated by self-gain
- Impulsivity and lack of behavioral control

Psychomotor Acceleration (Ma_2)

High scores on the Ma_2 subscale may be associated with the following:

- Attraction to risk-taking and sensation-seeking activities
- High need for excitement and stimulation
- Restlessness and overactivity
- Acceleration of speech or thought processes

Imperturbability (Ma_3)

High scores on the Ma_3 subscale may be associated with the following:

- Denial of social anxiety
- Freedom or independence from the influence of others
- Tendency to seek out excitement

Ego Inflation (Ma₄)

High scores on the Ma_4 subscale may be associated with the following:

- Resentment of expectations and demands placed by others
- Tendency to overvalue the self; feelings of self-importance and grandiosity

Si Subscales

As previously noted, Harris and Lingoes did not develop subscales for several of the MMPI basic scales, including scale *0*. Ben-Porath and colleagues (1989) developed *Si* subscales for the MMPI-2 based upon their analysis of the responses of normal college men and women. These subscales were initially developed based on the factor structure of scale *0* and refined through the use of item selection procedures designed to maximize internal consistency values found for the subscales. The *Si* subscales for the MMPI-2, developed by Ben-Porath and his colleagues, were carried over to the MMPI-A without modification and are presented on the same profile sheet with the Harris-Lingoes subscales. These three subscales are used to refine the interpretation of scores found for the MMPI-A basic scale *0*.

Shyness/Self-Consciousness (Si₁)

High scores on the Si_1 subscale may be associated with the following:

- Shyness in interpersonal situations
- Discomfort in new situations

Social Avoidance (Si₂)

High scores on the Si_2 subscale may be associated with the following:

- Avoidance of social events or dislike of social situations
- Interpersonal withdrawal and avoidance of contact with others

Alienation—Self and Others (Si₃)

High scores on the Si_3 subscale may be associated with the following:

- Fear, apprehension, and distrust of others
- Low self-esteem and poor self-image
- Lack of self-confidence
- Self-criticism

APPROACHES TO INTERPRETING MMPI-A BASIC SCALE DATA

Individual Clinical Scale Interpretation

An extensive body of research literature is available on the correlates or descriptors of the basic clinical scales for the original MMPI in clinical samples. Research findings based on the original form of the MMPI are relevant and applicable to the MMPI-A because very few changes occurred in the basic scales in their transformation from the original to the revised instrument, and studies indicate that individuals who produced a particular basic scale pattern on the original form are likely to produce the same pattern on the MMPI-A. Furthermore, the results of at least two studies have shown that items that were reworded in the MMPI revision process appear psychometrically equivalent in terms of the response frequencies produced to those items in the original and revised forms (e.g., Archer & Gordon, 1994). In addition to the correlate literature developed for the original instrument, however, a substantial body of research literature is also available on the MMPI-A basic clinical scales as described in the MMPI-A test manual and in Archer (1997). The MMPI-A manual, for example, provides extensive descriptions of the correlates found in research studies specifically conducted on the MMPI-A basic scales in both the normative and clinical samples. Thus, the correlate patterns and meanings of the MMPI-A basic scales are anchored in research conducted with both the original MMPI and with the MMPI-A in both normal and clinical samples. In general, the clinical correlates found for the basic scales of the MMPI-A provide the bedrock for any interpretive approach to this test instrument.

The interpretation of individual MMPI-A basic clinical scales is related to both the degree of elevation and definition found for particular basic scales. In general, elevation refers to the relative rareness of a score as reflected in the T-score value obtained on a particular scale. As we have noted, T scores in the range of 60 to 64, inclusive, reflect marginal range elevations associated with some, but not all, of the characteristics commonly found for clinical elevations on that scale. Thus, a T score of 63, for example, on MMPI-A basic scale *4* is likely to be found for adolescents who have some problems in terms of impulsivity or lower frustration tolerance, but adolescents in this range are unlikely to show a history of extreme conduct problems or delinquency associated with more elevated T-score values on this scale. Definition refers to the degree of T-score difference found between the most elevated clinical scale in the basic profile and the second most elevated basic scale, expressed in T-score points. For example, if the most elevated basic scale T score for a given MMPI-A profile occurs on scale *2* with a T-score value of 68, and the second most elevated score occurs on scale *4* with a T-score value of 63, that MMPI-A profile is said to display 5 T-score points of definition between the first and second most elevated basic scales. The higher a T-score elevation found for a particular basic scale, and the greater the degree of definition associated with that elevation, the more the correlates or descriptors associated with that scale are likely to apply to the adolescent respondent. As previously noted, interpreting the MMPI-A basic scales that are marginally to moderately elevated is particularly facilitated through the use of the Harris-Lingoes subscales and the *Si* subscales. While the interpretation approach of utilizing correlates from individual basic scale findings is always used when an adolescent produces only one basic scale value elevated within clinical ranges (sometimes referred to as a "spike" profile, or a "one-point" codetype), this approach may also be used in cases in which multiple clinical scales are elevated within clinical ranges. In these latter cases, the correlates derived from the elevated scales are added together in the report narrative, generally placing heavier emphasis on correlates described from the more elevated clinical scales.

Two-Point Codetype Interpretation

A two-point codetype classification for the MMPI-A is based on the two clinical scales that show the greatest degree of clinical elevation in the basic scale profile, typically with the restriction that each of these scales must be $\geq T$ score of 60 in order to be classified as an interpretable two-point code. The two-point codetype literature for adolescents on the original form of the MMPI may be found in the work of Marks, Seeman, and Haller (1974) and the extrapolation of this literature to the MMPI-A is described in Archer (1997). In contrast to the adult codetype literature, the available literature on codetype in-

terpretation for adolescents is relatively limited and subject to some controversy. For this reason, the MMPI-A test manual recommends that clinicians
use caution in interpreting two-point codes with adolescents; it also underscores the need for more empirical research on this issue with the MMPI-A.
Nevertheless, the test manual also notes that many practitioners find the use
of codetype interpretation with the MMPI-A to be informative, and illustrates
the use of this approach in one of the two clinical examples provided in the test
manual. Other examples of MMPI-A two-point codetype interpretation may
be found in Archer (1997), and in Archer, Krishnamurthy, and Jacobson
(1994).

In general, MMPI-A two-point codes are often used interchangeably, for
example, a *4-9* codetype is typically seen as equivalent, in terms of interpretive
correlates, to a *9-4* codetype. As in the case of single-scale interpretation, the
confidence in the descriptors derived from two-point code interpretation are
related to the issues of elevation and definition. In general, the greater the magnitude of the adolescent's *T*-score elevations on both of the scales involved in
the two-point code, the greater the likelihood that the adolescent is accurately
described by the correlates associated with elevations for that codetype. In addition, the degree of definition manifested by the adolescent's two-point code
should be evaluated. Two-point codetype definition refers to the degree of *T*-
score elevation difference found between the second and third highest elevations within the basic clinical scale profile, typically expressed in *T*-score
points. The greater the degree of definition found for the two-point code, the
more likely it is that the correlate or descriptive statements associated with that
codetype provide an accurate description for the particular adolescent respondent. The MMPI-A test manual recommends a minimum of 5 *T*-score
points difference between the second and third most elevated scales in order
to have confidence in using the correlates associated with a particular two-
point code. However, it should be noted that the majority of adolescents evaluated with the MMPI-A do not produce codetypes that meet the 5 *T*-score
point recommended criterion for definition, and are nevertheless subject to
two-point codetype interpretations by many clinicians. In the case of these less
well-defined codetypes, it is certainly prudent for the clinician to exercise increased caution in applying descriptors derived from that codetype classification. While the current text provides sample narratives for nine commonly occurring two-point codes, Archer (1997) has presented more detailed data on

29 two-point codetypes that are exhaustive of the available literature on correlates of two-point codes for adolescents.

MMPI-A CODETYPES

Similar to the interpretive approach used with the MMPI and MMPI-2 with
adults, interpretation of an adolescent's MMPI-A includes examining the profile pattern produced by the basic clinical scales. When MMPI-A profiles are
classified into groups based on the highest two clinical scales, this practice is
referred to as two-point codetype interpretation. Correlates for the two-point
codetypes are typically obtained by collecting groups of adolescents or adults
who produce similar codetypes and studying their behavioral characteristics as
revealed in their self-reports on other test instruments and in ratings obtained
from their therapists, teachers, treatment staff, and family members. In the
case using the MMPI with adolescents, the primary source of empirical data
concerning codetype interpretation is provided by Marks, Seeman, and Haller
(1974) and based on their extensive studies of adolescents in clinical treatment
settings.

A high-point codetype is usually referred to by a numerical designation of
the two scales that are most elevated in the profile, with convention indicating
that the most elevated scale be designated first in the codetype sequence, followed by the second most elevated scale. Additionally, the assignment of a
codetype classification usually requires that all of the scales designated in the
codetype produce clinical range elevations, that is, T scores ≥ 65. Thus, if an
adolescent produced his or her highest clinical range T-score elevations on
scales 4 and 9 (in that order), the profile would result in classification as a 4-9
two-point codetype. This approach also follows the widely accepted practice
of referring to scales by numerical designation rather than labels or alphabetic
abbreviations, because our understanding of what is measured by several of
the basic clinical scales has changed over the years and no longer corresponds
to the original scale title. For example, as noted under the discussion of scale 7,
the term "psychasthenia" is now largely archaic and does not adequately en-
compass our understanding of the symptomatology presented in scale 7. Thus,
when addressing codetype classifications in this chapter we use numerical des-
ignations consistent with the preferred practice among clinicians experienced
with the MMPI-2 or MMPI-A.

In applying clinical correlates derived from individual scales or two-point codetypes with adolescents it is imperative that the clinician bear in mind that the accuracy of clinical correlates to a particular adolescent always entails probability estimates. These estimates of likelihood that a correlate accurately applies vary greatly depending upon the source and generalizability of the origins of the descriptive statement (the soundness of the research methodology and the characteristics of the sample used in the study), as well as the individual characteristics of the adolescents being assessed, including such issues as age, gender, ethnicity, and setting. Additionally, it is also important to underscore that the likelihood that a particular set of characteristics will be found accurate for the description of a specific adolescent is also influenced by the extent to which the relevant scales are more elevated (T-score elevation) and the degree to which the single-scale or two-point code is substantially more elevated than the scores derived from the remainder of the clinical scale profile (T-score definition). The greater the elevation and the definition associated with either single-scale or two-point codetypes, the greater the likelihood that correlates derived from this information accurately describe an individual adolescent. The remainder of this section provides some empirical correlates for the 10 most frequently occurring MMPI-A codetypes in a manner meant to illustrate this approach to interpretation. For a more extensive discussion of MMPI-A codetypes, see Archer (1997).

No-Code or Within-Normal-Limits Codetypes

A "no-code" or "within-normal-limits" (WNL) profile is not strictly a form of single-scale or two-point codetypes, but rather reflects an MMPI-A Basic Scale Profile that shows no clinical range elevations on any of the 10 basic scales. This profile classification is presented first in this section because it is technically the most frequently occurring classification found for adolescents in psychiatric settings. Surprisingly, research findings have consistently shown that somewhere between 20 and 33% of adolescents receiving mental health services produce MMPI-A Basic Scale Profiles characterized by the absence of any clinical range elevations. The reasons for the relatively high frequency of occurrence of WNL profiles among adolescents in psychiatric settings are not well understood, but may potentially be related to the absence of a useful K-correction procedure with the MMPI-A. In other words, teenagers in treatment, in general, may be endorsing symptoms at similar rates to adolescents in the MMPI-A normative sample and there is no current method to correct for their relative underreporting of problems. It seems likely that the relative difference between normal and abnormal functioning in adolescence is more difficult to discern accurately than the successful discrimination of normal versus abnormal functioning in adulthood. Stated differently, the degree of overlap between normal and abnormal psychological functioning in adolescence may be more marked, rendering it more difficult to categorize normal and abnormal behavior on the MMPI-A. Regardless of the causes of this phenomenon, the MMPI-A interpreter should be aware of the relatively high frequency of WNL profiles produced by adolescents in a wide variety of outpatient, and even inpatient, clinical settings. This observation underscores the importance of the clinical psychologist employing a variety of other assessment instruments, as well as independent sources of information including psychiatric history findings, clinical interview results, and parental and teacher interviews, in forming an overall picture of the adolescent's psychological adjustment and functioning.

1-3/3-1 Codetype

Among both adolescents and adults, the *1-3/3-1* codetype typically represents individuals who complain of physical illness and poor health. The types of physical complaints reported by these individuals often include headaches, chest pain, dizziness, abdominal pain, nausea, insomnia, blurred vision, and eating disturbances. These physical symptoms typically increase during periods of psychological stress, and there is often evidence that the adolescent client experiences some desired outcome (i.e., secondary gain) as a result of this symptomatology (e.g., a school-avoidant adolescent who presents with physical symptoms is allowed to stay at home rather than attend school).

The primary defense mechanisms associated with this codetype consist of denial, externalization, and somatization. Teenagers who receive this codetype classification are more frequently seen for treatment because of problems and concerns in their school setting. Many of the adolescents who receive this codetype classification appear to be afraid of receiving poor grades. In addition, these adolescents also are rated as having strong needs for attention, displaying little insight into their psychological problems and being unwilling to acknowledge the role of psychological factors in their physical complaints.

2-3/3-2 Codetype

Both adolescents and adults who are classified with the *2-3/3-2* codetype are often described as emotionally overcontrolled, passive, docile, and dependent. They are also described as unassertive, inhibited, self-doubting, and insecure. While these adolescents tend to set high goals for their own performance and achievement, these aspirations are often unrealistic and lead to a sense of inferiority and depression. Defense mechanisms typically involve somatization and hypochondriasis, and physical complaints involving weakness, fatigue, and dizziness appear common. The majority of these adolescents are typically referred for treatment because of poor peer relationships and social isolation. They have few friends outside the school environment and are perceived by others as "loners." In contrast to other codetypes, adolescents with the *2-3/3-2* codetype do not typically engage in acting-out behaviors, and drug abuse and sexual acting out are relatively uncommon problems with these adolescents.

2-4/4-2 Codetype

Both adolescents and adults who produce a *2-4/4-2* codetype are often described as having difficulty with impulse control and behaving in a socially inappropriate manner. These adolescents are typically described as depressed, angry, and rebellious, and often have problems with authority figures. Acting out, displacement, and externalization appear to be primary defense mechanisms. The impulsivity and conduct-disordered behaviors exhibited by these adolescents often lead to legal problems, including histories of arrests and convictions. In addition, these adolescents are also at higher risk for substance abuse or alcohol problems. Indeed, the *2-4/4-2* profile is characteristic of drug or alcohol abusers both in adolescent and adult populations. In addition, acting out behaviors often extend to sexual promiscuity, truancy, and running away from home. These adolescents often perceive their parents as unaffectionate and inconsistent, and their family lives as conflictual and hostile.

3-4/4-3 Codetype

Adolescents and adults with the *3-4/4-3* codetype appear to present hypochondriacal or somatic complaints, often involving symptoms of fatigue, weakness, loss of appetite, and headaches. Additionally, adolescents with this codetype typically do not report high levels of emotional distress, but do manifest problems with impulse control and often have histories of antisocial behaviors including theft, school truancy, and running away from home. In psychiatric inpatient settings, adolescents with this codetype often present an elopement risk from the hospital unit, and many of these adolescents report extensive drug use histories. Additionally, adolescents with the *3-4/4-3* codetype have been described as angry and impulsive. These teenagers are typically referred to treatment for sleep difficulties and for suicidal thoughts, gestures, or attempts. Therapists of these teenagers frequently describe them as depressed and also note that they have temper control problems. In school they are often perceived as bullies or roughnecks with explosive tempers.

4-6/6-4 Codetype

Adolescents with the *4-6/6-4* codetype are often referred to treatment for symptomatology involving disobedience, negativism, and defiance. Treatment referrals for these adolescents are often made by court agencies. These adolescents are generally suspicious of the motives of others, and often make excessive demands on others for attention and sympathy. Typical defense mechanisms involve projection and rationalization, and these adolescents tend to externalize responsibility for their problems and behaviors. This codetype is very frequently associated with child-parent conflicts that often take the form of intense, chronic struggles. Recent research has associated the occurrence of this codetype with acting-out behaviors, including sexual acting out, while earlier researchers associated this code with drug abuse. Therapists tend to view adolescents with this codetype as provocative, aggressive, deceitful, hostile, and quarrelsome.

4-8/8-4 Codetype

The *4-8/8-4* codetype is often produced by adolescents with marginal social adjustment. They are frequently perceived by others as odd, peculiar, and immature and have problems in terms of interpersonal conflict and impulse control. Adolescents with this codetype are frequently described as being evasive in psychotherapy, and may display patterns of poor academic achievement and exhibit chaotic and conflictual family lives. Rare among adolescent codetypes, it appears that there may be some correlate differences related to the specific ordering of the two primary scales. Specifically, adolescents with the *8-4* codetype appear to be more regressed and primitive in their psychological functioning than adolescents with the *4-8* codetype.

4-9/9-4 Codetype

The *4-9/9-4* codetype occurs very frequently among adolescent psychiatric patients, particularly in boys. These adolescents are typically referred for treatment because of defiance, disobedience, provocative behaviors, impulsiveness, and school truancy. In many cases, the misbehaviors of these adolescents lead to constant conflict between the teenagers and their parents, but some original research on the families of these adolescents indicate a high rate of adoption or foster home placements. Many of these adolescents are placed on probation or in detention facilities, and acting out is a primary defense mechanism. Therapists describe adolescents with this codetype as socially extroverted, egocentric, narcissistic, and demanding, and resentful of authority figures. Additionally, this group is seen as impatient, impulsive, restless, pleasure-seeking, and undercontrolled. These adolescents tend to combine social extroversion and a gregarious nature with a tendency toward provocative and manipulative behaviors, including lying, stealing, and other antisocial actions. This combination of gregarious and antisocial features led Marks and his colleagues (1974) to refer to adolescents who receive the *4-9/9-4* codetype as "disobedient beauties."

6-8/8-6 Codetype

The *6-8/8-6* codetype indicates serious psychopathology for both adolescents and adults. This codetype has been associated with paranoid symptomatology, delusions of grandeur, feelings of persecution, hallucinations, poor reality testing, and hostile or aggressive outbursts. Adolescents with this codetype appear to be socially isolated and withdrawn, and their behavior is often unpredictable and inappropriate. These adolescents are typically referred for treatment in response to bizarre behaviors or difficulties in distinguishing fantasy from reality. They also appear to have aggression-control problems, and may express hostility or anger physically by hitting others or throwing objects. They are not liked by their peers and often are the target of teasing or are picked on by other adolescents. These teenagers report moderate levels of depression and feelings of guilt and shame. Adolescents with this codetype may be delusional or display grandiose ideas. Most of the teenagers with this codetype classification display little or no insight into their psychological problems.

7-8/8-7 Codetype

The 7-8/8-7 codetype appears to be related to the occurrence of inadequate defenses and poor stress tolerance. These adolescents are frequently described as anxious, depressed, withdrawn, and socially isolated, and they report feel-

---

≡Rapid Reference 4.2

Key Features of Nine Most Common MMPI-A Codetypes

Codetype	Behavioral/Emotional Correlates
1-3/3-1	Multiple physical complaints, attention-seeking actions, conformity, insecurity, poor insight
2-3/3-2	Emotional overcontrol, passivity, dependence, insecurity, poor peer relationships
2-4/4-2	Poor impulse control, substance abuse, depression, elopement risk
3-4/4-3	Somatic complaints, suicide risk, hostile/aggressive impulses, denial of emotional distress
4-6/6-4	Demands of attention/sympathy, resentment, suspiciousness, parent-child conflicts, hostility
4-8/8-4	Marginal social adjustment; seen as impulsive, odd, and peculiar by others; chaotic family lives and poor school adjustment
4-9/9-4	Defiance, disobedience, acting out, impulsivity, authority conflicts, drug abuse, truancy, running away from home
6-8/8-6	Serious psychopathology including paranoid symptoms, delusions, hallucinations, hostile outbursts, unpredictable behavior
7-8/8-7	Anxiety, depression, social withdrawal, strong feelings of inadequacy and insecurity, possible thought disorder symptoms including hallucinations

ings of inadequacy and insecurity. They have substantial difficulty in expressing their emotions in appropriate ways, and are described as inhibited and conflicted in their interpersonal relationships. Many of these teenagers have school difficulties in terms of academic failure and are seen as quite deviant in their thoughts and behavior patterns. In the landmark work conducted by Marks and his colleagues (1974), a relatively high percentage of these adolescents (nearly one half) reported experiencing either auditory or visual hallucinations.

Rapid Reference 4.2 provides a summary of the behavioral and emotional correlates for these common MMPI-A codetypes.

REFINING ASSESSMENT WITH THE CONTENT AND SUPPLEMENTARY SCALES

MMPI-A Content Scales

As described in the MMPI-A manual (Butcher et al., 1992), the MMPI-A content scales were created in a series of five discrete stages. The first, or preliminary, stage involved initially identifying MMPI-2 content scales and items within those scales that were appropriate for adaptation to the MMPI-A. The second stage involved refining the MMPI-A content scales by adding or deleting specific items designed to improve the reliability of the scale. The third stage involved rationally reviewing the scale content in order to ensure that each of these items appeared relevant to the construct or variable measured by that scale. The fourth stage involved statistically refining the scales further, including eliminating those items that showed higher correlations with content scales other than the content scale in which the item was initially scored. The final stage involved selecting narrative descriptors for each of the content scales using the combination of empirical research findings and logical inferences based on the item content of the scale.

Of the 15 MMPI-A content scales, 11 overlap heavily with the MMPI-2 content scales in terms of both constructs and item membership. For this reason, all of the MMPI-A content scales are preceded by the "A" prefix in order to distinguish this set of scales from their MMPI-2 counterparts. There are, however, a number of content scales unique to the MMPI-A: *Alienation (A-aln), Low Aspirations (A-las), School Problems (A-sch),* and *Conduct Problems (A-con).*

The MMPI-A content scales, like their counterparts on the MMPI-2, are composed exclusively of items that are face valid and obvious in terms of their representation of psychopathology. Therefore, the MMPI-A content scales are easily influenced by an adolescent's conscious or unconscious desire to underreport or overreport symptomatology. For these reasons, the MMPI-A interpreter should always carefully evaluate the validity of the MMPI-A protocol prior to interpreting the results of the MMPI-A content scales.

Empirically derived content scale descriptors have been reported by both Williams, Butcher, Ben-Porath, and Graham (1992) and by Archer and Gordon (1991). Similar to other MMPI-A scales, T scores ≥ 65 may be regarded as clinically elevated, while T scores between 60 and 64 may be described as marginally elevated. In contrast to the MMPI-A basic scales, however, little is known concerning the correlate meaning of low scores on the MMPI-A content scales, and thus, this chapter does not provide low-score interpretations for the content scales. The following is a brief description of each of the 15 content scales developed for the MMPI-A.

Anxiety (A-anx) Scale

The MMPI-A *A-anx* scale consists of 21 items related to symptoms of anxiety, apprehension, and rumination. Adolescents who produce elevated scores on this scale report confusion, problems in concentration, and difficulty with staying on task. They also report difficulties in sleeping and the occurrence of nightmares. These adolescents may have a sense that their lives are "going to pieces" and feel that something terrible or dreadful is about to happen. Adolescent girls who produce elevations on this scale often report low endurance and fatigue, domination by peers, obsessional thoughts, and anxiety and timidity, while boys with elevated T scores report problems in concentration, sadness, depression, and possible suicidal ideation.

Obsessiveness (A-obs) Scale

The *A-obs* scale consists of 15 items, all of which are scored in the *True* direction. This scale contains items related to ambivalence and difficulty in making decisions, excessive rumination and worry, and the occurrence of intrusive thoughts. Empirical data reveal that boys who produce elevations on this scale may be described as anxious and dependent, with higher levels of maladjustment, whereas girls are more likely to have histories of suicidal ideation or suicidal gestures.

Depression (A-dep) Scale

The *A-dep* scale consists of 26 items related to depression and sadness, apathy, low energy, and poor morale. Adolescents who produce elevations on this scale often feel dissatisfied with their lives and are unhappy. They have many self-deprecating thoughts and feel hopeless or apathetic concerning their futures. They report feelings of loneliness and despondency, and suicidal ideation is possible. Empirical evidence has related elevations on the *A-dep* scale to a higher incidence of suicidal ideation for girls and to a greater frequency of suicidal attempts for boys.

Health Concerns (A-hea) Scale

The *A-hea* scale includes 37 items, 23 of which also appear on the MMPI-A basic clinical scale *1*. Adolescents who produce elevations on this content scale endorse physical symptoms across a wide variety of areas including gastrointestinal, neurological, cardiovascular, sensory, respiratory, and dermatologic problems. These adolescents feel ill and unhealthy and are prone to worry about their health. Adolescents who produce elevations on this scale are described by their parents as being fearful of school and as having numerous physical problems or complaints. In addition, parents of these boys describe them as anxious and worried, accident-prone, clinging, fearful, perfectionistic, and guilt-prone. Girls who produce elevations on this scale are reported to have problems with weight gain, few or no friends, and an increased frequency of tiredness and fatigue.

Alienation (A-Aln) Scale

The *A-aln* scale contains 20 items selected to identify adolescents who are interpersonally isolated and alienated, and who maintain a considerable emotional distance from others. These adolescents typically feel pessimistic about social interactions and tend to believe that others do not understand them or are unsympathetic to them. Girls who produce higher scores on the *A-aln* scale tend to be socially withdrawn and irritable, and have smaller peer groups, while boys who produce higher scores show social skills deficits and lower levels of self-esteem.

Bizarre Mentation (A-biz) Scale

The *A-biz* scale consists of 19 items related to the occurrence of strange or unusual experiences, which may include auditory, visual, or olfactory hallucinations. Adolescents who produce elevations on this scale believe that something may be wrong with their minds, and are seen by others as strange. These adolescents often have paranoid ideations, including the belief that they are being plotted against or controlled by others. Empirical evidence associates higher scores on the *A-biz* scale with the occurrence of bizarre sensory experiences and psychotic symptoms. Additionally, higher scores for girls are related to the occurrence of hallucinations, poor emotional control, and poor reality testing, whereas higher scores for boys are associated with fighting, legal difficulties, hallucinations, and poor reality testing. In addition, boys in treatment settings who score high elevations on the *A-biz* scale are more likely to display strange behaviors and mannerisms.

Anger (A-ang) Scale

The *A-ang* scale consists of 17 items relevant to anger control problems. Adolescents who produce elevations on this scale are irritable, grouchy, and impatient, and their anger-related problems may extend to the potential for physical assaultiveness. In general, these adolescents feel like swearing, smashing things, starting fights, and may get into trouble because of temper tantrums. They are hot-headed and aggressive.

Empirical evidence indicates that adolescent boys who produce elevations on the *A-ang* scale are more likely to have drug abuse problems, symptoms of hyperactivity, and histories of threatened assaultiveness, whereas girls who produce elevations on this scale are more likely to have histories of truancy, defiance and disobedience, anger, poor parental relationships, assaultiveness, and court appearances. Furthermore, these girls are more likely to dress provocatively and to engage in promiscuity.

Cynicism (A-cyn) Scale

The *A-cyn* scale includes 22 items, and adolescents who produce elevations on this scale may be described as cynical, distrustful, and suspicious of others. They tend to believe that everyone is manipulative and selfish, and they expect others to lie, cheat, and steal. Empirical data for this scale relate girls' higher scores to the occurrence of sexual abuse and poor parental relationships, and these girls are typically perceived by treatment staff as resistant and negative in attitude. For boys, however, research has established few meaningful correlates related to elevations on this scale. Overall, one would expect both boys and girls with elevations on the *A-cyn* scale to be guarded and suspicious of the motives of others and to be hostile and unfriendly in interpersonal relationships.

Conduct Problems (A-con) Scale

The *A-con* scale is composed of 23 items developed to identify adolescents who report a variety of problem areas, including impulsivity, risk-taking behaviors, and antisocial behaviors. Adolescents who produce elevations on this scale are likely to have histories of legal violations or school suspensions, and they are more likely to receive conduct-disorder diagnoses. These adolescents see no problems with trying to get around the law and taking advantage of others. Behavioral problems are likely to include stealing, shoplifting, lying, destruction of property, and swearing.

Empirical evidence has related higher *A-con* scores for boys with presenting problems such as theft, truancy, drug abuse, legal difficulties, alcohol abuse, and assaultive behaviors. Elevations among girls have been related to a higher incidence of running away from home, truancy, defiance, and disobedience. Treatment staff of girls who produce higher scores on this scale note that these girls have multiple behavioral problems that include lying, unpredictability, moodiness, cheating, and anger control problems; these girls are seen as provocative, impulsive, and impatient.

Low Self-Esteem (A-lse) Scale

The *A-lse* scale consists of 18 items useful in identifying adolescents who have low self-esteem and little self-confidence. Adolescents who produce elevations on this scale feel inadequate, useless, and less capable and competent than others. They recognize many real and imagined flaws and faults in themselves, and are often unable to identify any areas of strength or skill. Empirical evidence has related higher scores among boys to poor social skills, passivity, self-blame or condemnation, and higher incidence of suicidal ideation. Among girls, higher scores on the *A-lse* scale have been related to depression, low self-esteem, social withdrawal, and tiredness and fatigue.

Low Aspirations (A-las) Scale

The *A-las* scale is composed of 16 items and is useful in identifying adolescents who have few educational or life goals. They do not apply themselves, they tend to procrastinate, and they give up quickly when faced with a difficult or frustrating task. They do not like to study or read, they dislike science, and they let other people solve problems whenever possible. Unsurprisingly, empirical evidence has related higher scores on the *A-las* scale to poor grades in school and a lower level of participation in school-based activities. Among boys, higher scores in the *A-las* scale are related to a higher incidence of legal difficulties and arrests and to a greater incidence of school truancy and running away from home. Girls with elevations on this scale are more likely to display a defiant and resistant attitude, to be sexually provocative, and to respond to difficulties with frustration and anger.

Social Discomfort (A-sod) Scale

The *A-sod* scale consists of 24 items, 16 of which also appear on the MMPI-A basic clinical scale *0*. Adolescents who produce elevations on the *A-sod* scale tend to be introverted, shy, and uncomfortable in social situations. They dislike having people around them, actively avoid social events, and find it difficult to interact with others. Empirical evidence shows that both boys and girls with higher *A-sod* scores tend to experience social withdrawal and discomfort. Among girls, higher scores have been related to depression, eating disorder problems, social withdrawal, apathy, fatigue, shyness, and avoidance of competition with peers. Among boys, higher *A-sod* scores have been related to a greater incidence of anxiety and nervousness, suicidal thoughts, and a lower level of participation in school activities.

Family Problems (A-fam) Scale

The *A-fam* scale includes 35 items related to the presence of substantial family conflict and discord. Adolescents who produce elevations on this scale have frequent quarrels with family members, report little love or understanding within their families, and feel misunderstood and unjustly punished by family members. These adolescents may wish to run away or escape from their homes and family, and may view their families as physically or emotionally abusive. Family discord, jealousy, fault-finding, and anger characterize the communication patterns within these families.

Empirical evidence has associated higher scores on the *A-fam* scale with a higher incidence of running away from home and physical abuse for boys, and a higher incidence of sexual abuse for girls. Additionally, high-scoring boys are seen as clinging and dependent, resentful, and anxious about their futures; girls are more likely to be seen as sexually provocative or promiscuous, angry, loud, and boisterous. They also tend to have a higher frequency of running away from home.

School Problems (A-sch) Scale

The *A-sch* scale consists of 20 items relevant to difficulties encountered in the school setting. Adolescents who produce elevations on this scale do not like school and are likely to display a number of academic and behavioral problems; they may also experience developmental delays or learning difficulties. These adolescents often get upset by things that occur at school, and may have a history of truancy and school suspensions. They tend to avoid participation in school activities or sports and view school as a waste of time.

Empirical evidence has related higher scores on the *A-sch* scale to a variety of academic and behavioral problems, including poor grades, course failures, disciplinary actions and probations, and suspensions. Girls who produce elevations on this scale have histories of academic underachievement and failure, truancy, learning disabilities, and defiance, whereas boys with *A-sch* scale elevations are more likely to have histories of legal difficulties, drug abuse and fighting, and running away from home.

Negative Treatment Indicators (A-trt) Scale

The *A-trt* scale consists of 26 items useful in identifying adolescents who present initial barriers to treatment that stem from apathy and despondency concerning their ability to change, or from a general suspiciousness and distrust of help offered by others (particularly mental health professionals). These adolescents may feel uncomfortable in making significant changes in their lives, or they may feel that working with others in a change process is useless and a sign of weakness. They do not believe that others are capable of understanding or caring about them, and they report a general unwillingness to discuss problem areas. They may not feel capable of planning their own futures and may be reluctant to accept responsibility for negative events or outcomes in their lives.

It is important to note that elevated scores on *A-trt* do not necessarily predict poor psychotherapy outcomes, but rather indicate the presence of some initial barriers to treatment involving negative attitudes and beliefs. Thus far, empirical evidence has associated higher *A-trt* scores among boys with poor sibling relationships and a tendency to physically threaten peers, whereas higher scores among girls have been related to poor physical coordination and odd physical movements. More useful and meaningful clinical correlates of the *A-trt* scale await careful investigations of this content scale in relation to a variety of treatment processes and outcome measures.

MMPI-A Supplementary Scales

In contrast to the numerous MMPI-2 supplementary scales, the MMPI-A presents a series of only six supplementary scales. Three of the supplementary scales were adapted from the original MMPI, while three were specifically developed for the MMPI-A. In contrast to the MMPI-A content scales, all supplementary scales are converted to *T*-score values based on linear *T*-score transformation procedures. Similar to the MMPI-A content scales, all MMPI-A supplementary scales have a "gray or shaded zone" denoting marginal range elevations that occur between *T* scores of 60 to 64, inclusive. Also similar to the MMPI-A content scales, the MMPI-A supplementary scales require a full-length administration of the MMPI-A and cannot be scored if administration is stopped after the first 350 items.

MacAndrew Alcoholism Scale–Revised (MAC-R)

The first three supplementary scales to appear on the Content and Supplementary Scale Profile focus on the issue of substance abuse, with the *MAC-R* the first of these scales. The original *MacAndrew Alcoholism Scale (MAC)* was created for the MMPI by MacAndrew in 1965 by contrasting or comparing the item responses of 300 male alcoholics with those of 300 male psychiatric patients. Prior to the development of the MMPI-A, the *MAC* scale received a significant amount of research attention for its use with adolescents. This literature generally shows that higher *MAC* scores were related to higher levels of adolescent substance abuse for both alcohol and a variety of drugs. The *MAC* scale was revised for both the MMPI-2 and MMPI-A, with four of the original items deleted and replaced with other items more useful in discriminating individuals with and without substance abuse histories. The MMPI-A *MAC-R* scale contains 49 items, with higher scores indicating a greater likelihood that the adolescent is similar to adolescents who have histories of alcohol or drug problems. In addition to indicating the use and abuse of a wide variety of drugs, higher scores on the *MAC-R* scale also appear to be associated with a variety of personality characteristics, including impulsivity, social extroversion, and general willingness to engage in risk-taking or sensation-seeking activities.

The following correlates have been associated with high ($T \geq 65$) scores on the MMPI-A *MAC-R:*

- Increased likelihood of use or abuse of alcohol and a wide variety of drugs
- Interpersonal assertiveness, dominance, and boldness
- Impulsive, unconventional, and sensation-seeking behaviors

Alcohol/Drug Problem Acknowledgement (ACK) Scale

The *Alcohol/Drug Problem Acknowledgment* (*ACK*) scale is a new scale developed specifically for the MMPI-A and is designed to assess an adolescent's willingness to acknowledge alcohol- or drug-use related symptoms, attitudes, behaviors, or beliefs. The *ACK* scale consists of 13 items that were selected because the item content appeared directly relevant to alcohol or drug use, and the scale was further refined, based upon the use of statistical criterion, to increase scale reliability and validity. Elevations on the *ACK* scale indicate the degree to which the adolescent is willing to admit drug or alcohol use. Adolescents who elevate the *ACK* scale openly acknowledge the use of alcohol, marijuana, and other drugs, and endorse a number of attitudes, beliefs, or behaviors that are associated with drug use. In summary, *T*-score elevations ≥ 65 are associated with the following features or characteristics:

- Willingness to acknowledge the use of alcohol or marijuana and other drugs
- Impulsivity and poor judgment

Alcohol/Drug Problem Proneness (PRO) Scale

The *Alcohol/Drug Problem Proneness* (*PRO*) scale is an empirically derived, 36-item scale that covers a wide range of content including family characteristics, peer group features, antisocial behaviors and beliefs, and academic interests and behaviors. The items for the *PRO* scale were empirically selected based on item endorsement differences shown by adolescents in alcohol and drug treatment programs versus adolescents receiving inpatient psychiatric services. Thus, the "contrasting groups" construction method used to develop the *PRO* scale was quite similar to the methodology used by MacAndrew in creating the

MAC scale. In general, the following characteristics are associated with *T*-score values of 65 or greater on the *PRO* scale:

- Proneness to use or abuse alcohol or drugs
- Involvement in a negative peer group
- Behavioral and disciplinary problems at home and in school

Immaturity (IMM) Scale

The *Immaturity* (*IMM*) scale was developed for the MMPI-A to measure psychological maturation during adolescence. The scale was based on Loevinger's (1976) concept of ego development, particularly those developmental stages characterized as pre-conformist and conformist. Preliminary item selection was based on correlations between MMPI-A items and a measure of ego development, and raters were subsequently used to determine the extent to which preliminary items were related to the concept of ego development. In the final stage of item development, researchers retained or eliminated items based on their overall effects on the internal reliability of the *IMM* scale.

The final form of the *IMM* scale consists of 43 items that cover a variety of areas, including lack of self-confidence, externalization of blame, lack of insight and introspection, interpersonal and social discomfort and alienation, egocentricity and self-centeredness, and hostility and antisocial attitudes. Adolescents who produce elevations on this MMPI-A scale could be described as impulsive and having a limited capacity for self-awareness. They tend to be egocentric and view life in a simplistic and concrete manner. They are opportunistic, exploitive, and demanding in their interpersonal relationships, and, in the Loevinger model, they are operating at the pre-conformist stage of development. In general, the following features or correlates are associated with adolescents who produce high ($T \geq 65$) *IMM* scores:

- Easily frustrated and impatient attitude
- Tendency to be loud, boisterous, and quick to anger
- Untrustworthy and bullying with others
- Likely to have histories of academic and social difficulties
- Uncooperative, defiant, and resistant stance

Welsh's Anxiety (A) Scale and Repression (R) Scale

Welsh's (1956) *Anxiety* and *Repression* scales are derived from factor analyses of the original MMPI. The first factor derived from these analyses has been assigned a variety of labels, including *General Maladjustment;* Welsh termed this factor *Anxiety.* The 35 items in the MMPI-A *A* scale are associated with a variety of forms of emotional or affective distress, and high scores on this scale reflect maladjustment, anxiety, depression, pessimism, general emotional discomfort, and distress. Research with adolescents and the *Anxiety* scale has associated elevations on this scale with fearfulness, anxiety, self-criticism, and a tendency to be guilt-prone. In general, the following features are associated with elevations on the *A* scale:

- Tense and anxious state
- Fearfulness and rumination
- Presentation as maladjusted and emotionally distressed
- Tendency to be self-critical and guilty

Welsh developed the *Repression* scale to assess the second dimension that emerges when the MMPI is subjected to factor analysis. The MMPI-A *R* scale consists of 33 items, all of which are scored in the *False* direction. Individuals who produce elevations on the *R* scale present themselves as conventional, submissive, and agreeable. Significant correlates for elevations on the *R* scale include the following characteristics:

- Overcontrolled and inhibited nature
- Passivity and compliance
- Less likelihood of employing acting-out or exhibiting conduct-disorder behaviors
- Tendency to be pessimistic and cautious

DEVELOPING AND APPLYING THE MMPI-A STRUCTURAL SUMMARY

Our previous presentation of the single-scale and two-point codetype approaches to interpretation have concentrated on information yielded from the MMPI-A basic clinical scales. However, the MMPI-A contains many more standardly used scales and subscales that require careful integration in the process of test interpretation. However, this integration and interpretation process is complicated by the observation that there is a substantial degree of intercorrelation or overlap among the 69 scales and subscales that comprise the MMPI-

A. Part of the reason for areas of significant correlation relate to overlapping items within MMPI scales, reflected in the numerous items that appear on more than one scale. This structural redundancy leads to a significant amount of intercorrelational redundancy. MMPI-A scales are also highly intercorrelated because they often measure similar underlying constructs. Thus, the relationship between clusters of MMPI-A scales may be due both to shared item content and to shared construct overlap. For example, the high intercorrelation found between MMPI-A basic scale *1* and scores derived from content scale *A-hea* ($r \geq .90$) reflects both a substantial shared item pool and a common measurement focus. In contrast, other MMPI-A scales that appear, at least in name, to measure similar constructs do not produce high levels of intercorrelation. For example, the MMPI-A basic clinical scale *2* (*Depression*) and the MMPI-A *A-dep* scale are only moderately correlated ($r = .54$ for males in the normative sample), and these scales are clearly involved in measuring substantially different constructs or variables. Thus, the MMPI-A scales and subscales present a significant challenge in terms of integrating all of this data in order to provide an overall summary regarding the adolescent's psychological functioning.

The best statistical method available for reducing the 69 MMPI-A scales and subscales to a smaller number of underlying dimensions is represented in the factor analytic approaches to the test instrument. Factor analyses have been conducted with the MMPI and the MMPI-A on both the item level and scale level, but it is the scale-level factor analyses that have particularly important implications for interpretation practices. The results of factor analysis of MMPI-A scales indicate that nearly all of the variance in scale and subscale raw scores can be related to eight underlying dimensions. These structural dimensions provide very important and useful information that permit accurate inferences concerning the adolescent's basic psychological functioning. A major advantage to this approach is that it promotes a comprehensive assessment of an adolescent's functioning while eliminating the largely arbitrary distinctions that occur in our typical classification of MMPI-A scales (into categories of basic, content, and supplementary scales or Harris-Lingoes and *Si* subscales). The structural perspective provided by factor-analysis results underscores that the MMPI-A is a highly interrelated instrument reflecting broad underlying dimensions of psychological functioning and psychopathology. The eight factor dimensions developed for the MMPI-A Structural Summary were originally based on factor analyses conducted by Archer, Belevich, and Elkins (1994) with the MMPI-A normative sample; more recently, Archer and Krishna-murthy (1997b) replicated the factor-analytic findings in clinical samples.

Archer and Krishnamurthy (1994) have provided an extensive array of empirical correlates for each of the Structural Summary factors based on data from the 1,620 adolescents in the MMPI-A normative sample and an additional sample of adolescent inpatients (also detailed in Archer, Krishnamurthy, & Jacobson 1994). These correlates are based on information derived from adolescent self-reports, parental ratings, staff ratings, and presenting problems for adolescents in inpatient settings.

At this time, the MMPI-A Structural Summary is best used as a means of effectively focusing the interpreter's attention on the basic dimensions of overall importance in describing an adolescent's psychological functioning. The clinician should restrict factor interpretation to only those factors for which more than half of the scales and subscales received check marks (i.e., $T \geq 60$ or $T \leq 40$, as described in Chapter 3), indicating that the clinician should emphasize that dimension as salient in describing the adolescent's functioning. Furthermore, it currently appears reasonable to assume that the higher the percentage of scales or subscales within a factor that produce critical values, the greater the role of that particular factor dimension in providing a comprehensive description of the adolescent. Thus, the following two guidelines are provided in terms of utilizing the MMPI-A Structural Summary:

- A majority of scales and subscales within a factor must reach critical values ($T \geq 60$ or $T \leq 40$) in order to emphasize that factor in the interpretation process.
- The greater the relative percentage of scales and subscales that produce critical values within a factor, the greater the relative salience of that dimension and the greater the interpretive emphasis that should be placed on that dimension.

THE MMPI-A STRUCTURAL SUMMARY FACTORS

General Maladjustment Factor (23 Scales and Subscales)

The First Factor of the MMPI-A Structural Summary has received substantial research attention and is commonly found in all factor analyses of the test instrument. This factor accounts for the largest component of variance in the test instrument, and is perhaps labeled most accurately as a "General Maladjustment" or "General Distress" dimension. Welsh referred to this factor as "Anxiety," and Welsh's (1956) *Anxiety* scale serves as the best single marker for this factor. Adolescents who produce elevations on this dimension might be expected to show the following characteristics:

- Substantial adjustment problems at home and at school
- Self-consciousness, social withdrawal, timidity, dependency
- Sadness, depression, rumination
- Low competence in social activities
- Avoidance of competitive situations
- Higher likelihood of reporting symptoms of fatigue, tiredness, and sleep difficulties

Immaturity Factor (15 Scales and Subscales)

The second dimension reflected in the MMPI-A Structural Summary has been labeled "Immaturity," and the primary marker of this dimension is the *Immaturity (IMM)* scale. Adolescents who produce elevations on the *Immaturity* scale might be expected to show the following characteristics:

- Egocentricity and self-centeredness
- Limited self-awareness and psychological insight
- Poor judgment and poor impulse control
- School problems including suspensions, disobedience, and poor academic grades
- Peer relationships marked by threats, bullying, and physical aggressiveness
- Increased likelihood of hyperactive, delinquent, and aggressive behaviors

Disinhibition/Excitatory Potential (12 Scales or Subscales)

The third dimension of the Structural Summary relates to disinhibition and excitatory potential and appears to reflect the adolescent's propensity to engage in poorly controlled and impulsive behaviors. The best markers for this dimension are MMPI-A basic clinical scale *9* and the Harris-Lingoes subscale

Ma$_2$ (Psychomotor Acceleration). Adolescents who produce critical *T*-score values on most of the scales and subscales of this factor are likely to display the following characteristics:

- Impulsivity leading to disciplinary problems
- Boastful, loud, talkative, and attention-seeking behavior
- History of poor school work and failing grades
- Greater likelihood of drug or alcohol abuse
- Dominance and aggression in interpersonal relationships
- Conflicts with authority figures and peers

Social Discomfort Factor (8 Scales and Subscales)

The Fourth Factor was labeled "Social Discomfort" and is characterized by elevations on scales related to social introversion, social discomfort, low self-esteem, and interpersonal or social anxiety. Adolescents who produce critical *T*-score values on most of the scales and subscales of this factor are likely to display the following characteristics:

- Social withdrawal and self-consciousness
- Tendency to be dominated by peers and viewed as fearful, timid, and docile
- Lower probability of acting-out behaviors and an increased probability of internalizing behaviors

Health Concerns Factor (6 Scales or Subscales)

The fifth dimension of the Structural Summary was labeled "Health Concerns" but also might have been termed "Somatization." Among the basic clinical scales, the best measures of this factor are scales *1* and *3;* among content scales, the *A-hea* scale serves as a valuable marker for this dimension. Adolescents who produce critical range elevations on the majority of the scales and subscales related to the Health Concerns factor are likely to display the following characteristics:

- Tendency to tire quickly and to have low levels of endurance
- Likelihood of reporting sleeping difficulties, academic problems, and histories of weight loss

- Likelihood of displaying lower levels of social competence and of being socially isolated
- Dependence, shyness, sadness, and preoccupation with health functioning

Naivete Factor (5 Scales or Subscales)

The Sixth Factor was labeled "Naivete" because the Harris-Lingoes subscale by this label (Pa_3) served as a useful and valuable marker for this dimension. Adolescents who produce critical T-score values on the majority of scales and subscales of this factor are likely to display the following characteristics:

- Presentation of self as trusting, socially conforming, and optimistic
- Tendency to deny the presence of hostile or negative feelings or impulses
- Emphasis on conventional behavior and lower probability of provocative or antisocial actions

Familial Alienation Factor (4 Scales or Subscales)

The Seventh Factor identified in the MMPI-A Structural Summary was labeled "Familial Alienation" but might also have been captured by a designation of "Family Conflict." The best markers of this dimension are the *Family Problems* (*A-fam*) content scale and the *Familial Discord* (Pd_1) Harris-Lingoes subscale. Adolescents who produce elevations on three or more of the scales on this factor are likely to display the following characteristics:

- Likely to be seen by parents as hostile, delinquent, or aggressive
- Higher likelihood of having poor parent relationships involving frequent or serious conflicts
- Higher likelihood of having disciplinary problems at school resulting in school suspensions or probations
- Loud, threatening, verbally abusive, and disobedient behavior

Psychoticism Factor (4 Scales or Subscales)

The final factor or dimension on the Structural Summary has been labeled "Psychoticism" because all four of the scales and subscales that define this factor are heavily influenced by psychotic symptomatology. Adolescents who produce elevations on three or more of these four subscales are likely to show the following characteristics:

- Higher likelihood of being teased or rejected by their peer groups
- Subject to sudden mood changes and poorly controlled expressions of anger
- Socially disengaged or schizoid presentation

INTERPRETING THE MMPI-A STRUCTURAL SUMMARY

Archer and Krishnamurthy (1994) have recommended that an interpreter emphasize an MMPI-A Structural Summary dimension as salient in describing an adolescent's functioning only under conditions in which more than half of the scales and subscales associated with the particular factor reach critical values. In order to evaluate this guideline, more recent research findings have suggested that simply placing a check-mark next to critically elevated scales and deriving a simple total of the elevated scales and subscales serve as effective mechanisms for deriving the percentage of markers that show critical values for a particular dimension or factor. For example, if eight of the scales or subscales associated with the Immaturity factor produced T-score values ≥ 60, then this factor meets the criterion of having over 50% of the dimension producing critical values and therefore would be emphasized in the interpretation of the test findings for this adolescent.

It is also possible to examine the specific pattern of scales and subscales elevated within a dimension and to use this information in refining a more precise description of the adolescent. For example, if the eight subscales reaching critical values on the Immaturity dimension involved MMPI-A scales F, 8, 6, Pa_1, Sc_2, Sc_6, A-biz, and A-aln, it would seem appropriate to discuss immaturity characteristics that emphasize alienated and schizoid qualities with disturbed interpersonal relationships. In contrast, if the eight scales and subscales producing critical range elevations on the Immaturity factor involved MMPI-A scales IMM, F, ACK, MAC-R, A-sch, A-con, A-fam, and A-trt, it would appear likely that the Immaturity dimension reflected by this adolescent would emphasize poor judgment and impulse control, aggressiveness, delinquency, and externalizing behaviors. In contrast to the former pattern, this latter pattern is more likely to reflect a conduct-disordered type of symptomatology marked by behavioral difficulties in both the school and home environment. Obviously, this type of refinement in interpreting the Structural Summary dimension (by examining the individual scales and subscales reaching critical value) is likely to be more useful for the larger and more complex factors such as General Maladjustment, Immaturity, and Disinhibition/Excitatory Potential, in contrast to smaller and less involved factors such as Familial Alienation and Psychoticism.

A final guideline in terms of MMPI-A Structural Summary utilization involves the recommendation that greater interpretive emphasis should be placed on those factors and dimensions producing the highest percentage of scales or subscales reaching critical values. Thus, if 18 of the 23 scales and subscales defining the General Maladjustment factor (78%) reach critical values and 8 of the 15 scales and subscales defining the Immaturity dimension (53%) are similarly elevated, then the general characteristics and correlates associated with the General Maladjustment dimension would receive greater emphasis in the interpretation of test data than the features related to the Immaturity dimension. Rapid Reference 4.3 provides a summary of the key

≡ Rapid Reference 4.3

Key Features of the MMPI-A Structural Summary Factors

Factor	Central Characteristic
General Maladjustment	Emotional distress, poor overall adjustment
Immaturity	Self-focus, limited self-awareness or insight, poor judgment
Disinhibition/ Excitatory Potential	Poor impulse control, disciplinary problems, behavioral/legal problems
Social Discomfort	Withdrawal and timidness, domination by others
Health Concerns	Dependence, isolation, somatization
Naivete	Denial of negative impulses, optimism, conformity
Familial Alienation	Disobedience, delinquency, aggressiveness, disciplinary problems
Psychoticism	Obsessiveness, social disengagement, poorly modulated emotions

characteristics associated with each of the eight dimensions of the MMPI-A Structural Summary.

PUTTING IT ALL TOGETHER: STEPS IN THE MMPI-A INTERPRETATION PROCESS

The ability to derive meaningful and useful information from the MMPI-A is a function of the clinician's overall interpretive skills and knowledge combined with his or her ability to successfully integrate and synthesize a large body of complex data. This process begins with an evaluation of extra-test factors that might influence the MMPI-A results, including the setting in which the MMPI-A was administered and the purposes of the evaluation. For example, a very different MMPI-A protocol might be expected from an adolescent screened in a juvenile detention facility as part of a pretrial evaluation, as compared to an adolescent evaluated in a psychiatric treatment unit as part of a discharge planning process, or assessed in a public school system as part of a determination for eligibility for special education services. Furthermore, the adolescent's health status, history of psychiatric symptoms and treatment, family history, ethnic or cultural background, and socioeconomic status might all be expected to influence MMPI-A test findings and the accuracy and utility of inferences derived from the MMPI-A. As previously noted, while it is possible to interpret an MMPI-A profile in a "blind" manner without considering the adolescent's background or history, such a practice is never desirable and is always substantially less accurate than interpretation based on a comprehensive knowledge of the adolescent's background and the testing context.

The next step concerns the evaluation of the technical validity of the MMPI-A profile through an examination of the validity scales and indicators. As we have noted, this process involves reviewing the number of items omitted and evaluating variables related to response consistency and response accuracy. As reflected in the upper portion of the MMPI-A Structural Summary profile labeled "Test-Taking Attitudes," item omissions are reflected in the *Cannot Say* scale value, response consistency is best evaluated through the MMPI-A *VRIN* and *TRIN* scales (and, to a lesser degree, by examining the T-score elevation difference between MMPI-A F_1 and F_2 subscales), and the accuracy of the adolescent's response pattern may be evaluated by using validity scales *F, L,* and *K.* Overreporting is most clearly illustrated by MMPI-A profiles that contain an *F* *T*-score value ≥ 90 and a "floating" clinical scale pattern involving the clinical range elevation on all the basic scales with the exception of the nonclinical scales of *Mf* and *Si*. In contrast, underreporting is best exemplified by an MMPI-A protocol showing *T*-score values ≥ 65 on validity scales *L* and *K,* and *T*-score values of < 60 on all basic clinical scales (except *Mf* and *Si*) produced by an adolescent with a history of psychopathology.

The next step in MMPI-A profile interpretation involves examining the data presented in the basic or standard clinical scales and determining the most useful approach in interpreting these data. For MMPI-A Basic Scale Profiles with only one clinical scale elevation (*T* ≥ 65), the approach will obviously center on single-scale interpretation in which the symptoms or psychopathological characteristics associated with a specific MMPI-A basic scale are emphasized in the interpretation of the adolescent's test findings. However, when two or more MMPI-A basic scales show clinical range elevations, the clinician must choose whether to use the single-scale interpretation or a two-point codetype interpretation approach. If the clinician retains the single-scale approach, he or she would simply accumulate or aggregate the characteristics or correlates generated by each of the elevated clinical scales, placing greatest weight on those scales that are most elevated. In contrast, if the clinician uses a two-point codetype interpretation he or she would seek to classify the adolescent into a two-point codetype classification based on the degree to which the adolescent's specific MMPI-A profile corresponds to one of the basic two-point codes presented in Archer (1997). The degree of usefulness of the MMPI-A codetype is likely to be related to both the extent of elevation of the two primary scales and the degree of definition exhibited in the two-point codetype for a given adolescent.

For MMPI-A Basic Clinical Scale Profiles that contain three or more clinically elevated scales (*T* ≥ 65), a combination of two-point codetype and individual scale interpretation would be the preferred interpretive approach, with correlates and descriptors associated with the two-point codetype combined with correlates and descriptors generated from all other basic clinical scales that produce clinical range elevations. Again, the interpretive principle guiding this process would be that the correlates and adjectives derived from the most elevated scales are given greater weight in the description of the adolescent.

Regardless of whether the interpretation of the MMPI-A basic scales is undertaken through an individual scale approach, a two-point codetype approach, or a combination of these approaches in cases of multiply elevated profiles, the use of the Harris-Lingoes and *Si* subscales is very effective in helping to refine the interpretation of the MMPI-A basic scale elevations, particularly for those basic scales that are elevated in a marginal to moderate range. However, the Harris-Lingoes and *Si* subscales should not be interpreted unless a clinical range elevation has occurred on the corresponding MMPI-A basic scales. For example, the Harris-Lingoes subscales for scale *4* should not be reviewed and interpreted unless the adolescent produces an elevation of $T \geq 60$ on scale *4*. These cautions are necessary because many of the subscales are extremely short and, therefore, of reduced reliability, and because the interpretation of subscales in the absence of a clinical range elevation on the basic scale often "over-pathologizes" an adolescent in terms of rendering an interpretation that overemphasizes psychopathological characteristics or traits.

Following the review of the MMPI-A basic scales and refinement of interpretation through the Harris-Lingoes and *Si* subscales, the clinician should evaluate the information derived from the MMPI-A content and supplementary scales and integrate it into test findings. A review of the MMPI-A supplementary scales provides important information concerning the adolescent's overall level of emotional distress, ego maturation, and use of repression as a primary defense mechanism; it also provides extensive information concerning the degree to which the teenager's problems are likely to include alcohol and drug abuse issues. The 15 MMPI-A content scales provide a very extensive amount of information concerning the adolescent's functioning, but until more research is available on these scales, it is prudent not to interpret these scales independently but only in conjunction with data derived from the MMPI-A basic scales. The results of findings with the *A-anx, A-obs, A-dep, A-aln,* and *A-biz* scales provide the interpreter with much information concerning the adolescent's emotional functioning and overall adjustment, while results from the *A-ang, A-cyn,* and *A-con* scales provide important data concerning the likelihood that an adolescent will display behavioral problems and come into conflict with others in a manner found for adolescents employing externalizing defenses. Finally, the results of the *A-lse, A-las, A-sod, A-fam, A-sch,* and *A-trt* scales provide the interpreter with rich data concerning the adolescent's functioning in a variety of specific areas, including his or her social environment, school environment, family environment, and probably his or her initial attitude toward the psychotherapy process (*A-trt*). For both the supplementary and content scales, clinical range elevations are defined by T scores $\geq$ 65 and indicate that the symptoms or behaviors assessed by a particular scale are likely to be descriptive of the adolescent's functioning, while marginal or transitional range elevations are defined by T scores of 60 to 64, inclusive. Adolescents who produce these marginal elevations on MMPI-A clinical or supplementary scales are likely to have fewer of the symptoms or problems associated with higher elevations, and less confidence should be placed in interpretive statements generated by marginal range elevations.

The MMPI-A interpreter may wish to utilize the Structural Summary form as a method of organizing MMPI-A scale data in a final stage of profile analysis. As we have noted, the MMPI-A Structural Summary form attempts to organize and simplify the adolescent's overall MMPI-A test findings in a manner that emphasizes the most salient and comprehensive aspects of the adolescent's functioning and de-emphasizes the largely arbitrary distinction between categories of scales. The MMPI-A Structural Summary identifies those features that most reflect the adolescent's functioning, based on the proposition that a majority of scales or subscales associated with a particular factor must reach critical values ($T \geq 60$ or $T \leq 40$, depending on the scale or subscale) before the interpreter should emphasize that dimension as important in the ado-

DON'T FORGET

Steps to Follow in Interpretation

- Consider the role of extra-test factors, such as the evaluation setting, purposes of testing, and the examinee's history and background, on MMPI-A results to refine interpretation and improve accuracy.
- Use the validity scales to evaluate whether the profiles are interpretable.
- Consider if a two-point codetype interpretation (versus single-scale interpretation) is suitable based on codetype elevation and definition.
- Use Harris-Lingoes and *Si* subscale elevations to determine the source of basic scale elevations when applicable.
- Augment the basic scale findings with information from content and supplementary scales.
- Examine Structural Summary factor patterns to determine overarching trends.

lescent's personality functioning. Furthermore, when more than one dimension or factor has a majority of scales or subscales reaching critical values, the higher the percentage of scales or subscales within a factor that produce critical values, and the greater the role of that particular factor or dimension in providing a comprehensive description of the adolescent.

COMPUTER-BASED TEST INTERPRETATION APPROACHES

An overview of the interpretation approaches to the MMPI-A would not be complete without some discussion of the uses of computer technology in the interpretation of this test instrument. Because of the extensive empirical literature available on the MMPI and the strong conceptual basis for actuarial interpretation of the test instrument, the MMPI served as the first focus for computer scoring and computer interpretation programs. Since the original development of the early MMPI computer interpretation systems, the use of computer-based test interpretation has spread to many diverse assessment instruments including objective, projective, intellectual, and neuropsychological tests.

The first application of computer interpretation for the MMPI was developed at the Mayo Clinic in the early 1960s in order to handle the large volume of patients seen at the Mayo Clinic. The first widespread commercially available computer interpretation service for the MMPI was developed by Raymond Fowler and distributed by the Roche Corporation in 1963. Today, there are numerous MMPI-2 interpretive programs commercially available, and at least three programs marketed for the interpretation of the MMPI-A. These computer packages include an MMPI-A Adolescent Interpretive System developed by Archer and distributed by Psychological Assessment Resources (PAR), the Minnesota Report: Adolescent Interpretive System developed by Butcher and Williams and distributed by National Computer Systems (NCS), and the Marks Adolescent Interpretive Report by Marks and Lewak and distributed by Western Psychological Services (WPS). The output from the PAR MMPI-A program is illustrated in Chapter 7.

Automated-computer interpretive reports for various forms of the MMPI are based on combinations of research findings and clinical experience, resulting in what has been described as the *actuarial-clinical approach* to test interpretation. Specifically, on the basis of published research combined with the author's clinical hypotheses and clinical experiences, a series of interpretive statements are generated to match particular sets of test scores. When the computer interpretive package is accessed, the memory function is reviewed to find interpretive statements that are judged to be appropriate for a particular set of test scores or patterns, and these statements are then selected for printout. The accuracy of the computer-based interpretations depends on the knowledge and skill of the individual who generated the interpretive statements, and his or her ability to translate this knowledge successfully into a format compatible with a computer code.

Research has shown that the overall quality and accuracy of computer-based test interpretation programs vary widely. The American Psychological Association (APA) has published a set of guidelines for the development and use of computer-based test interpretation (CBTI) products (APA, 1986). These guidelines include the provision that professionals limit their use of CBTI products to those instruments with which they are familiar and competent, and that such reports only be used in conjunction with professional judgment. Research has shown that even the best CBTI programs are rated by clinicians as only moderately accurate, and CBTI programs should never be used as the sole basis for providing interpretive descriptions of the patient. Butcher (1987) has suggested several advantages to the use of computer-based test interpretations, noting that such approaches often are cost-effective and a rapid way of obtaining an objective and reliable "outside" opinion on an MMPI protocol. CBTI products, for example, can typically be generated within a few minutes after data is entered into the system and are not subject to interpreter bias based on the characteristics of the client. However, Butcher also noted several disadvantages associated with CBTI products, including the confusing abundance of packages currently available, the possibility of excessively generalizing interpretive statements to protocols that are not closely matched to those used by the computer for the interpretation, and an increased potential for misuse because of the wide availability of CBTI products. It is important to note that the APA guidelines make it very clear that clinicians are responsible for the use of computer-based test interpretation approaches, and that CBTI users must be sufficiently familiar with the test, test interpretation package, and the client in order to judge the applicability of CBTI statements to a particular respondent.

Graham (2000) has suggested several guidelines for clinicians when selecting and using CBTI products. First, all CBTI products represent a combination of the author's clinical judgment and research findings that have been established for a particular test instrument. Therefore, the potential test user must be aware of the identity and expertise of the individual or individuals who have developed the CBTI package in order to accurately judge the usefulness of this product. The clinician acquiring the CBTI product is, in a very real sense, purchasing or leasing the clinical and scientific judgment of the individual writing the interpretive output. Related to this point, it is important for the clinician to understand the ways in which the CBTI report has been created and written. How broad was the empirical research base used in the development of the test instrument, and to what degree are CBTI-generated statements based on empirical findings? The clinician should carefully review the CBTI manual for this type of information prior to the purchase and use of computerized interpretive reports. In purchasing a CBTI product, it is also reasonable for the clinician as consumer to request samples of the interpretive output for the report, and to examine the degree to which the company provides adequate support for the use and application of the CBTI product. Does the company provide an 800-number available for product users, and is the manual detailed and "user-friendly?." Does it have sufficient information to meaningfully assist the clinician in both the technical and clinical aspects of the interpretive report? Is the CBTI periodically revised and updated to reflect changes in the scientific literature and in interpretive approaches to the test instrument? This point is particularly important for instruments such as the MMPI-A, which are relatively new and hence subject to rapid changes as the research literature changes and expands over time. Finally, to what extent has the computer-based test interpretation been subject to research studies establishing the empirical validity of the product? This type of research might include consumer satisfaction studies, but also should include validity studies involving external criteria in which the accuracy of CBTI-based descriptors are evaluated by external clinician-raters.

In summary, automated computerized reports for the MMPI-A (as well as other assessment instruments) are best thought of as professional consultations to be integrated with other sources of information available about the adolescent. CBTI products are never a substitute for a comprehensive psychological assessment of the adolescent, nor do they provide shortcuts for the clinician in terms of developing competency with a particular test instrument.

CAUTION

Points to Remember in the Use of Computerized Assessments

- All CBTIs are a combination of an author's clinical judgment and research findings. Be aware of the identity and expertise of the developers of the CBTI package.
- Know how the CBTI report was written. To what extent is it based on research findings and how broad was the empirical base used in the development of the CBTI?
- Companies vary in the degree to which they provide user support services. To what degree does the company marketing the CBTI support its use and application? Is there a detailed and user-friendly test manual? Is an 800-number available to support product use?
- All CBTI products should be periodically revised and updated. Is the CBTI systematically revised or updated to reflect changes in interpretation practices?

As repeatedly emphasized in this chapter, even though the MMPI-A is relatively easy to administer and score, the interpretation of this instrument is a relatively complex process that involves a high degree of expertise and skill on the part of the clinician. This chapter has emphasized the technical knowledge concerning the MMPI-A that is most useful in the test interpretation process. In addition to psychometric sophistication concerning the MMPI-A, it is also important that the clinician have an extensive familiarity with personality structure, development, and psychopathology as found in adolescence. Thus, the formation of useful diagnostic or treatment recommendations for any adolescent involves a detailed knowledge of the MMPI-A combined with a broad understanding of the complexities of adolescent development and psychopathology. The test interpretation principles and processes presented in this chapter are illustrated in more detail in Chapter 7, which provides several case examples of MMPI-A interpretations as well as an illustration of the application of the PAR computerized test interpretation package for the MMPI-A.

🖋 TEST YOURSELF 🖋

1. **Somatic complaints are most likely for which of the following codetypes?**

   (a) 1-3/3-1

   (b) 4-9/9-4

   (c) 6-8/8-6

   (d) 7-8/8-7

2. **The ACK and PRO scales are useful in identifying**

   (a) anger problems.

   (b) school problems.

   (c) substance abuse problems.

   (d) eating disorder problems.

3. **Interpretation of subscales is recommended when the parent clinical scale**

   (a) is part of a codetype.

   (b) shows a spike elevation.

   (c) is in a subclinical range.

   (d) is in a marginal or clinical range of elevation.

4. **A thought disorder is most likely indicated when**

   (a) scale 8 and A-biz are both elevated.

   (b) scale 8 is elevated but A-biz is not.

   (c) scale 9 and A-trt are both elevated.

   (d) scale 8 and IMM are both elevated.

5. **An overreporting bias in test-taking is reflected in**

   (a) high F, high L and K configuration.

   (b) high F, low L and K configuration.

   (c) low F, high L, and moderate K configuration.

   (d) jointly elevated F, L, and K configuration.

Answers: 1. a; 2. c; 3. d; 4. a; 5. b

Five

STRENGTHS AND WEAKNESSES OF THE MMPI-A

From the date of its release, the MMPI-A has benefited from its continuity with the original MMPI. The two forms of the test share a common empirical foundation and test structure, a remarkable comprehensiveness in evaluating psychological and behavioral disorders in adolescents, and a vast research literature that has supported and enhanced their use. Currently nearing its first decade of use, the MMPI-A's advantages and disadvantages have become more discernable when compared to the use of the original MMPI with adolescents and in relation to other existing personality measures for adolescents. Test reviews of the MMPI-A published since its inception have been largely favorable. For example, Claiborn (1995) remarked that the new normative sample is "admirably diverse" (p. 626), the new content and supplementary scales are "clearly relevant to understanding adolescent development and symptomatology" (p. 628), and the test overall is "an impressive inventory, sure to become a preeminent tool for assessing adolescent psychopathology" (p. 628). Lanyon (1995) concurred that the newly developed content scales are likely to have high clinical utility. He further stated that the MMPI-A test developers' goals of maintaining similarity to the MMPI while addressing several of its limitations have been achieved. Lanyon concluded that "the life of the MMPI has thereby been enhanced and significantly extended" (p. 629) in the MMPI-A and that the test "would appear to have no serious competition" (p. 629). However, not all of the features of the MMPI-A have received praise from reviewers. For example, Claiborn commented that the retention of the archaic names for the clinical scales is "unfortunate" (p. 627), and Lanyon observed that the test-construction approach used for the scales retained from the original MMPI is "simplistic by today's standards" (p. 629). In this chapter, we discuss what we consider to be the salient strengths and limitations of the MMPI-A, incorporating findings from recent research investigations and observations from clinical use of the instrument. Our evaluative impressions are also summarized in the Rapid Reference and Caution boxes in this chapter.

STRENGTHS

Norms

The development of updated and expanded norms is perhaps the single most important feature of the MMPI-A and forms the essential foundation for its advantages. MMPI-A norms meet the standards of national representation, stratification of the sample in terms of major demographic variables, and achieving a reasonable match to national census data. Specifically, the inclusion of individuals from African-American, Hispanic, Asian, and Native American minority groups in the normative sample has rendered the test more appropriate for use with diverse adolescent populations. The provision of a single set of "official" norms has also succeeded in standardizing the use of the test, and has eliminated the confusion associated with the availability of multiple adolescent MMPI norm sets that transferred the burden of selecting the appropriate norms to the test user. It should be noted, however, that the MMPI-A norms are not without flaws. For example, the average parental education of the normative sample was noticeably higher than that for the population represented in the 1980 census, which raises questions about the relative sophistication of the normative sample in responding to test items as compared to the typical adolescent evaluated in a clinical setting. Moreover, the actual number of participants from ethnic minority groups was less than 50 for Hispanic, Native American, and Asian groups, separately, warranting further evaluation to determine fully the accuracy of the norms for minority group adolescents. It is also important to note that the clinical sample used for developing MMPI-A content scales was considerably smaller than the normative sample and was collected entirely from Minneapolis treatment facilities. However, the test manual (Butcher et al., 1992) reports that the clinical scale profiles generated from this sample were congruent with those produced by adolescents in Marks et al.'s (1974) MMPI sample. In general, the MMPI-A norms are well developed, offer a clear improvement over MMPI adolescent norm sets, and should prove useful for several decades.

Test Structure and Psychometric Adequacy

As discussed in Chapter 1, the process of revising the MMPI to the MMPI-A involved specific goals of retaining the basic structure of the test, improving items, and developing new scales to measure disturbances specific to the adolescent developmental phase. The MMPI-A item pool represents a significant improvement over MMPI items in terms of greater relevance for adolescents, improved grammar, and relative nonintrusiveness of the revised items. For example, MMPI-A items such as "I am a slow learner in school," "My friends often talk me into doing things I know are wrong," and "My parents do not really love me" directly address feelings and experiences of troubled adolescents. Original MMPI items that lack a meaningful context for recent generations of teenagers, or that are frequently not comprehended by modern-day adolescents, have largely been deleted. Although some test items continue to have words and phrases that may be considered awkward or antiquated and the use of double negatives in test items has not been eliminated completely, MMPI-A items are typically more straightforward and comprehensible. Moreover, the shortening of the test from 566 to 478 items renders it more amenable to successful completion by adolescents, and the audiocassette version makes it usable with adolescents who have reading and concentration difficulties.

The MMPI-A continues to measure the broad array of psychopathological disturbances assessed by the MMPI. Moreover, the development of a new set of content scales and the maintenance of, and addition to, the set of supplementary scales has successfully augmented and enhanced the measurement of various domains of adolescent psychopathology. Specifically, scales such as *Conduct Problems, School Problems, Low Aspirations,* and *Immaturity* assess areas that were previously not addressed for adolescents evaluated with the MMPI. The designation of a standard set of six supplementary scales instead of a plenitude of insufficiently evaluated research and supplemental MMPI scales has also helped to standardize the method of assessing adolescents with this measure.

The MMPI-A manual (Butcher et al., 1992) provides extensive information on the psychometric properties of the test with data presented in a series of well-organized tables. In general, these data attest to the instrument's psychometric soundness. Test-retest stability and internal consistency figures are quite respectable. Other independent studies have also upheld the reliability of the instrument with reference to the stability of the items modified from the MMPI to the MMPI-A, in terms of strong similarity in item response patterns (Archer & Gordon, 1994) and test-retest stability over a one-year time span in nonclinical adolescents (Stein, McClinton, & Graham, 1998). Evidence of test validity in the MMPI-A manual also includes factor-analytic findings revealing similarities between the factor structures underlying MMPI-A and MMPI basic scales. More recent studies have also provided factor-analytic support for the structural underpinnings of MMPI-A items and scales in normative and clinical samples, respectively (Archer, Belevich, & Elkins, 1994; Archer & Krishnamurthy, 1997b; McCarthy & Archer, 1998), for the convergent and discriminant validity of selected MMPI-A content scales (Arita & Baer, 1998), and for the concurrent validity of the MMPI-A in assessing juvenile offenders (Toyer & Weed, 1998). The overall psychometric soundness of the MMPI-A is further supported by a recent study indicating that variance in MMPI-A scale scores is based on actual psychopathology and is not significantly affected by demographic characteristics of sex and ethnicity (Schinka, Elkins, & Archer, 1998). With reference to the accuracy of MMPI-A codetypes in reflecting clients' symptoms, psychosocial histories, and underlying psychodynamics, a study by Janus, Tolbert, Calestro, and Toepfer (1996) found that accuracy ratings for profiles based on MMPI-A norms were comparable to those using the Marks and Briggs (1972) adolescent norms. Moreover, nearly half of the raters in their study considered the overall accuracy of the MMPI-A as favorable (i.e., generally accurate to totally accurate), particularly with respect to accuracy of symptom description.

Research Foundation

Because the MMPI-A is a revision of the MMPI that retains the latter's central features, particularly with reference to the basic validity and clinical scales, use of this instrument is supported by more than five decades of research investigation. As mentioned in Chapter 1, no other personality assessment measure has received more research attention than the MMPI. Empirical studies of the MMPI with adolescents have revealed the most appropriate uses of the test by identifying optimal cutting scores for determining clinical significance of scale elevations, providing clinical correlates of scale scores for adolescent populations, and examining a host of issues related to accurate interpretation of adolescent psychopathology (to name a few areas). For example, studies by Archer, Gordon, Anderson, and Giannetti (1989) and Archer, Gordon, Giannetti, and Singles (1988) revealed that correlates of selected basic scales and supplementary scales, respectively, were similar for adolescents and adults, which offered support for the application of standard scale descriptors to adolescent populations. Williams and Butcher (1989a) similarly found that single-scale descriptors for adolescents were consistent with those previously reported for adults. These studies suggest that reliance on the vast correlate literature of the MMPI derived from adolescent and adult studies is justifiable for MMPI-A interpretation. However, Williams and Butcher (1989b) reported that several codetype descriptors previously identified by Marks et al. (1974) for adolescents did not replicate in their study, which caused them to offer cautions in using MMPI codetype descriptions for the MMPI-A.

An independent research literature is beginning to develop, albeit somewhat slowly, for the MMPI-A that includes attention to the content and supplementary scales such as *ACK, PRO,* and *IMM,* and that examines the effectiveness of the validity scales in detecting response biases. For example, in an investigation of the relative contributions of MMPI-A scales and Rorschach indices in classifying adolescents into diagnostic groups, Archer and Krishnamurthy (1997a) reported a hit rate of .68 using either MMPI-A scale *2* or the *A-dep* content scale for identifying depression-group membership. For diagnoses related to conduct disorder, scales *A-con* and *A-cyn* yielded hit rates of .61 and .66, respectively, using a *T*-score cutoff of ≥ 65. Both sets of results were found to be superior to those involving the Rorschach. These types of studies have begun to amplify the utility of MMPI-A scales, singly or in combination with each other, in the task of adolescent diagnostic assessment.

In addition to published research, a review of *Dissertation Abstracts Online* reveals that the MMPI-A has been the subject of approximately 70 doctoral-dissertation research investigations conducted between 1991 and 1999 and of numerous other master's thesis studies, which reflects a perpetuation of strong research interest in the MMPI to its adolescent revision.

Evaluation of Response Sets and Profile Validity

The MMPI is one of the first personality inventories that incorporated a method for gauging overall profile validity and detecting response biases that interfere with the accuracy of the resulting profiles. This is an important issue, because inconsistent responding and inaccurate self-representation are relatively common among both adolescents and adults. For example, the MMPI-2 research literature indicates that motivation to overreport or exaggerate distress may be present for adults involved in personal injury litigation (e.g., Lees-Haley, 1991), and underreporting or problem-minimizing trends may be found in cases involving determination of suitability for child custody (e.g., Bagby, Nicholson, Buis, Radovanovic, & Fidler, 1999). Among forensic populations, either type of response distortion (i.e., overreporting or underreporting) may occur depending on the type of perceived advantages associated with them (see Ben-Porath, Graham, Hall, Hirschman, & Zaragoza, 1995). Various forms of psychopathology may also contribute to an inaccurate portrayal of one's psychological disturbance, and psychological and neuropsychological disorders involving states of confusion and distracted thinking may result in inconsistent responding to items that are conceptually similar in meaning. As noted in Chapter 2, adolescents with poor reading comprehension, attention deficits, or learning disabilities may respond in contradictory ways to test items, and unmotivated teenagers' hasty or careless responding may produce profiles that are essentially uninterpretable. Although the clinician can anticipate and attempt to reduce the likelihood of response distortions, problems with profile validity are inevitable in clinical assessment situations. The validity scales of the MMPI-A are therefore crucial in detecting these distortions.

Preliminary evaluation of the new *VRIN* and *TRIN* validity scales suggested that they were useful in detecting inconsistent responding and reliance on acquiescent or nay-saying response sets, respectively (Butcher et al., 1992). The test manual also suggests that comparing scores on F_1 and F_2 scales could help identify changes in the test-taking approach as the adolescent progressed from the first half to the second half of the test. Recent investigations have furnished support for the utility of these scales in detecting inconsistent responding. For example, Archer (1997) reported that a random response pattern, created by endorsing equal numbers of items in true and false directions, produced a profile with clinical elevations on *VRIN*, F, F_1, F_2, and L, and a normal-range *TRIN T* score below 60. Based on this finding, the clinician obtaining such a profile pattern could readily identify it as a random response pattern and refrain from interpreting it.

Baer, Ballenger, Berry, and Wetter (1997) also evaluated random responding on the MMPI-A using a sample of normal adolescents. Responses obtained in a standard administration were compared with those from four random response conditions, each involving a different degree of randomness based on different starting points in the test for implementing random responding. Results demonstrated a striking pattern of increasing scores on scales F_1, F_2, F, and $VRIN$ with increasing degrees of random responding, and an effect size of at least 1 standard deviation difference between the random response groups and the standard instruction group was obtained. The results also indicated that the discrimination between random and standard profiles was successfully achieved by F_2, F, and $VRIN$ for all levels of randomness, and by scale F_1 for the first half of the test. Archer and Elkins (1999) similarly found that MMPI-A validity scales F, F_1, F_2, and $VRIN$ were effective in discriminating between random and nonrandom responding using test protocols from a clinical sample of 354 adolescents and computer-generated random protocols. All of these studies underscore the utility of scales $VRIN$, F, F_1, and F_2 in detecting random responding with adolescents in psychiatric settings.

Validity scales F, L, and K that were retained from the original form of the MMPI to the MMPI-A have been extensively evaluated in research studies involving the original test instrument and found to be useful in detecting inaccurate responding. Recent studies specifically involving the MMPI-A have reinforced these findings by indicating that these scales are sensitive to under- and overreporting of symptoms. For example, a study by Baer, Ballenger, and Kroll (1998) compared community and clinical samples of adolescents who were instructed to portray themselves as having excellent psychological adjustment by means of underreporting symptoms. Results indicated significantly higher scores for the underreporting groups on scales L and K, reflective of denial and defensiveness, which permitted accurate discrimination between underreported profiles and standard profiles. Baer, Kroll, Rinaldo, and Ballenger (1999) further demonstrated that overreporting on the MMPI-A can be detected using the validity scales with clinical and nonclinical adolescent samples. Specifically, they found that scale F was elevated at a T score $\geq$ 80 for adolescents who overreported psychopathological symptoms. Moreover, F was sensitive to both random responding and overreporting of symptoms, whereas $VRIN$ was elevated only by random responding. The authors proposed that random responding could be inferred when F and $VRIN$ scales are jointly elevated, whereas an F scale elevation without a $VRIN$ elevation suggests an overreporting pattern.

A recent development in MMPI-A validity assessment consists of the development of an *Infrequency-Psychopathology* scale for the MMPI-A (*Fp-A;* Mc-Grath, Pogge, Stein, Graham, Zaccario, & Piacentini, 2000) mirroring the $F(p)$ scale developed by Arbisi and Ben-Porath (1995) for the MMPI-2. The original $F(p)$ scale was developed to facilitate interpretation of an elevated F scale, given that F can be elevated under several conditions including actual distress and disturbance, overreporting of symptoms or malingering, and random responding. Although the $VRIN$ scale has since aided the detection of random responding, discrimination of overreported profiles from actual distress profiles remained difficult under conditions of an elevated F score. The $F(p)$ scale consists of items endorsed infrequently by both nonclinical adults and psychiatric patients, such that an elevation in $F(p)$ points to overreporting as the basis of an F scale elevation. Using the same rationale and method, the $Fp-A$ was developed using participants from the MMPI-A normative sample, two inpatient clinical sample of adolescents for scale derivation and construct validation, respectively, and a high school sample for evaluating the effectiveness of $Fp-A$ in detecting overreporting. The authors reported that $Fp-A$ was less responsive to actual psychopathology than F, as was expected, and that it showed a modest but significant incremental contribution over F in the prediction of overreporting. These initial results are promising, and future investigations may demonstrate that the $Fp-A$ scale will serve to further enhance validity assessment processes on the MMPI-A. Collectively, the published research studies concerning MMPI-A validity scales suggest that validity assessment is a prominent strength of the MMPI-A, reflecting a continuation and expansion of the emphasis found in the original MMPI concerning accurate appraisal of profile validity.

Popularity and Frequency of Use

Similar to the original MMPI, the MMPI-A retains the position of being the most widely used self-report personality inventory for evaluating adolescents. A recent survey by Archer and Newsom (2000) polled 346 psychologists engaged in clinical practice in diverse settings—including independent practices, universities and medical schools, medical centers or hospitals, outpatient clinics, and school systems—to determine their frequency of usage of 36 psychological test measures. Survey results indicated that the MMPI-A was among the ten most frequently used instruments in adolescent assessment and was the only objective personality assessment measure in that set. Moreover, it was rated fifth (after intelligence and projective measures) in total mentions and in terms of a weighted score reflecting intensity of use. These results may be compared to those of Archer et al. (1991), who conducted a similar survey prior to the release of the MMPI-A, when the MMPI was used in evaluating adolescents. The earlier survey found that the MMPI was the third most frequently mentioned test instrument in adolescent assessment and the sixth most frequently used test measure with this population. Archer and Newsom's survey findings reflect the sturdiness of the MMPI and its revised form in a managed mental health practice environment characterized by reductions in the overall utilization of testing. Moreover, their results reflected clinicians' recognition of the test's ability to provide a comprehensive clinical picture, which was endorsed by survey respondents as one of its predominant strengths. The foreign-language translations in progress for the MMPI-A, mentioned in Chapter 2, are expected to amplify further the use of this test measure on an international scale.

Usefulness in Treatment Planning and Treatment Outcome Evaluation

The MMPI-A contains a number of scales that are directly useful to clinicians for developing an appropriate, individually tailored treatment plan based on the specific adolescent's difficulties as revealed in the test profiles. For example, a number of scales across the basic, content, and supplementary scale profiles shed light on whether the adolescent is expressing a plea for help, a strong reluctance to engage in psychotherapy, a need for structured and consistently applied limits, or ego-supportive measures. Using this information, the clinician can evolve a plan of treatment that represents a good fit to the salient and unique aspects of the adolescent's difficulties. Additionally, retesting with the MMPI-A during the course of treatment offers opportunities to examine whether any changes in treatment plan or treatment approach need to occur, and testing at the point of termination enables evaluation of treatment progress. MMPI-A results can also be combined with findings from other test measures at the initiation or termination of treatment to obtain a sense of the adolescent's functioning from multiple perspectives. These issues are discussed in greater detail in the next chapter. The treatment-relevant information provided by the MMPI-A is, in our view, one of the strongest and most useful features of the test. Rapid Reference 5.1 summarizes the strengths of the MMPI-A.

⪉ Rapid Reference 5.1

Strengths of the MMPI-A

Breadth
- The test provides a broad-band assessment of adolescent problem areas.

Norms
- It has contemporary norms based on a representative national sample.

Items
- The number of items has been reduced from 566 to 478.
- New test items have been added to reflect adolescent-relevant areas of concern.
- Many poorly worded or objectionable items have been deleted or modified in the revision process.

Scales
- There is a standard set of supplementary scales.
- The new set of content scales addresses adolescent-specific problem areas.
- The provision of validity scales enables detection of response sets and profile invalidity.

Foundations
- A large research base supports its applications.
- The test is psychometrically sound.

Usage
- It continues to be one of the most popular and widely used measures for evaluating adolescents.
- It is useful for planning, directing, and evaluating treatment.
- The test is available in audiocassette form and foreign language translations.

LIMITATIONS

The limitations of the MMPI-A described in this section underscore aspects of the structural and psychometric features of the test that may present barriers to a complete and accurate evaluation. It should be noted that other perceived limitations of the test may have more to do with test users' relative unfamiliarity with the test and insufficient knowledge of its appropriate uses. Although the MMPI-A can be immensely useful for a diagnostic assessment, the test user should be aware that test scales are not intended to correspond directly to *DSM-IV* diagnoses. Since multiple scales can be elevated in a profile and the test scores are primarily descriptive, the clinician would need to integrate test findings with other sources of information about the client to form a diagnostic impression. In particular, certain diagnostic conditions such as Post-Traumatic Stress Disorder (PTSD) and Bipolar Disorder are not easily gauged from a single administration of the MMPI-A and would require multiple assessments combined with non-test findings to render an accurate diagnosis. The MMPI-A, similar to other psychological tests, also cannot identify whether suicidal or homicidal behavior is imminent. Although data from the MMPI-A and other test findings concerning degree of impulse control, occurrence of hopeless or despairing attitudes, and presence of anger, humiliation, or rage are important aids in risk assessment, the ultimate determination of imminent risk still depends on the keen judgment of the clinician.

Another constraint that the MMPI-A shares with all other personality tests concerns the prediction of future behavior. Although Hathaway and Monachesi's (1953, 1963) report suggested a predictive relationship between elevations on excitatory scales *4, 8,* and *9* and future delinquent behavior, psychological tests including the MMPI-A have limited effectiveness in prediction tasks and are best used for describing current functioning. This is exemplified in the reports of Gottesman and Hanson (1990) and Hanson, Gottesman, and Heston (1990), who conducted a follow-up investigation of Hathaway and Monachesi's adolescent sample more than 20 years after their initial ninth-grade MMPI assessment. The researchers identified a subgroup diagnosed with schizophrenia in adulthood whose ninth-grade profiles had been largely similar to those of matched cohorts who did not develop schizophrenia. Moreover, any differences between groups seen at the ninth-grade assessment were not of the kind that would predict later psychosis for one group. Potential changes in adolescents' profiles over time may also be expected based on the fact that the standard error of measurement of MMPI-A basic scales is approximately 4 to 6 T-score points. This indicates that an adolescent's score at immediate retesting would be expected to fall within a range of 5 T-score points above or 5 points below the original score only 50% of the time. When longer time intervals exist between initial testing and retesting, larger changes may be expected based on developmental changes in the adolescent's psychological functioning and intervening life events. These findings collectively suggest that any attempts to render long-term predictions of functioning from MMPI-A profiles are likely to be fraught with prediction errors.

It should also be noted that the MMPI-A is not intended to be used to judge the cognitive capacities or neuropsychological status of the adolescent client. Although several scales shed light on dysfunctional cognitive processes (e.g., the *A-obs* content scale and D_4 [*Mental Dullness*] Harris-Lingoes subscale), these descriptors are relevant in the context of psychological impairment and do not substitute for an intelligence test when the adolescent's cognitive skills are in question. In summary, awareness of the appropriate limits of test use should minimize erroneous conclusions based on MMPI-A results.

Test Length and Time Requirement

Despite the efforts undertaken to decrease the length of the MMPI-A relative to the MMPI and MMPI-2, the test continues to be rather long for the typical adolescent evaluated in a clinical setting. In comparison with other multidimensional personality inventories (e.g., the Millon Adolescent Clinical Inventory [MACI; Millon, 1993], which contains 160 items; the Personality Inventory for Youth [PIY; Lachar & Gruber, 1995], 270 items; and the Adolescent Psychopathology Scale [APS; Reynolds, 1998], 346 items), the 478 items of the MMPI-A are unquestionably more demanding of the adolescent's attention and time. Additionally, the adolescent version of the Personality Assessment Inventory (PAI-A), which is currently under development, is intended to contain 264 items—55% of the length of the MMPI-A (Morey, 2000). In terms of test administration time, the 60–90 minutes required for an MMPI-A administration compares somewhat unfavorably with the 45–60-minute period required for the APS, 45 minutes for the PIY, and 30 minutes required for the MACI, as reported by those test authors. These facts concerning test length and test-taking time are likely complemented by clinicians' experiences of having to expend much effort to ensure that the test is completed. Reliance on a 350-item abbreviated version of the test leads to the loss of crucial information, and, as discussed in Chapter 2, is not recommended except under extreme extenuating circumstances. The MMPI-A user therefore trades the extensiveness and usefulness of information derived from this test against the increased test-administration demands associated with the overall test length.

Requirements for Reading and Cognitive Maturation

In Chapter 2 we stated that a 7th-grade reading level is recommended for MMPI-A administration. As noted previously, the reading difficulty level of MMPI-A test items varies quite considerably from a 1st-grade level for the easiest items up to the 15th- and 16th-grade levels for the few most difficult items. In addition to the analysis of item difficulty level reported in the test manual, a study by Dahlstrom, Archer, Hopkins, Jackson, and Dahlstrom (1994) evaluated the reading difficulty of the MMPI-A in comparison with the MMPI and MMPI-2. The authors reported that MMPI-A test booklet instructions and test items were slightly easier to read compared to those on the other two forms of the test. However, these differences were relatively small in magnitude, and the average difficulty level for all forms of the MMPI, found to be at a 6th-grade level, was comparable. Dahlstrom et al. also found that approximately 6% of MMPI-A items required at least a 10th-grade reading level. These results suggest that several MMPI-A items may be difficult for most adolescents to read. When the reading level of the MMPI-A is compared to those of the three other personality tests mentioned earlier, the MACI is seen to be somewhat comparable by requiring a minimum 6th-grade level, but the APS and PIY have items written at a 3rd-grade level. Furthermore, the multitude of behavioral checklists and symptom scales that are available for adolescent assessment are generally written at a lower reading level. Consequently, the reading demands of the MMPI-A may be considered to be a significant limitation of the test.

The issues of reading comprehension and cognitive maturation may further complicate the ability of adolescents to grasp the meaning of items and deliver accurate responses. Some of the items retained from the original MMPI continue to be problematic for contemporary teenagers due to their wording or content. Several MMPI-A items dealing with characteristics such as sociability, irritability, tension, or sensitivity require the capacity to evaluate oneself in terms of these features, which, in turn, requires a substantial level of cognitive maturity and capacity for abstract thinking. Such factors may interfere with adolescents' ability to produce accurate profiles.

Codetype Congruence between the MMPI and MMPI-A

The generalizability of the MMPI research literature on basic-scale codetypes to the MMPI-A is constrained by the relative problems with codetype congruence between the two forms of the test. *Codetype congruence* refers to the frequency with which a given two-point codetype obtained on the MMPI-A basic scale profile matches the codetype that would have been obtained if the original MMPI had been administered. A codetype match would indicate that the correlates of that codetype can be applied without reservation in describing the MMPI-A basic scale profile. The MMPI-A manual (Butcher et al., 1992) reports congruence rates of 67.8% for boys and 55.8% for girls in the MMPI-A normative sample. Congruence rates of 69.5% and 67.2% were found for boys and girls, respectively, in the clinical sample described in the test manual. These rates may be considered acceptable from the perspective that more than 55% of MMPI-A profiles are likely to have no significant problems with use of codetype descriptors. However, in approximately one-third of cases, the lack of codetype congruence would render codetype interpretation suspect, and the practicing clinician would generally be unaware of when the obtained codetype is reliable for interpretation. One factor that may assist in this judgment concerns the issue of codetype definition described in the preceding chapter. The codetype congruence rate is considerably higher for well-defined profiles, as indicated by rates of 95.2% for boys and 81.8% for girls in the MMPI-A normative sample, and rates of 95% and 91% for boys and girls, respectively, in the clinical sample, who produced codetypes that met the 5-point definition standard (Butcher et al., 1992). Consequently, the MMPI-A user can have more confidence that codetype descriptors would accurately describe the adolescent when a well-defined basic scale profile is obtained. Conversely, the clinician should consider giving greater emphasis to single scale descriptors and content and supplementary scale findings when the basic scales' codetype features do not meet the criterion of definition. It should be noted, however, that a substantial number of MMPI-A profiles obtained in clinical settings tend not to be well defined. For example, Pena, Megargee, and Brody's (1996) study of 162 delinquent boys found that 57.4% of the interpretable codetypes (i.e, those with scores at the clinical range of elevation) were not defined. This further complicates the clinician's decision-making strategy for interpreting the basic clinical scales using a configural approach, and suggests that many MMPI-A profiles are not suitable for codetype interpretation.

Undersensitivity to Detecting Psychopathology

A fundamental problem with the MMPI-A as a function of the new norms concerns the issue of the test's relative undersensitivity in identifying psychopathology. Specifically, MMPI-A profiles tend to be less elevated compared to profiles on the original MMPI, and produce a relatively high rate of false-negative or normal-range profiles for adolescents who are known to be psychologically disturbed. This is a by-product of the fact that the MMPI-A normative sample produced higher scores than those produced by the original MMPI's norm group. Although the existence of false negatives is not unique to the MMPI-A, the awareness of this issue on the original MMPI prompted the MMPI-A test developers to lower the T-score cutoff demarcating the beginning of the clinical range of elevation from 70 to 65 and to designate the range from T score 60 to 64 as a marginal but interpretable range of elevation. Despite these adjustments, the MMPI-A appears to have continued problems with sensitivity, which has become evident in recent research studies. For example, Pena et al. (1996) found that mean T scores on several basic scales produced by their male delinquent sample were within 1 standard deviation from the normative mean and, in some cases, below the average for normal adolescents. All basic scale mean scores were uniformly below the cutting-score level of 65 T. Archer and Krishnamurthy (1997a) similarly found that the mean basic scale T scores for their adolescent clinical samples ranged from 50 to 64 for teenagers diagnosed with depression and from 48 to 61 for adolescents diagnosed with conduct disturbances. Clinicians across several treatment settings may have observed a relatively high frequency of within-normal-limits (WNL) profiles obtained by adolescents whose histories clearly point to psychological or behavioral difficulties. The relatively low sensitivity of the MMPI-A is undoubtedly a significant issue that may come to affect clinicians' willingness to use the test in diagnostically difficult or complicated clinical assessments.

Additional Expense of Separate MMPI-A Test Materials

Prior to the revision of the MMPI into the MMPI-2 and MMPI-A, assessment using the MMPI required the purchase of a single set of test materials that could be used for evaluating individuals in all age groups at or above the age of 16. The practicing clinician could therefore test a broad range of clients in adolescent and adult age groups using the same test booklet and answer sheets, only needing to purchase separate profile sheets for adolescents and adults in order to use the appropriate norms for profiling and interpretation. One disadvantage of that situation, as discussed in Chapter 1, was that clinicians were often testing teenagers in the absence of having an appropriate understanding of the developmental and normative differences between adults and adolescents and without recognizing the interpretive errors arising from using adult norms for adolescents. However, the use of a single test for adolescents and adults also presented some cost-related advantages to the practicing clinician, who could get considerable usage from the MMPI test materials. Additionally, advancements in the assessment of adolescents with the MMPI, and research on the MMPI with adolescents, may have been facilitated by the relative inex-

≡Rapid Reference 5.2

Limitations of the MMPI-A

- The test is rather lengthy and time consuming.
- A relatively high reading level is required for the test.
- Some of the items retained from the original MMPI continue to be problematic for contemporary teenagers due to wording or content.
- Rates of MMPI/MMPI-A codetype congruence are less than optimal.
- The new norms have caused MMPI-A scales to be undersensitive to the detection of psychopathology.
- Test examiners have increased costs related to purchasing test materials that can be used only with adolescent clients.

CAUTION

Issues Insufficiently Addressed by the MMPI-A

- Presence of Post-Traumatic Stress Disorder
- Presence of Bipolar Disorder
- Imminence of suicidal or homicidal behavior
- Prediction of adult functioning
- Cognitive capacities

pense of MMPI testing materials. The revision of the MMPI into the MMPI-A for adolescents and MMPI-2 for adults necessitated that clinicians purchase separate sets of test materials for evaluating the two age groups, representing an increase in the commercial costs of conducting personality assessments. This is likely an issue of heightened concern in the current practice environment governed by managed care organizations in which payments for assessment services have been markedly curtailed. For clinicians whose practices do not predominantly involve adolescent clients, the ensuing costs of purchasing MMPI-A materials may serve as a deterrent. Rapid Reference 5.2 summarizes the limitations of the MMPI-A.

 TEST YOURSELF

1. **The MMPI-A is the shortest of several multidimensional personality tests available for evaluating adolescents.** True or False?

2. **Adolescent maladjustment may be somewhat underestimated on the MMPI-A due to the reduced clinical sensitivity of scales.** True or False?

3. **Validity assessment has become less reliable on the MMPI-A compared to the MMPI.** True or False?

4. **Using the MMPI-A is valuable for guiding treatment planning and evaluating treatment outcome.** True or False?

5. **Interpretation of MMPI-A scales is largely based on newly derived scale correlates.** True or False?

Answers: 1. False; 2. True; 3. False; 4. True; 5. False

Six

CLINICAL APPLICATIONS OF THE MMPI-A

The description of MMPI-A scale correlates and the interpretive process delineated in Chapter 4 underscore the point that the MMPI-A is predominantly intended for use in the clinical/psychodiagnostic evaluation of adolescents in treatment settings, rather than for the description of normal adolescents' personality styles. In addition to the general evaluation of psychopathology in inpatient, residential, and outpatient settings, the MMPI-A has utility in evaluating specific subgroups of adolescents and particular types of presenting problems, which has support from the developing research literature on this test instrument. In this chapter, we begin by discussing findings concerning the appropriateness of the MMPI-A for evaluating adolescents from ethnic minority groups. We also discuss the applications of the MMPI-A in evaluating adolescents with problems frequently found in treatment settings, including juvenile delinquents and conduct-disordered teenagers, adolescent substance abusers, eating disordered adolescents, and sexually abused teenagers. The last section of this chapter describes the utility of the MMPI-A in treatment planning and evaluation of progress and outcome.

SUITABILITY FOR ETHNIC MINORITIES

The applicability of the MMPI for evaluating individuals from ethnic minority groups is an issue that has been debated for several decades. Questions and cautions in this regard have been based on the fact that the normative sample for the original MMPI consisted entirely of Caucasians. Moreover, the multitude of supplemental MMPI scales developed in the decades following the test's publication were also typically based on predominantly Caucasian samples. Efforts to address this problem were evident in the goal of obtaining nationally representative and ethnically diverse samples in the development of the MMPI-2 for adults and the MMPI-A for adolescents. Although these efforts were largely successful, the MMPI-2 normative sample underrepresented Hispanic and Asian-American adults (see Nichols, 2001), and the majority (approximately 76%) of the adolescents in the MMPI-A normative sample were of Caucasian descent (see Butcher et al., 1992).

The research literature concerning the impact of ethnic background on MMPI profile patterns has produced mixed results. Some investigations conducted with the original MMPI showed that African-American adults obtained higher scores than Caucasian adults on scales *F, 8,* and *9,* which caused them to appear more maladjusted (e.g., Gynther, 1972). Early MMPI studies with adolescents yielded a similar direction of results. For example, a study by Ball (1960) showed that Black ninth-graders scored higher than their White counterparts on scale *1* among boys and scales *F, 8,* and *0* among girls. Other studies suggested that differences in socioeconomic status may be the determining factor in racial differences on MMPI profiles. Dahlstrom, Lachar, and Dahlstrom (1986), for example, reported that differences between Black and White groups on the MMPI were considerably smaller and frequently nonsignificant when the groups were equated on demographic characteristics such as level of education. Archer (1987) found minimal differences in the MMPI profiles of Black and White adolescents in a sample obtained from a predominantly middle-class public high school. Greene (2000) underscored the point that moderator variables, including socioeconomic status (SES), education, and intelligence, are important factors to consider in research on MMPI ethnic-group differences. Greene also concluded, based on his review of the MMPI research on Black-White, Hispanic-White, Black-Hispanic, Native American–White, and Asian American–White comparisons, that no consistent or reliable patterns of differences are discernable across samples.

Recent MMPI-2 studies involving adult samples have generally failed to find meaningful Black-White differences in profile elevations. Timbrook and Graham (1994) compared the responses of 75 Black men and 65 Black women with those of 725 White men and 742 White women from the MMPI-2 normative sample. They found that mean differences on MMPI-2 basic scales between ethnic groups were small in magnitude for both genders, and were further reduced when the groups were matched for age, education, and income levels. An important finding from their study was that there were no systematic differences in the accuracy of scale correlates for Black and White individuals.

The research literature available at the time of this writing suggests that the adult and adolescent forms of the MMPI may be used in assessing individuals from ethnic minority groups using the standard norms available for these test instruments. However, several cautions are warranted in using the MMPI-A with adolescents from ethnic minority groups. First, the bulk of the MMPI research studies involving adults and adolescents have been focused on comparing the profiles of Black and White groups, and relatively little is known about Hispanic, Native American, Asian American, and other minority groups' profile patterns. Second, minimal information is available that is specific to the MMPI-As of ethnic minority groups. One recent study by Gumbiner (1998) examined the MMPI-A's of 14- to 18-year-old Hispanic youths. This study, however, focused on comparing scale elevation patterns for boys versus girls and did not involve comparisons with adolescents from other ethnic groups. A comparative study by Gomez, Johnson, Davis, and Velasquez (2000) examined the MMPI-A scale elevations of African-American and Mexican American youthful offenders. The authors found no significant multivariate results as a function of ethnicity. Among individual scales, they found only one scale, *Repression,* on which African-American adolescents scored significantly higher than Mexican-American teenagers. These two studies represent steps toward studying ethnic-group differences on the MMPI-A but are not sufficient to form any firm conclusions. A third caution concerns the evidence that use of the *MAC-R* scale with ethnic minority groups may produce higher rates of false positive errors than with White individuals (e.g., Gottesman & Prescott, 1989). Wrobel and Lachar (1995) also cautioned that content scale elevations produced by African-American and White adolescents may require different interpretations. They reported significant differences on four Wiggins content scales of the MMPI between African-American and White psychiatric patients from a predominantly lower-SES background. Notably, they also found greater validity of some content scales for White adolescents and some differences in scale correlates for the two ethnic groups. Extrapolating from the Wiggins scales to the MMPI-A content scales, the authors cautioned that the MMPI-A content scales may overpathologize African-American adolescents in certain areas such as psychotic, somatic, and phobic symptoms, and underidentify prob-

≡ *Rapid Reference 6.1*

Evaluating Adolescents from Ethnic Minority Groups with the MMPI-A

- The literature generally supports using caution in interpreting the MMPI-A profiles of adolescents from ethnic minority groups.
- The *MAC-R* scale, in particular, may yield higher false positive errors for ethnic minority groups and should be interpreted with caution.
- Moderator variables such as socioeconomic status, education, and intelligence may account for much of the observed ethnic group differences in scale elevations.

lems in other areas such as conflicts with family and authority figures. At the present time, and until more is known about the impact of race, ethnicity, and socio-demographic characteristics on MMPI-A scale elevations, we recommend that clinicians be appropriately conservative in interpreting the MMPI-A profiles of ethnic minority adolescents. (See Rapid Reference 6.1.)

APPLICATIONS WITH SPECIAL POPULATIONS

Juvenile Delinquents

The identification and assessment of juvenile delinquents with the MMPI has a rich history, beginning with the landmark studies of Capwell (1945) and Hathaway and Monachesi (1952, 1953, 1957, 1963) in evaluating MMPI patterns in this population. Capwell identified the effectiveness of scale *4* in discriminating between delinquent and nondelinquent girls. Hathaway and Monachesi's longitudinal investigations showed that elevations on scales *4, 8,* and *9* were useful in identifying juvenile delinquents, and that scales *4* and *9* were particularly effective in predicting delinquency. These authors also found a pattern of low scale *5* scores for delinquent boys and low scale *3* scores for delinquent girls. Since those pioneering efforts, a number of investigations have been conducted using the original MMPI on various samples of institutionalized and non-institutionalized delinquents and on other conduct-disordered adolescent samples, and a parallel literature is beginning to develop for the MMPI-A. Among studies conducted in the last 6 years, one study replicated Hathaway and Monachesi's finding by identifying that scales *4, 6,* and *9* and the *4-9* codetype on the MMPI-A define the profiles of adolescent boys (Pena et al., 1996). Another investigation (Hicks, Rogers, & Cashel, 2000) found that although elevations on the configural or codetype patterns created by MMPI-A scales *4, 8,* and *9* were not useful in predicting total infractions among institutionalized male juvenile offenders, individual scale elevations on scales *9* and *6* were important in predicting violent infractions. A study comparing male juvenile delinquents with and without a history of sexual offenses showed that elevations on scales *4* and *8* were more frequent among sex offenders, and elevations on scales *3* and *7* were a salient feature among nonsex offenders (Losada-Paisey, 1998).

The research studies just cited converge in indicating that MMPI-A scales *4, 6,* and *9,* traditionally labeled "excitatory" scales for their association with acting-out tendencies, play a central role in the MMPI-A profiles of juvenile delinquents. The co-occurrence of elevations of scales *4* and *9,* forming the *4-9* codetype, is also a defining characteristic for delinquent populations. It should be noted that the *4-9* codetype is the most commonly occurring codetype among adolescent boys in psychiatric settings and is therefore not unique to teenagers who have been adjudicated delinquent. Nonetheless, descriptions of individuals with this codetype have considerable relevance in understanding juvenile delinquency. For example, Gilberstadt and Duker (1965) noted that the histories of individuals with the modal MMPI *4-9* pattern were marked by family experiences in childhood whereby the father figure was disparaged, and which instilled a contempt for male authority figures that found expression in adolescence. Marks et al. (1974) described *4-9* adolescents as frequently neglected by their mothers, unafraid of their father's discipline, and in continual conflict with their parents over misbehavior, including lying. They were more likely to have been raised in foster homes or adoptive homes than adolescents with other codetypes. Approximately half of these teenagers had come to the attention of law enforcement and had been placed on probation or in detention. Notably, *4-9* adolescents tended to report boredom when they felt sad, and did not experience psychophysiological distress.

The new content and supplementary scales of the MMPI-A offer additional means of evaluating juvenile delinquents and, more generally, conduct-disordered youth. Pena et al. (1996) reported that their sample of 162 delinquent boys produced their lowest mean supplementary scale score on the *Repression* scale and their highest score of any of the MMPI-A scales on the *MAC-R* scale, reflective of an uninhibited, sensation-seeking orientation. These delinquent boys also scored higher than nondelinquent boys on supplementary scales *MAC-R, ACK, PRO,* and *IMM* that are associated with impulsive, acting-out tendencies often involving alcohol or drug abuse. Content scales *A-ang, A-cyn, A-sch,* and *A-con* were also prominent in the delinquents' profiles, as were elevations on scales *A-trt* and *A-sod.* A recent investigation by Moore, Thompson-Pope, and Whited (1996) examined the MMPI-A profiles of adolescents boys with histories of fire-setting, and reported greater pathology in the fire-setting group than a comparison non–fire-setting group. Specifically, basic scales *7, 8,* and *9,* and eight content scales representing a blend of emotional distress, disturbed thinking, and acting out, were found to be significantly higher for fire-setters.

In summary, the currently available literature indicates that the MMPI-A profiles of juvenile delinquents show prominent externalizing characteristics reflected in elevations on several basic, content, and supplementary scales related to behavioral acting out. The Disinhibition/Excitatory Potential and Immaturity dimensions of the MMPI-A Structural Summary contain the majority of these scales and are therefore recommended for examination in the course of profile interpretation. In some conduct-disordered subgroups, elevations on scales related to emotional maladjustment and disordered thinking may also be found, which helps to identify the unique components of the adolescent's overall maladjustment. (See Rapid Reference 6.2.)

≡Rapid Reference 6.2

Evaluating Juvenile Delinquents with the MMPI-A

- Early MMPI studies found that scales 4, 8, and 9 were useful in identifying juvenile delinquents.
- Recent studies have found that scales 4, 6, and 9, and the 4-9 codetype, are frequently found in male juvenile delinquents' MMPI-A profiles.
- Elevations on supplementary scales MAC-R, ACK, PRO, and IMM, and content scales A-ang, A-cyn, A-sch, A-con, A-trt, and A-sod may also be expected in the profiles of juvenile delinquents.
- The overall profile pattern of juvenile delinquents typically reflects strong externalizing tendencies.

Substance Abusers

Adolescent substance abusers share many of the characteristics of conduct-disordered and delinquent youth, and may be viewed as a subgroup whose behavioral acting out includes reliance on alcohol or drugs as a means of rebellion, as a possible mechanism to self-medicate, and as a method of achieving an optimal level of psychophysiological arousal. The link between substance abuse and delinquency is exemplified in a recent report by Komro et al. (1999), who found that alcohol use and acknowledgement of alcohol- and drug-related problems were statistically associated with delinquent and violent behaviors in a large sample ($N = 937$) of eighth- and ninth-grade adolescents. The authors concluded that alcohol use represented an independent risk factor for delinquent and violent behaviors among adolescents.

On the original MMPI, the *MAC* scale received extensive research focus for its utility in detecting substance abuse problems accurately among adolescents in hospital, residential, and drug treatment programs, and in non-treatment public school settings. Many of these studies were directed toward identifying the optimal cutting score for effective discrimination between substance abusers and non–substance abusers. For example, Gantner, Graham, and Archer (1992) found that a *MAC* raw score of 28 for boys and 27 for girls provided the best discrimination between adolescent substance abusers and psychiatric inpatients, whereas raw scores of 26 for boys and 25 for girls maximally differentiated adolescent substance abusers from normal high school students. Archer and Klinefelter (1992) further found that elevated *MAC* scores were frequently associated with the occurrence of a *4-9* codetype in adolescent MMPI profiles. High *MAC* scores have also been found to be associated with the abuse of various drugs, such as amphetamines, barbiturates, cocaine, hallucinogens, marijuana, and alcohol (Andrucci, Archer, Pancoast, & Gordon, 1989).

Other studies conducted with the original MMPI have attempted to discern the typical profile characteristics of adolescent substance abusers. One important finding from a study by Walfish, Massey, and Krone (1990) concerned the overall absence of psychopathological features in the profiles of 243 adolescents presenting for chemical dependency treatment in a residential setting, suggesting notable differences between this group and adolescents in general psychiatric settings. However, the profiles of the chemically dependent adolescents were characterized by a significant elevation on scale *4* and a relatively low score on scale *2,* which were interpreted in terms of low motivation for recovery due to the relative absence of depression and emotional distress. A follow-up study by Massey, Walfish, and Krone (1992) involved a cluster analysis of the MMPI profiles of 250 adolescents receiving substance abuse treatment. Three salient clusters were identified, characterized by (a) evidence of a significant level of psychopathology, (b) an impulsive, acting-out style, and (c) lack of significant psychopathology reflected in the absence of clinical-level scale elevations. Adolescent substance abusers therefore appear to be a heterogeneous group who, nonetheless, produce some identifiable or characteristic MMPI scale patterns.

The newly developed *ACK* and *PRO* supplementary scales of the MMPI-A, which were empirically constructed to facilitate the identification of adolescent substance abusers, show considerable promise for use with this population. Weed, Butcher, and Williams (1994) reported greater accuracy in differentiating adolescent substance abusers from nonabusers using *ACK* and *PRO* than the MMPI-A *MAC-R* scale. Their findings were based on an initial evaluation of these scales using the 1,620 adolescents in the MMPI-A normative sample, 251 adolescents receiving psychiatric treatment, and 462 adolescents in alcohol and drug treatment units as contrasting groups.

Two research studies based specifically on the MMPI-A with substance abuse populations are noteworthy. Gallucci (1997b) evaluated the contributions of specific MMPI-A scales in classifying 180 adolescent substance abusers into three groups: a primary substance abuse group characterized by behavioral undercontrol, a secondary group showing the absence of behavioral undercontrol, and a combined group that displayed features of under- and overcontrol. Results of a discriminant function analysis revealed that scales *MAC-R, 2, 4, 9, 3, PRO,* and *ACK,* respectively, made significant contributions to the discrimination task and collectively produced a 79.4% rate of accurate classification. Across the three groups some important differences were found that supported earlier findings concerning the heterogeneity of adolescent substance abuse profiles. For example, mean *T* scores for *MAC-R* were in the clinical range of elevation for the primary and combined groups but not for the secondary group, and the same elevation pattern was found for scale *4. PRO* was elevated in all three groups, but *ACK* fell in the clinical range of elevation only for the primary, undercontrolled group. Gallucci concluded that the MMPI-A is valuable in evaluating substance abuse in adolescents, largely due to its ability to measure a broad range of psychopathological features—an ability that also serves to differentiate different types of adolescent substance-abusing subgroups. In a second study, Gallucci (1997a) examined the correlates of 16 substance-related MMPI-A scales in a sample of 180 adolescent boys and girls receiving substance abuse treatment in inpatient psychiatric- and day-hospital facilities. The scales selected for examination included *MAC-R, ACK,* and *PRO,* and a variety of substance abuse–related scales developed for the MMPI. Gallucci stated that his results supported the description of *ACK* as a specific measure of willingness to admit problematic substance use patterns, and affirmed that *PRO* and *MAC-R* reflected a broad pattern of behavioral undercontrol, of which substance abuse is a component.

The converging evidence concerning the use of the MMPI-A in evaluating adolescent substance abusers provides support for the effectiveness of the *MAC-R, ACK,* and *PRO* scales in this endeavor, and also points to the importance of examining basic scale profile patterns for the presence of excitatory scale elevations. The clinician conducting the evaluation would therefore look for general signs of behavioral disturbance characterized by marked impulsiveness and externalizing tendencies, with additional indicators of substance abuse revealed in elevations on *MAC-R* and *PRO* and in drug- or alcohol-use acknowledgment on the *ACK* scale. (See Rapid Reference 6.3.)

Adolescents with Eating Disorders

Despite the prominence of eating disorders in adolescence and its potential continuity into adulthood, there has been relatively little research conducted on the MMPI patterns of individuals, particularly

Rapid Reference 6.3

Evaluating Substance Abusing Adolescents with the MMPI-A

- High *MAC* scale scores on the original MMPI have been associated with drug and alcohol abuse among adolescents.
- A high scale 4 and presence of the 4-9 codetype are also common for this population.
- MMPI-A supplementary scales *ACK* and *PRO* facilitate the identification of adolescent substance abusers.

adolescents, with eating disorders. Two reasons may be proposed for the gap in this research area. First, the larger body of literature on the original MMPI has typically found an absence of distinctive profile patterns for specific diagnostic conditions. Second, the original MMPI lacked items directly pertinent to disordered eating patterns or body image distortions. However, a few MMPI/MMPI-2 investigations have examined the profiles of adult women with eating disorders and have commonly found indications of high distress and psychopathology in these individuals. For example, two studies reported a significant relationship between severity of eating disorder and overall general psychopathology at long-term follow-up in adult women treated for Anorexia Nervosa (Schork, Eckert, & Halmi, 1994; Sunday, Reeman, Eckert, & Halmi, 1996). One study found that recovered anorexic patients showed a greater decrease in MMPI scores at a 10-year follow-up compared with anorexic patients with poor outcome (Dancyger, Sunday, Eckert, & Halmi, 1997). A recent MMPI-2 study by Cumella, Wall, and Kerr-Almeida (2000), using a large sample of 550 adult eating-disordered women, found their highest mean elevations on scales *2, 7,* and *3,* and the presence of a *2-7* profile pattern as the modal codetype. MMPI-2 scales were also found to be useful in distinguishing between eating disordered subgroups in terms of patients with restricting Anorexia Nervosa displaying lesser psychopathology than other subgroups. In contrast, Pryor and Wiederman (1996) found no significant differences in the MMPI-2 profiles of adult women in four diagnostic subgroups of (a) Anorexia Nervosa, restricting type, (b) Anorexia Nervosa, binge eating/purging type, (c) Bulimia Nervosa, purging type, and (d) Bulimia Nervosa, nonpurging type. Studies on patients with bulimia have generally found multiple scale elevations, in contrast to the subclinical profiles often found of restricting anorexics. Dacey, Nelson, and Aikman (1990) reported that scales *6, 3, 5,* and *8* discriminated effectively between bulimics and nonbulimic controls.

The adolescent-relevant items of the MMPI-A render it more applicable for evaluating various types of disturbances, including eating disorders, in adolescents. Although the test contains an insufficient number of items relating specifically to eating disorders to develop an eating disorder scale (Williams, et al., 1992), eating problems are found as correlates of such scales as *2* and *A-sod*. To date, there has been a single published study evaluating the MMPI-A profiles of eating disordered adolescents. The study by Cumella,

Wall, and Kerr-Almeida (1999) is notable for using a large sample of 245 adolescents receiving inpatient treatment for eating disorders. Their sample included four subgroups of adolescents diagnosed with (a) Anorexia Nervosa, restricting type, (b) Anorexia Nervosa, binge-eating/purging type, (c) Bulimia Nervosa, purging type, and (d) Eating Disorder, Not Otherwise Specified. Results indicated that all four subgroups showed clinically interpretable mean scores at $T \geq 60$ on scales *2, 3,* and *1,* respectively. Furthermore, five profile types (*1-2, 1-3,* spike *2, 2-3,* and *2-0*) accurately classified 60% of the profiles in the overall eating-disordered sample. The *2-3* codetype was the modal two-point pattern found for the bulimic and anorexic groups. However, bulimic patients showed higher scores than the anorexic subgroups on scales *9* and *4,* several content scales including *A-ang, A-con, A-las, A-fam, A-sch,* and all three substance abuse scales. A stepwise regression analysis was also conducted to evaluate the incremental contributions of MMPI-A scales in differentiating anorexic and bulimic patients. This analysis showed that four scales (*PRO, ACK, A-trt,* and scale *4*) contributed significantly to the differential prediction and accounted for 39% of the variance in diagnosis. The authors concluded that the MMPI-A successfully distinguishes between anorexics and bulimics, and between unspecified and specified eating disorders, although it does not effectively discriminate between Anorexia Nervosa subgroups.

Based on the studies just cited, some conclusions can be reached concerning the MMPI-A profiles of eating disordered adolescents. These teenagers' profiles, with the possible exception of the profiles of restricting anorexics, are generally likely to show several signs of emotional distress and psychopathology. Specifically, their MMPI-A profiles are likely to be characterized by elevations on scales *1, 2, 3, 7,* and *0,* and we may expect that their General Maladjustment factor score would be significantly elevated. Additionally, bulimics may also show elevations on scales *4, 6, 8,* and *9,* and on content and supplementary scales related to anger, poor impulse control, low frustration tolerance, family and school conflicts, and overall externalizing tendencies. As a concluding point, we note that the utility of the MMPI-A in evaluating eating disordered adolescents relates largely to its ability to identify broad areas of dysfunction. However, attempts to diagnose specific forms of eating disorders from MMPI-A profile patterns are not recommended. (See Rapid Reference 6.4.)

≡ Rapid Reference 6.4

Evaluating Eating Disordered Adolescents with the MMPI-A

- Elevations on MMPI-A scales *2* and *A-sod* have been associated with eating problems.
- Elevations on scales *1, 2, 3, 7,* and *0,* and presence of the *2-3* code-type, are often found for eating-disordered adolescents.
- Adolescents with Bulimia Nervosa may show greater externalizing tendencies, involving elevations on scales *4, 6, 8,* and *9,* than adolescents with Anorexia Nervosa.

Sexually Abused Adolescents

The MMPI profiles of individuals who have been sexually abused share some common features with the MMPIs of eating-disordered individuals. In general, both sets of profiles contain multiple scale elevations often involving distress-related symptoms. Sexually-abused individuals are also likely to produce scale elevations reflecting feelings of alienation, interpersonal sensitivity, and social withdrawal, and show levels of overall psychological disorganization similar to those seen in a broad range of psychiatric samples.

Among studies involving the original MMPI, Roland, Zelhart, Cochran, and Funderburk (1985) reported that scales *3, 5, 1,* and *4* accurately identified 73% of adult women who reported childhood experiences of sexual abuse. Engels, Moisan, and Harris (1994) reported differences on global psychopathological indicators of the MMPI between adult female outpatients who reported histories of abuse (sexual, physical, or both) and those who reported no abuse history. Belkin, Greene, Rodrigue, and Boggs (1994) added that the MMPI profiles of sexual abuse survivors were characterized by elevated scores on scales *4* and *8.* MMPI-2 studies of adult women with child sexual abuse histories have found, for example, significantly higher scores for this group on scales *1, 2, 4, 6, 7, 8,* and *9* compared to women without abuse histories (Griffith, Myers, Cusick, & Tankersley, 1997). Differences on scales *F, 1, 2, 3, 4, 6, 7,* and *8* have also been reported for substance-abusing women who reported childhood sexual abuse compared to those without reported sexual abuse histories (Knisely, Barker, Ingersoll, & Dawson, 2000). One interesting study by Elhai, Frueh, Gold, Gold, and Hamner (2000) compared the MMPI-2 profiles of combat veterans seeking treatment for combat-related PTSD with those of adults seeking treatment for PTSD related to childhood sexual abuse. Differences on several

MMPI-2 scales were initially found that, however, dwindled when the analyses were controlled for age effects. The authors concluded that the MMPI-2 profiles of sexual abuse survivors and combat veterans were more similar than dissimilar, a result that underscores the absence of a characteristic profile linked to sexual abuse. Efforts directed toward developing sexual abuse scales for the MMPI-2 (e.g., Griffith, Myers, & Tankersley, 1996; Korbanka, 1997) have also been largely unsuccessful. Cluster-analytic results have additionally identified that women reporting childhood sexual abuse are a heterogeneous group (Follette, Naugle, & Follette, 1997).

MMPI studies of sexually abused adolescents have typically found evidence of depression and anxiety (e.g., Hillary & Schare, 1993), although elevations on scales *8* and *9* are also common. Scott and Stone (1986) compared the MMPI profiles of adolescents and adults receiving psychotherapy who had been molested by their fathers or stepfathers. They found that the adolescent sample scored higher than the adult sample on scale *9,* whereas adults obtained higher scores than adolescents on scale *2.* Both groups had elevated scores on scale *8.* The adolescent findings were interpreted as reflecting characteristics of excitability, mood elevation, and transient depression that are typical of the adolescent phase, in addition to reflecting feelings of alienation and social withdrawal related to their sexual abuse.

The clinical correlates of several MMPI-A content scales involve histories of abuse. Williams et al. (1992) reported that scales *A-dep, A-ang, A-lse,* and *A-sch* were associated with sexual abuse for boys, and *A-fam* was correlated with sexual abuse for girls and physical abuse for boys. Additionally, sexually abused boys are likely to have elevations on basic scales *7* and *8,* and sexually abused girls are likely to obtain high scores on scales *4* and *8* (Butcher & Williams, 2000). A recent MMPI-A investigation by Forbey and Ben-Porath (2000) predicted that 14 MMPI-A scales, which were either correlated with a history of sexual abuse or with characteristics common to sexually abused adolescents, would show higher scale elevations for sexually abused than nonabused adolescents. The researchers used a sample of 107 adolescents, aged 13 through 18, who were receiving residential treatment. Results indicated significant differences on 9 of the 14 predicted scales (*F, 2, 4, 8, 0, A-dep, A-lse, A-sod,* and *A-fam*) and on 2 unexpected scales (scales *6* and *A-aln*). The authors concluded that sexually abused adolescents report depression, feelings of hopelessness and worthlessness, distrust, low interest and initiative,

≡Rapid Reference 6.5

Evaluating Sexually Abused Adolescents with the MMPI-A

- The profiles of sexually abused adolescents typically reveal characteristics of depression and anxiety.

- Elevations on MMPI-A content scales A-dep, A-ang, A-lse, A-sch, and A-fam have been associated with histories of abuse.

- The profiles of sexually abused adolescents are likely to contain multiple scale elevations in contrast to a specific codetype found for this population.

≡Rapid Reference 6.6

Sample References on Clinical Applications of the MMPI-A

- *Juvenile Delinquents*
  Pena, Megargee, & Brody (1996)
- *Adolescent Sexual Offenders*
  Losada-Paisey (1998)
- *Adolescent Substance Abusers*
  Gallucci (1997a, 1997b)
- *Eating-Disordered Adolescents*
  Cumella, Wall, & Kerr-Almeida (1999)
- *Sexually Abused Adolescents*
  Forbey & Ben-Porath (2000)

and withdrawal from others. These adolescents are also likely to have self-injurious thoughts and to engage in runaway behaviors.

In summary, the MMPI-A profiles of sexually abused teenagers are likely to contain several elevations across the entire set of available scales. There is, however, no single profile pattern that identifies sexual abuse, and any attempt to diagnose sexual abuse based solely on the MMPI-A is apt to be misguided. The clinician should obtain a detailed history from multiple sources to gather information about abuse, and should use that information to create a meaningful context for understanding the MMPI-A profile characteristics of a given adolescent client. (See Rapid References 6.5 and 6.6.)

TREATMENT-RELATED APPLICATIONS

Treatment Planning

The MMPI-A is most typically administered as part of an intake assessment procedure to obtain information relevant to treatment planning. There are several issues to consider in formulating a suitable treatment plan for an adolescent. These include potential knowledge of unobserved or unreported characteristics such as pent-up anger or deep pessimism, and awareness of underlying personality dynamics such as psychological resistance and interpersonal sensitivity. These features, which are very important for designing an appropriate intervention, often are not revealed in an intake interview and may never be verbally discussed by an adolescent. In an MMPI-A evaluation, however, teenagers are sometimes able to express feelings and experiences that they cannot or will not report in a face-to-face interview. Use of the MMPI-A can therefore help the clinician become cognizant of important aspects of the teenager's functioning.

Initial Barriers to Treatment

One of the central issues to examine in designing a treatment plan is the amenability of the adolescent to psychotherapy. On the original MMPI, several scales were found to be useful prognostic indicators. For example, Archer, White, and Orvin (1979) found that high scores on validity scales L and K, indicative of a defensive stance at initial evaluation, were also associated with a longer term of treatment among adolescents in psychiatric hospitals. On the MMPI-A, these scales continue to identify adolescents who are reluctant to reveal perceived personal failings and disturbances in their psychological functioning, and who would therefore avoid active engagement in the process of therapy. Elevations on Welsh's R supplementary scale, which has been found to be strongly correlated with scales L and K, further identifies teenagers who would likely participate minimally in treatment as a result of having constricted affect and an overcontrolled self-presentation. In addition, the *A-trt* content scale holds promise for detecting adolescents with low motivation for treatment, due either to skepticism about the ability of mental health professionals to be helpful or to a core apathy and a disbelief in the adolescent's own ability to be helped. Identifying these issues at the onset of treatment permits the clinician to put additional time and effort into building confidence and trust, and into developing a treatment plan that is not contingent on high levels of disclosure in the early phase of psychotherapy.

Indicators of Need for Limit Setting

A common presenting problem for adolescents in treatment settings involves conduct disturbance. A variety of MMPI-A scales, such as scale *4, A-ang, A-con, A-cyn, A-sch, MAC-R, ACK, PRO,* and *IMM,* can help identify the potential of the adolescent to engage in a variety of acting-out behaviors. Harris-

Lingoes subscales could additionally clarify the predominant areas of behavioral difficulty. For example, elevations on Harris-Lingoes subscale Pd_1 reveal the pressure of conflicts centered within the family, in contrast to Pd_2 elevations which indicate a more general rebellion against societal rules and expectations. Codetypes including *4-6, 4-9,* and *2-4* also expand and enrich the clinician's understanding of the adolescent's negativism and defiance. The MMPI-A Structural Summary dimensions of Immaturity and Disinhibition/Excitatory Potential offer a broader perspective on the externalizing aspects of the adolescent's behavioral disturbance and draw attention to the magnitude of his or her conflicts across home and school settings. Awareness of these difficulties might assist a clinician in determining that a firm limit-setting approach within a supportive framework would be necessary for treatment to be effective, and may suggest the need for involving juvenile law enforcement agents (such as probation officers) as adjunctive supports to the treatment process. Elevations on the *MAC-R, ACK,* or *PRO* scales would additionally suggest that substance abuse issues present an important initial target for intervention. Early identification of substance abuse problems is critical for soliciting the assistance of the adolescent's parents or legal guardians in monitoring the adolescent's activities when the treatment is conducted in an outpatient setting, and in alerting staff to conduct appropriate checks for illicit substances in inpatient settings.

Markers of Degree of Acute Emotional Distress

Many adolescents are significantly distressed when they present to, or are referred for, treatment. These teenagers will often obtain elevations on the basic clinical scales *2* and *7* and on Welsh's *A* supplementary scale, which reflect components of depression, anxiety, and reactivity that are experienced as affective distress. Harris-Lingoes subscales such as D_1 (*Subjective Depression*) or D_5 (*Brooding*) would further elucidate the forms taken by the depression or distress, as would the content scales *A-dep, A-anx, A-obs,* and *A-lse.* A pattern of scale elevations on the General Maladjustment factor of the MMPI-A Structural Summary would reveal that the teenager's distress would likely disrupt many areas of his or her functioning. Such MMPI-A profile patterns suggest that the treatment focus should be centered around providing symptomatic relief as a first priority, improving the adolescent's level of daily functioning, actively monitoring for suicide risk as needed, and examining the need for hospitalization and other crisis services. Although the MMPI-A does not contain very many items related to suicidal ideation, the clinician could nonetheless examine responses to items such as "I sometimes think about killing myself" (Item 177) as a starting point of an in-depth suicide-risk assessment. Recent research by Archer and Slesinger (1999) has also found higher endorsement frequencies of suicide-related items 177, 283 ("Most of the time I wish I were dead"), and 399 ("The future seems hopeless to me") among adolescents who produce single scale elevations on scales *2* or *8,* or who produce *4-8* or *8-9* codetypes.

Interpersonal Functioning

Teenagers who experience interpersonal discomfort and detachment from others often produce elevations on scales *0, A-sod,* or *A-aln,* and on the Social Discomfort factor of the MMPI-A Structural Summary. A starting point of intervention with these adolescents may consist of relationship-building within an individual therapy format, and group therapy options may be deferred until the development of an adequate level of social comfort and skill in relating to others. In the contrasting scenario, teenagers producing a low score on scale *0* could be expected to be comfortable with group psychotherapy interventions and may be less likely to drop out of treatment prematurely when their need for social contact is accommodated by this treatment placement. An elevated score on scale *3* sensitizes the clinician to the teenager's need for interpersonal attention and approval, and dependency features would be accentuated when the high *3* is combined with an elevated scale *1*. Such an adolescent would likely respond well to the attention provided in an individual therapy context, provided the therapist does not demand self-reflection or challenge the authenticity of the adolescent's physical complaints. The therapist would, however, need to be alert to signs of excessive dependency and may seek to develop a task-oriented treatment plan that permits frequent successes while emphasizing self-reliance in treatment progress. A clinician would also need to consider whether an interpersonally manipulative style exists, as may be found when scales *4* and *9* are elevated and when scale *0* is considerably low, which would help the therapist avoid becoming an unwitting party to the client's maneuvers. This is an important consideration in inpatient and residential settings where the clinician is often consulted in decisions concerning granting privileges for "good" behavior that may include allowances of un-supervised or off-site activities.

Specific Concerns

The MMPI-A can also aid the identification and targeting of specific problem areas such as those within the family (e.g., *A-fam* scale, Pd_1 subscale, and the Familial Alienation factor). Specifically, if the test results indicate strong feelings of alienation from family members (as might be seen in significantly elevated scores on the Familial Alienation dimension of the Structural Summary profile), the need for providing family therapy interventions in addition to, or in place of, individual psychotherapy would be indicated. Correlates of the MMPI-A scales and factors related to family problems also highlight the likelihood of actions such as running away from home that may place the adolescent at substantial physical risk. Marked difficulties in school are indicated by elevations on content scales *A-sch* and *A-las* that may be further evidenced by low self-esteem problems (*A-lse*) and feelings of estrangement from peers (*A-aln*). These indicators permit consideration of school-based interventions to buttress and extend therapeutic interventions into the adolescent's learning environment. Concerns about health and the presence of physical symptoms ranging from fatigue to somatic stress reactions are revealed most directly by scales *A-hea, 1,* and *3,* which are strongly intercorrelated, and the Health Concerns factor of the Structural Summary. However, a variety of other scales and subscales dealing with internalizing tendencies (e.g., *A-anx, A-dep*) also contribute to the identification of health-related symptoms, including feelings of reduced energy and low endurance. Consistent and strong problems in the health domain remind the clinician to inquire whether a physical examination has been recently conducted and to incorporate methods of stress management in the psychotherapy treatment plan. Evidence of a thought disorder is best revealed through elevations on scales *8, 6,* and *9* and their subscales Sc_6 (*Bizarre Sensory Experiences*) and Pa_1 (*Persecutory Ideas*). Thought disorder symptomatology is also reflected by the *6-8* and *8-9* codetypes and the *A-biz* content scale, and is supported by an examination of the Psychoticism dimension on the MMPI-A Structural Summary. These findings are particularly useful in instances when an incipient psychotic process is not easily discernable by behavioral observations. Evidence of a thought disorder during the pretreatment assessment phase enables the therapist to optimize the treatment approach by

DON'T FORGET

....

Treatment Guidelines Based on MMPI-A Profile Patterns

- MMPI-A indicators of defensiveness or low motivation for treatment (scales L, K, R, A-trt) point to a need for emphasizing relationship building and making minimal demands for disclosure in the early stages of treatment.
- Evidence of significant behavioral disturbance (scales 4, A-ang, A-con, A-cyn, A-sch, IMM, 4-9 codetype, 4-6 codetype, Disinhibition/Excitatory Potential factor) underscores the importance of limit-setting interventions.
- Suicide-risk assessment, crisis intervention, and hospitalization should be considered when severe and acute distress is evident (scales 2, 7, A, A-dep, A-anx, A-obs, A-lse, General Maladjustment factor). Stabilization and symptomatic relief should be treatment priorities.
- Selection of psychotherapy format should be guided by whether there is interpersonal discomfort (scales 0, A-sod, individual psychotherapy preferred) or need for social contact (low 0, group psychotherapy preferred). The therapist should also attend to issues of dependency (scales 1, 3) or manipulative tendencies (scales 4, 9) in designing the treatment plan.
- The treatment plan should address the following specific areas when the relevant scales are elevated on the profile:

Family	A-fam, Pd_1, Familial Alienation factor
School	A-sch, A-las, A-lse, A-aln
Health	1, 3, A-hea, A-anx, A-dep, Health Concerns factor
Thought Disorder	8, 6, Sc_6, A-biz, 6-8 and 8-9 codetypes, Psychoticism factor
Substance Abuse	MAC-R, ACK, PRO

engaging psychiatric or pharmacologic interventions concurrent with psychological therapies.

Monitoring Treatment Progress and Evaluating Treatment Outcome

In addition to its initial application for treatment-planning purposes, the MMPI-A can be administered at multiple points during the course of treatment to examine changes in the adolescent's functioning, and at the completion of treatment to evaluate the degree to which treatment goals were met. Examination of such changes is made possible using the MMPI-A because the test has reasonably good temporal stability, as revealed in psychometric evaluations of its test-retest reliability over relatively short time periods. In other words, given that unsystematic changes in scores are minimized as a function of the test's psychometric structure, changes seen in the MMPI-A profile at retesting can be used to infer actual changes in the adolescent's functioning.

Evaluation of change is further facilitated by the fact that several MMPI-A scales are sensitive to situational distress and disturbance, such that they could be expected to show reduction in T-score elevations when treatment progresses successfully. For example, the higher the elevation on scales of affective distress (such as scales 2, A-dep, and A-anx) at the time of initial evaluation, the greater the likelihood that acute affective problems exist that should show reduction over the course of treatment, assuming that the adolescent is reasonably responsive to the treatment interventions. On the other hand, scales such as 5 and 0, which measure trait characteristics, typically show much less change at retesting.

Interpretation of the stability or change in the adolescent's codetype in a retest profile should include consideration of the standard error of measurement (SEM) of MMPI-A scales. As noted in Chapters 1 and 5, the average SEM of 4 to 6 points for MMPI-A basic scales suggests that changes of 5 T-score points or less may be related to measurement error and therefore should not be interpreted as reflecting meaningful change. The SEM range is also relevant to codetype analysis because small changes in T-score elevation related to measurement error may alter the codetype in the subsequent testing, particularly when the original codetype was not well defined. To illustrate this point, an initial profile with scale 4 at a T-score elevation of 69, scale 8 at $T = 67$, and scale 6 at $T = 65$ would have been classified as a 4-8 codetype. The retest MMPI-A profile may appear as follows: scale 4 = 64, scale 8 = 65, and scale 6 = 66, which would reclassify it as a 6-8 codetype. However, the small shifts in the scale elevations in this example do not necessarily reflect substantive changes in functioning, and the clinician should not misinterpret this finding as indicative of a progression from marginal social adjustment (4-8) to serious psychopathology (6-8).

Another important consideration in the accurate interpretation of retest findings concerns the observation that positive changes do not involve only reductions in T-score elevation. Rather, treatment progress may also be reflected in *increases* on certain scales. For example, a markedly low scale K at initial testing indicates impaired coping ability and low resilience to stress, and a low scale *9* indicates apathy and insufficient energy to contend with day-to-day tasks. Increases in the *T*-score level of these scales during treatment or at the completion of treatment would indicate that the adolescent has developed healthy coping resources and psychomotor energy sufficient to improve daily functioning. This interpretation should, however, be tempered by the knowledge that scale *K*, which loads on the Second Factor (Repression) commonly found in MMPI factor-analytic studies, is strongly and negatively correlated with several MMPI-A scales measuring First Factor (General Maladjustment) distress. Consequently, increases in *K* and other Second Factor scales should be expected to accompany reductions in First Factor scales in a retest profile.

The guidelines and examples offered in the preceding paragraphs should remind the reader that a sound knowledge of the characteristics measured by MMPI-A scales, scale correlates, and psychometric properties of the test is necessary for the clinician to interpret changes observed in MMPI-A profiles with accuracy. Despite the complexity inherent in this area, retesting with the MMPI-A during the course of treatment is a crucial means of evaluating whether treatment goals have been met, in determining whether adjustments are indicated in the treatment plan, and in estimating the point at which the maximum treatment benefit has been revealed and treatment termination may be appropriate.

Combining with Other Data Sources

In the typical course of a clinical assessment, MMPI-A results are interpreted in the context of historical and background information about the client and in consideration of expected base rates for the occurrence of specific types of behaviors or problems, given the setting in which the evaluation takes place. In fact, MMPI-A testing should *always* be accompanied by a clinical interview as a means of cross-validating test findings and obtaining information that permits more accurate MMPI-A interpretation. Additionally, there are many assessment referral questions and scenarios that indicate that MMPI-A testing should occur as part of a larger testing battery. For example, the examiner may need to address broad questions concerning the adolescent's capacities for stress tolerance and affective regulation, and the accuracy of his or her reality-testing processes. In the context of this referral question, a Rorschach could usefully supplement MMPI-A testing. Similarly, assessment questions regarding the adolescent's interpersonal perceptions and relationships may be addressed by including the Thematic Apperception Test (TAT) in the test battery. Another useful assessment battery approach may involve combining the adolescent's self-report on the MMPI-A with parent-reported or teacher-reported data, as might be obtained from the relevant versions of the Child Behavior Checklist (CBCL; Achenbach & Edelbrock, 1983). These approaches have the advantage of using multiple methods of assessment, which offers opportunities for evaluating personality dynamics and processes from different perspectives. Empirical evaluations of MMPI and Rorschach interrelationships in adolescent samples (see Archer & Krishnamurthy, 1993; Krishnamurthy, Archer, & House, 1996) have shown that the relationship between conceptually similar scales and indices on the two tests (e.g., MMPI-A scale 2 and Rorschach Depression Index (DEPI) are typically quite minimal. These findings suggest two possibilities: that the constructs measured by the two tests are substantially dissimilar, or that very different facets of similar constructs are evaluated by indices on the two tests. Either possibility would indicate that the clinician would not be obtaining redundant information from the use of both tests in a test battery. The research literature on parent- versus child-report inventories has similarly found poor associations between the two sets of reports. For example, parent-reported CBCL results are often divergent from Youth Self-Report (YSR) findings, and a similar discrepancy is seen between YSR and CBCL teacher-reported profiles. For the clinical assessor, these findings suggest that multiple sources of information may be crucial in obtaining a broader picture of the adolescent's functioning.

MMPI-A testing can also be integrated with data from intellectual, achievement, and neuropsychological testing, which provide unique or nonoverlapping types of information concerning an adolescent's functioning. This is particularly important when the adolescent is suspected of having a neurologically based disorder such as Attention-Deficit Hyperactivity Disorder (ADHD) or Specific Learning Disability, or has a history of head injury. Intelligence test scores may, for example, account for inconsistent or random responding to MMPI-A items in an invalid or marginally valid profile, or provide a fuller explanation of behaviors reflecting poor judgment or impulsivity. Reading comprehension scores from achievement testing can also serve as a useful context for understanding MMPI-A findings concerning school-related problems or low aspirations, in addition to determining whether the adolescent's endorsement of test items was based on an adequate understanding of the items. Neuropsychological testing may reveal perceptual and cognitive deficits that help the therapist understand MMPI-A indications of confusion, low self-esteem, and emotional distress.

Another beneficial supplement to MMPI-A testing is a complementary evaluation of the adolescent's parents using the MMPI-2, which can provide a useful picture of the family context within which to understand the adolescent's difficulties more completely. The MMPI-2 profile may reveal, for instance, a high level of parental stress or parental psychopathology, from which the clinician can make important inferences about the parents' capacity to participate in, or benefit from, interventions such as family therapy.

A final point is that MMPI-A testing for treatment planning is actually a time-saving method of collecting the kinds of information needed to develop an effective treatment plan, particularly when one considers the amount of time that would be involved in obtaining a comparable range of data solely from clinical interviews. MMPI-A results also furnish greater objectivity and accuracy when interpreted utilizing contextual information, a sound psychometric understanding of the test, and knowledge of adolescent development and psychopathology. These features translate to cost effectiveness, an important governing principle in contemporary clinical practice, as well as to increased clinical effectiveness.

🖋 TEST YOURSELF 🖋

1. **The 4-9 codetype is commonly found in the MMPI-A profiles of juvenile delinquents but not substance abusers.** True or False?
2. **Bulimic adolescents are more likely than anorexics to show MMPI-A scale elevations reflecting acting-out tendencies.** True or False?
3. **Elevated scores on scales K, R, and A-trt in a pretreatment MMPI-A assessment suggest**
   (a) greater suitability for group psychotherapy.
   (b) greater suitability for individual psychotherapy.
   (c) reluctance to engage in psychotherapy.
   (d) openness to all forms of psychotherapy.

(continued)

4. Changes of 5 or fewer *T*-score points in retest MMPI-A profiles

(a) reflect a realistic amount of treatment-related change.

(b) may be due solely to measurement error.

(c) indicate treatment failure.

(d) none of the above.

5. Combining the MMPI-A with other tests in a battery

(a) can be helpful in addressing broad referral questions.

(b) produces only redundant information.

(c) is contraindicated in the current managed-care practice environment.

(d) should occur only if the other tests are parent-reported checklists.

Answers: 1. False; 2. True; 3. c; 4. b; 5. a

Seven

ILLUSTRATIVE CASE REPORTS

This chapter presents four MMPI-A case examples of adolescents who were referred for psychological testing for various presenting problems. The first case report of a 14-year-old girl evaluated in an inpatient psychiatric facility exemplifies how her MMPI-A profiles are essentially uninterpretable due to her defensive test-taking approach. The second case report concerns a 16-year-old boy referred to an outpatient psychiatric clinic after a precipitous decline in his school grades. His profiles are used to describe the process of single-scale interpretation of the basic scale profile, the addition of information from subscales, content scales, and supplementary scales, and the use of the MMPI-A Structural Summary in arriving at summary impressions. The third case report presents the profiles of a 17-year-old girl referred for evaluation and psychotherapy following a serious escalation of conflicts with her parents and increased use of alcohol and drugs. In this case, we discuss two-point codetype interpretation, and include a sample of the computerized interpretive report generated by use of the MMPI-A Interpretive System, Version 2, developed by Robert Archer and published by PAR. The fourth case report, that of a 16-year-old girl with a history of sexual abuse, is offered to illustrate a method for interpreting a basic scale profile with multiple elevations. The case reports (excluding the first case example) will demonstrate how MMPI-A findings are integrated with background information, behavioral observations, and other test results to produce descriptions of psychological functioning and arrive at diagnostic impressions. The cases present more detail concerning the specific source of interpretive comments than would typically be found in most professional test reports because of our primary focus on clearly illustrating interpretation practices and principles. The reader is also provided with guidelines concerning the format and essential components of a psychological test report through the "Rapid Reference," "Don't Forget," and "Caution" presentations.

DON'T FORGET

Sections of a Test Report

- *Identifying information:* Name, age, date of birth, sex, ethnicity, grade, date(s) of testing, date of report
- *Reason for referral:* Referral source, questions to be addressed in the evaluation
- *History/background:* Family constellation, developmental history, medical/psychiatric history, substance abuse history, educational history, previous treatments, recent stressors
- *Assessment methods:* Interview, mental status examination, and tests used
- *Behavioral observations:* Physical appearance and grooming, any additional noteworthy characteristics, alertness, orientation, memory, psychomotor activity, thought processes, speech, affect/mood, suicidal/homicidal ideation, attention/concentration, cooperation, interest/involvement in testing, task orientation, ability to follow directions
- *Test results and interpretation:* Profile validity, profile patterns and scale elevations, structural summary
- *Summary and diagnostic impressions:* Major findings, inferences, and conclusions, prognosis, five-axial diagnosis when requested
- *Recommendations:* Specific suggestions for treatment, referral, and placement

≡Rapid Reference 7.1

Useful Organizing Themes for MMPI-A Interpretation

- Overall adjustment level
- Predominant symptoms
- Defense mechanisms
- Affective features and stability
- Thought processes
- Behavioral functioning
- Interpersonal relationships
- Diagnostic impressions
- Prognosis
- Potential intervention modalities (e.g., individual, group, family therapy, inpatient vs. outpatient treatment, medications)

CAUTION

Common Errors to Avoid in Report Writing

- Excluding pertinent contextual information
- Using scale names as self-evident instead of descriptive information
- Using overly tentative language
- Making value judgments
- Providing contradictory statements
- Making the report test-centered rather than person-centered
- Making grammatical and typographical errors
- Failing to tailor the report style/language to the intended audience
- Failing to answer the referral question

DON'T FORGET

Ethical Considerations

- Obtain consent from the adolescent and his/her legal guardian before releasing the test report to another individual
- Do not release raw data to a nonpsychologist
- Provide test feedback to the adolescent in manner that is comprehensible and meaningful to him/her

CASE REPORT 1

Name:	Jenna B.
Age:	14
Sex:	Female
Ethnicity:	Biracial: Caucasian/Hispanic
Grade:	8

Reason for Referral

Jenna was admitted to the adolescent unit of a psychiatric facility following several incidents of uncontrollable and aggressive behaviors at home. Her parents felt unable to control her actions, which they viewed as increasingly unpredictable and violent. Recent episodes included her attempt to attack her mother with a pair of scissors and screaming that she wanted her dead. The psychological evaluation was conducted as part of the initial diagnostic evaluation and was intended for use in the treatment team's determination of length of hospital stay.

Background Information

Jenna was a first-born child of a couple who had been married for 15 years. Her father was a software salesman employed by a local computer business and her mother was a social worker employed by their state of their residence. Jenna's younger brother, age 10, had no reported behavioral or emotional difficulties. Jenna was described as a rather fussy infant in terms of being difficult to pacify, but met all major developmental milestones and had no unusual illnesses or medical complications. She was reported to have "settled down" in early and middle childhood, had an unremarkable academic history, and had no difficulty making friends.

The problems reportedly became evident around age 12 when Jenna began rebelling against parental authority and, in her parent's view, began demanding unreasonable levels of freedom. Her mother was the disciplinarian in the family, whereas her father was described as an indulgent parent who was often manipulated by Jenna into capitulating to her demands. In the preceding year, Jenna had also been suspended from school twice for cheating on a test and damaging school property, respectively. She maintained a C average in her classes and had no significant learning problems, but had a growing record of school truancy. She was a popular member of a peer group of eighth-graders who were identified by school officials as troublemakers and were suspected of drug use.

Jenna's parents had taken her to a therapist for outpatient treatment approximately six months earlier when incidents of angry outbursts and her refusal to comply with rules escalated, and because their efforts to impose consequences for her actions were unsuccessful. They had also begun to participate in family therapy sessions. However, Jenna frequently refused to go to her sessions and missed four consecutive appointments. Hospital admission became the last resort when all other attempted interventions failed to have a significant impact in placing effective limits on Jenna's aggressive and antisocial behaviors.

Assessment Methods

Clinical Interview and Mental Status Examination
Minnesota Multiphasic Personality Inventory–Adolescent (MMPI-A)

Behavioral Observations and Mental Status Examination

Jenna was angry and agitated during the interview, which was conducted a day after her hospital admission. Her initial refusal to answer questions was followed by a period of ranting against her parents and threats to run away from the hospital unit at the earliest opportunity. She agreed to take the MMPI-A only when she was told that her cooperation would help her to earn privileges toward using the snack machines. Jenna was dressed in black jeans and black T-shirt, and her long dark hair partially covered her face. Her speech was intense, rapid, and loud, and she restlessly swung her legs throughout the interview. The mental status examination showed no problems in orientation, attention, memory, or thought processes. She denied suicidal ideation and intent, but was nonresponsive to questions about harm to others. During the testing session, she gnawed on the back of her pencil and spat out the pieces she had chewed off, but remained on task. She completed the MMPI-A in 50 minutes.

Test Results and Interpretation

Jenna's basic scale profile is shown in Figure 7.1. The examination of profile validity, beginning with the *Cannot Say* score, shows that she answered all the test questions despite her displeasure about the testing process. Her *VRIN* scale T score of 43 indicates that her responses were at an acceptable level of consistency, which is further supported by the uniformity between F_1 and F_2 scale scores. The *TRIN* scale score of 53 is also within normal limits and reflects the absence of a response bias in either an acquiescence or nay-saying direction. However, evaluation of the accuracy of the profile, using scales F, L, and K, identifies that there is a problem with accurate self-presentation. The

Figure 7.1 Profile for Basic Scales for Jenna B.

Minnesota Multiphasic Personality Inventory–Adolescent (MMPI-A). Copyright © the Regents of the University of Minnesota 1942, 1943 (renewed 1970), 1992. Reproduced by permission of the publisher: "Minnesota Multiphasic Personality Inventory–Adolescent" and "MMPI-A" are trademarks owned by the University of Minnesota.

overall *F-L-K,* configuration is one of being unwilling to admit psychological problems, reflected by the clinical elevation on *K* indicating strong defensiveness and an average score on *F* that would suggest the absence of psychopathology. While these scores reveal that Jenna essentially denies having any psychological difficulties, her normal-range *L* scale score suggests that she is not necessarily attempting to present herself as a "good" or socially conforming teenager. Her approach to denial is therefore not crude, but involves a fairly sophisticated style of withholding information about psychological symptoms and problematic experiences while acknowledging common human failings or foibles. The level of defensiveness seen in this validity scale profile suggests a more difficult treatment process and also indicates that the resulting basic, content, and supplementary scale profiles do not accurately represent this client's level of functioning. The interpretive process would consequently end with the determination that the protocol is invalid due to substantial distortions in accuracy resulting from an underreporting response style.

A look at Jenna's clinical scale profile underscores the point that her MMPI-A results cannot be meaningfully interpreted. The profile shows an absence of clinical-range elevations on any of the clinical scales. In fact, 4 of the 10 basic scales are at least 1 SD below the mean, and her mean *T*-score elevation across the 10 scales is only 42. This basic scale profile reflects the impact of using a defensive responding style and should not be viewed as indicating the absence of psychopathology. The suppression effect of the high *K* score is seen more clearly on Jenna's content and supplementary scale profile (Figure 7.2), where virtually all content scales hover between the *T*-score levels of 30 and 40, producing a markedly low mean score of 38. Furthermore, all supplementary scales are also at average to low elevation ranges.

Concluding Comments

This case brings two important issues to light. First, psychological testing efforts using the MMPI-A or any other test instrument are prone to be unproductive when the adolescent is not engaged in the testing process and perceives no apparent benefits from it. Jenna felt coerced into hospitalization and the evaluative procedures that followed her hospital admission. It is therefore not surprising that she felt no need to cooperate with testing. Second, recognizing when not to proceed with testing may be as important as knowledge about

Figure 7.2 Profile for Content and Supplementary Scales for Jenna B.

Minnesota Multiphasic PersonalityInventory–Adolescent (MMPI-A). Copyright © the Regents of the University of Minnesota 1942, 1943 (renewed 1970), 1992. Reproduced by permission of the publisher. "Minnesota Multiphasic Personality Inventory–Adolescent" and "MMPI-A" are trademarks owned by the University of Minnesota.

conducting an accurate interpretation. Useful interpretations can not be forced out of an MMPI-A profile such as Jenna's because her level of defensiveness precludes deriving accurate or useful data about her personality functioning beyond the important observation that she is markedly guarded and defensive.

CASE REPORT 2

Name: Shawn M.
Age: 16
Sex: Male
Ethnicity: Caucasian
Grade: 11

Reason for Referral

Shawn's parents originally brought him to an outpatient psychiatric clinic to assess for possible attentional or emotional causes of a sudden decline in his school performance. Specifically, his grades had fallen from his usual B average to grades of D and F in most classes, with the exception of continued As in his art class. He was evaluated by a neuropsychologist and subsequently referred to another psychologist in the clinic for psychotherapy.

Background Information

Shawn had been identified as a gifted student in elementary school but was also found to be learning disabled in Spelling. He was attending a public high school at the time of this referral. An Individual Education Plan (IEP) was being implemented for him, and he was also attending some advanced placement classes. Shawn's school attendance was consistently good and no behavioral problems were reported in the school environment. However, Shawn was proud of doing no homework (he referred to this as his strict "no-homework policy") and managed to achieve barely passing course grades by balancing his Fs on homework assignments with good examination grades.

Shawn's mother reported that he had a fairly unremarkable childhood medical history. He had sustained a mild concussion at age 12 during soccer practice, but his MRI was negative and he had no residual symptoms. He did not take any prescription medications, and substance use was denied. There was no known family history of psychiatric illnesses.

Shawn's parents divorced when he was approximately 6 years of age and he was reared by his mother since the divorce. His biological father moved to the West Coast but maintained contact with him. Shawn described his father as an "eccentric but cool guy" with whom he identified very strongly, and they shared a binding interest in photography and computer graphics. In recent years, their twice-yearly face-to-face contact was supplemented with weekly e-mail exchanges. At the time of the testing, Shawn lived with his mother, his stepfather of 9 years, and his 8-year-old half-sister. He felt largely ignored by his mother and stepfather, whom he viewed as "in a rat race," and felt overly responsible for raising his younger half-sister. Both his mother and stepfather had advanced degrees and held high-level professional positions. His step-father had graduated from an Ivy League college and, together with Shawn's mother, had begun to talk to him about applying to his alma mater for college. Shawn had recently taken the PSAT and obtained a 1450 score, which was quite competitive for college admission.

Evaluative Techniques

Clinical Interview with Shawn and his mother
Mental Status Examination
Minnesota Multiphasic Personality Inventory–Adolescent (MMPI-A)
Beck Depression Inventory–II (BDI-II)
Rotter Incomplete Sentences Blank–High School Form
Wechsler Adult Intelligence Scale–Third Edition (WAIS-III)
Wide Range Achievement Test–Revision 3 (WRAT-3)
Stroop Neuropsychological Screening Test
Trail Making Test–Parts A and B
Brown Attention-Deficit Disorder Scales–Adolescent Form

Behavioral Observations and Mental Status Examination

Shawn was a tall, lanky, well-groomed teenager who appeared his stated age. He arrived on time for his interview and all testing appointments, accompa-nied by his mother on each occasion, and was fully cooperative with all procedures. He was alert and oriented in all spheres, displayed a normal range of affect, and exhibited no disorder in thought content or form. His speech was normal in tone, receptive language skills appeared intact, and his vocabulary appeared quite superior for his age. Shawn acknowledged having intermittent suicidal ideation that was passive in quality ("I sometimes think it would be so much easier if it were all over") but denied active suicidal intent or plans.

The testing sessions proceeded without difficulty. Shawn engaged well with the examiner, followed all test directions, and seemed sufficiently invested in all evaluative tasks to produce interpretable results. There were no signs of fatigue, distraction, or loss of concentration.

Summary of Other Test Results

The results of the cognitive, achievement, neuropsychological, and other personality testing and depression screenings are briefly and separately summarized here in order to place emphasis on the MMPI-A results that follow. Shawn's IQ scores were uniformly in the Superior range (Full Scale IQ = 128) with no significant discrepancy between verbal and visual-spatial skills. Verbal comprehension was, however, significantly better developed than nonverbal reasoning and speed of information processing. Shawn's Reading skills exceeded the high-school level, whereas his Arithmetic skills were at grade level. However, his Spelling ability was below grade level and was consistent with his earlier diagnosis of learning disability in this area. Evaluation of attentional abilities and executive functions generally indicated average to above-average levels of performance. Although Shawn reported experiences of restlessness and inattention, his responses did not meet the cutoff criteria for diagnosing ADHD. Shawn's total score on the BDI-II indicated mild depression. His responses to the Incomplete Sentences Blank revealed considerable apprehension about the future (e.g., "The future *is a gaping hole opening into a dark, bottomless pit*") and his ability to succeed ("My greatest worry is *failing*"; I can't *do the things that make for success in life*").

MMPI-A Results and Interpretation

Shawn's basic scale profile, presented in Figure 7.3, shows no item omissions, and his *VRIN* score reflects consistent responding to items across the 478 items of the test. A comparison of F_1 and F_2 scores supports the finding of

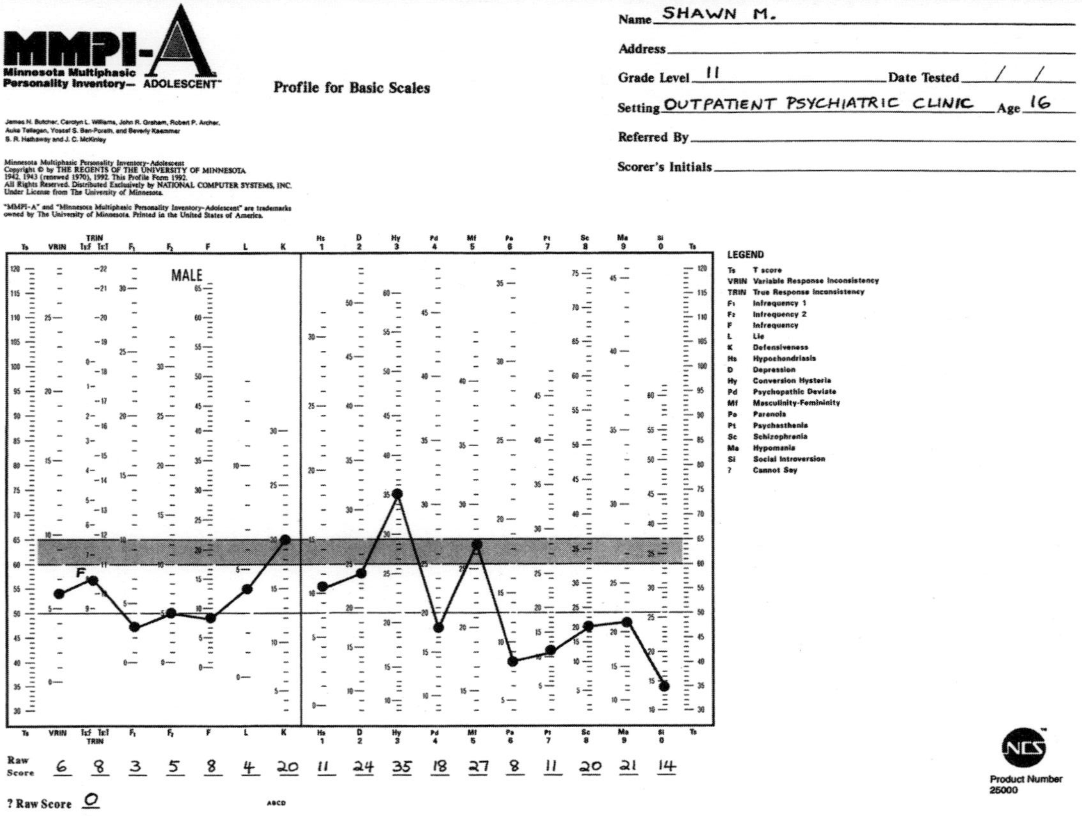

Figure 7.3 Profile for Basic Scales for Shawn M.

Minnesota Multiphasic Personality Inventory–Adolescent (MMPI-A). Copyright © the Regents of the University of Minnesota 1942, 1943 (renewed 1970), 1992. Reproduced by permission of the publisher: "Minnesota Multiphasic Personality Inventory–Adolescent" and "MMPI-A" are trademarks owned by the University of Minnesota.

consistent responding, and the normal-range *TRIN* score indicates an absence of acquiescent and nay-saying response tendencies. His *F-L-K* configuration suggests a tendency toward minimizing reports of psychological symptomatology. The *K* score of 65 further suggests that he maintains a self-reliant stance and would be reluctant to seek help from others. Shawn's test profiles are, nonetheless, interpretable because (a) the level of defensiveness shown on the *K* scale is not unacceptably high, and (b) some basic, content, and supplementary scale scores are at clinically significant levels. However, the examiner should be aware that the resulting interpretation is likely to be a conservative estimate of his difficulties.

Shawn's basic scale profile may be interpreted as a Spike *3* profile, and descriptors from the marginally elevated scale *5* and the low ($T \le 40$) scores on scales *6* and *0* would be added to the interpretive yield from scale *3*. Shawn's content scale profile has a single clinical range elevation on *A-dep*, and his supplementary scale profile has a marginal range elevation on scale *R* (see figure 7.4). Scales Hy_1, Hy_3, and Hy_5 on the Harris-Lingoes subscale profile can be interpreted to clarify the elevation on basic scale *3* (see figure 7.5).

High scale *3* scores have been associated with higher levels of intelligence and achievement, and have been found among well-behaved and intelligent children from middle-class homes. However, Shawn's profiles also indicate that he had some difficulties in adjustment. Teenagers with a high scale *3* tend to overreact to stress through the development of physical symptoms. Shawn's profiles further indicate the presence of moderate depression, seen in the elevated *A-dep* score and in the Hy_3 descriptors involving characteristics of sadness and despondency, and a sense of unhappiness. The Hy_3 subscale elevation also reflects feelings of weakness and fatigue, and suggests that he is functioning at a reduced level of physical and cognitive efficiency. Disruptions in sleep and appetite are also likely, as suggested by Hy_3, and the overall sense is likely to be one of lacking good health.

Teenagers with a high scale *3* tend to be psychologically naive and generally are not self-reflective, which accounts for their somatic rather than emotional expressions of distress. Their primary defense mechanisms consist of denial and repression. Shawn's profile also shows considerable underlying insecurity and a sense of inadequacy. Moreover, the elevations on scales *3* and *R* reveal to us that Shawn is emotionally overcontrolled and constricted, and the *A-dep* score suggests that he is likely to hold a strongly pessimistic view of the world.

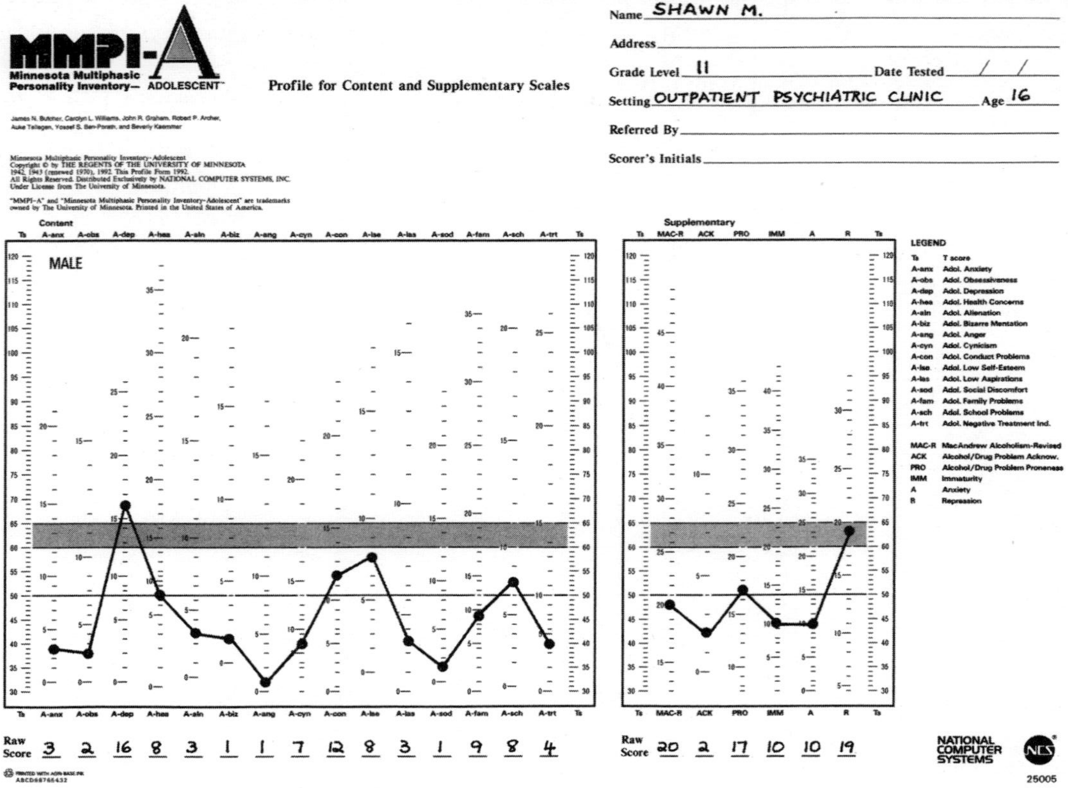

Figure 7.4 Profile for Content and Supplementary Scales for Shawn M.

Minnesota Multiphasic Personality Inventory–Adolescent (MMPI-A). Copyright © the Regents of the University of Minnesota 1942, 1943 (renewed 1970), 1992. Reproduced by permission of the publisher: "Minnesota Multiphasic Personality Inventory–Adolescent" and "MMPI-A" are trademarks owned by the University of Minnesota.

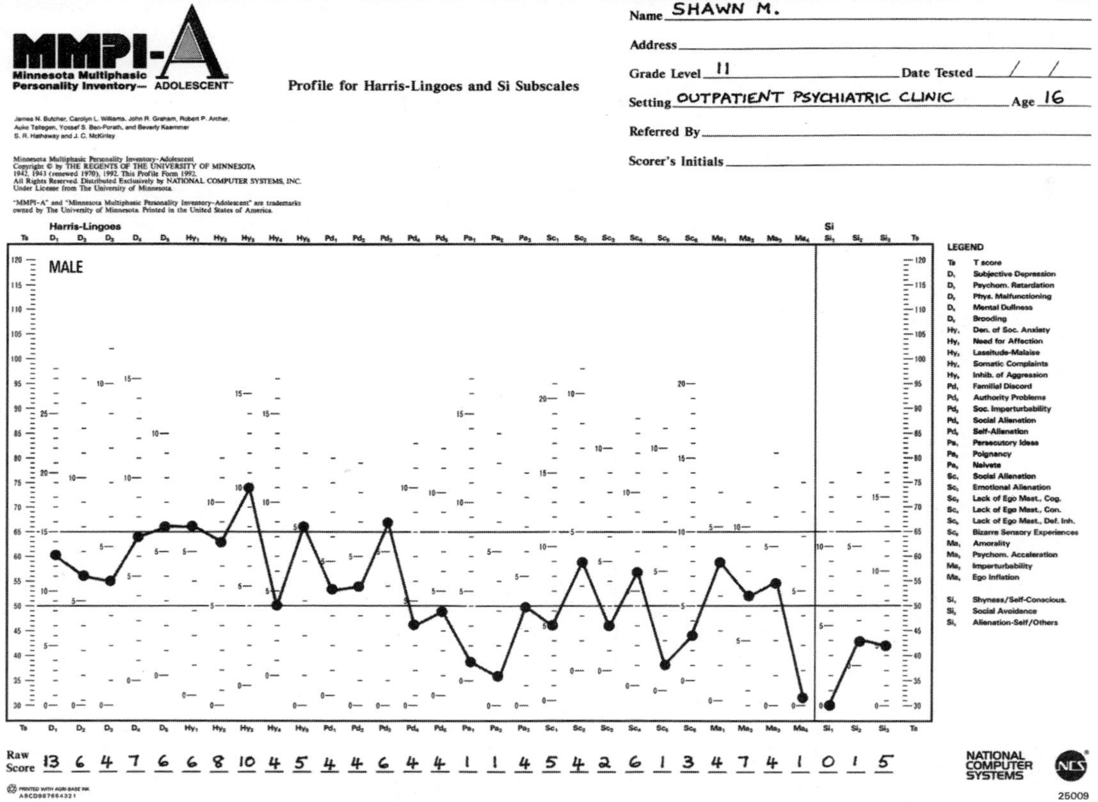

Figure 7.5 Profile for Harris-Lingoes and Si Subscales for Shawn M.

In the interpersonal realm, teenagers with a scale *3* elevation have strong needs for attention and affection from others. Shawn's markedly low scale *0* score suggests that strong affiliative needs exist that serve as a means of obtaining social approval, and such adolescents are often talkative and gregarious. There is likely to be considerable sensitivity to how others respond to him, and the elevation of the Hy_5 score suggests that Shawn would be unlikely to express angry or hostile feelings or impulses. On the other hand, his high scale *3* score in combination with a low scale *6* score indicate that Shawn may be more sensitive to his own needs than to the feelings and motives of others. The scale *5* score, elevated in the feminine direction, additionally suggest tendencies toward interpersonal passivity and withdrawal from others, and (in combination with the scale *3* elevation) a low likelihood of antisocial acting-out behaviors.

Shawn's MMPI-A Structural Summary, shown in Figure 7.6, underscores several important aspects of his personality and functioning. Interestingly, the most prominent dimension is that of Naivete, which reflects a strong denial of negative impulses and emphasizes a socially conforming presentation. This dimension is consistent with Shawn's overall history, which shows that he is generally well behaved and stays out of trouble, and that his homework refusals represent a very small-scale and circumscribed rebellion. This reluctance and difficulty in dealing directly with conflictual or angry feelings is a central feature of Shawn's current problems. The General Maladjustment dimension, which has 21% of its scales elevated at $T \geq 60$, adds some valuable information to the overall interpretation. On one hand, it offers greater clarity on Shawn's subjective feelings of depression and ruminative tendencies than was evident from the interpretation of individual scales, and underscores the cognitive and physical effects of his depression. On the other hand, it underscores that his depressive symptoms are not producing widespread affective distress or disruption. The Health Concerns dimension, with a 33% rate of scale elevation, also offers the perspective that although Shawn reports some somatic symptoms or complaints, these are not intense enough to be seen as a pervasive or central issue at this time.

Summary and Diagnostic Impression

Shawn's MMPI-A profiles reflect a teenager who feels essentially dissatisfied with himself, and who longs for acceptance from others but is unable to express

MMPI-A Structural Summary
Robert P. Archer and Radhika Krishnamurthy

Name: **SHAWN M.** Date: _____

Age: **16** Grade: **11**

Gender: **MALE** School: _____

Test-Taking Attitudes

1. Omissions (raw score total)

   0 ? (Cannot Say scale)

2. Consistency (T-score values)

   54 VRIN

   57F TRIN

   47 F_1 vs. **50** F_2

3. Accuracy (check if condition present)

Overreport

   _____ F scale T score ≥ 90

   _____ All clinical scales except 5 and 0 ≥ 60

Underreport

   _____ High L (T ≥ 65)

   ✓ High K (T ≥ 65)

   _____ All clinical scales except 5 and 0 < 60

Factor Groupings
(enter T-score data)

1. General Maladjustment

   _____ Welsh's A

   _____ Scale 7

   _____ Scale 8

   _____ Scale 2

   _____ Scale 4

   ✓ D_1 (Subjective Depression)

   ✓ D_4 (Mental Dullness)

   ✓ D_5 (Brooding)

   ✓ Hy_3 (Lassitude-Malaise)

   _____ Sc_1 (Social Alienation)

   _____ Sc_2 (Emotional Alienation)

   _____ Sc_3 (Lack of Ego Mastery – Cognitive)

   _____ Sc_4 (Lack of Ego Mastery – Conative)

   _____ Si_3 (Alienation)

   _____ Pd_4 (Social Alienation)

   _____ Pd_5 (Self-Alienation)

   _____ Pa_2 (Poignancy)

   ✓ A-dep

   _____ A-anx

   _____ A-lse

   _____ A-aln

   _____ A-obs

   _____ A-trt

   5 /23 Number of scales with T ≥ 60

2. Immaturity

   _____ IMM

   _____ Scale F

   _____ Scale 8

   _____ Scale 6

   _____ ACK

   _____ MAC-R

   _____ Pa_1 (Persecutory Ideas)

   _____ Sc_2 (Emotional Alienation)

   _____ Sc_6 (Bizarre Sensory Experiences)

   _____ A-sch

   _____ A-biz

   _____ A-aln

   _____ A-con

   _____ A-fam

   _____ A-trt

   0 /15 Number of scales with T ≥ 60

Figure 7.6 MMPI-A Structural Summary for Shawn M.

3. Disinhibition/Excitatory Potential

_____ Scale 9

_____ Ma$_2$ (Psychomotor Acceleration)

_____ Ma$_4$ (Ego Inflation)

_____ Sc$_5$ (Lack of Ego Mastery, Defective Inhibition)

_____ D$_2$ (Psychomotor Retardation) (low score)*

_____ Welsh's R (low score)*

_____ Scale K (low score)*

_____ Scale L (low score)*

_____ A-ang

_____ A-cyn

_____ A-con

_____ MAC-R

O /12 Number of scales with $T \geq 60$ or ≤ 40 for scales with asterisk

4. Social Discomfort

_____ Scale 0

_____ Si$_1$ (Shyness/Self-Consciousness)

_____ Hy$_1$ (Denial of Social Anxiety) (low score)*

_____ Pd$_3$ (Social Imperturbability) (low score)*

_____ Ma$_3$ (Imperturbability) (low scores)*

_____ A-sod

_____ A-lse

_____ Scale 7

O /8 Number of scales with $T \geq 60$ or $T \leq 40$ for scales with asterisk

5. Health Concerns

_____ Scale 1

✓ Scale 3

_____ A-hea

_____ Hy$_4$ (Somatic Complaints)

✓ Hy$_3$ (Lassitude-Malaise)

_____ D$_3$ (Physical Malfunctioning)

2 /6 Number of scales with $T \geq 60$

6. Naivete

✓ A-cyn (low score)*

_____ Pa$_3$ (Naivete)

✓ Hy$_2$ (Need for Affection)

_____ Si$_3$ (Alienation–Self and Others) (low score)*

✓ Scale K

3 /5 Number of scales with $T \geq 60$ or $T \leq 40$ for scales with asterisk

7. Familial Alienation

_____ Pd$_1$ (Familial Discord)

_____ A-fam

_____ Scale 4

_____ PRO

O /4 Number of scales with $T \geq 60$

8. Psychoticism

_____ Pa$_1$ (Persecutory Ideas)

_____ Scale 6

_____ A-biz

_____ Sc$_6$ (Bizarre Sensory Experiences)

O /4 Number of scales with $T \geq 60$

Note. The presentation of scales under each factor label is generally organized in a descending order from the best to the least effective marker. Within this overall approach, scales are grouped logically in terms of basic clinical scales, Harris-Lingoes and *Si* subscales, and content scales. The majority of scales included in this summary sheet were correlated ≥ .60 or ≤ –.60 with the relevant factor for the MMPI-A normative sample.

PAR **Psychological Assessment Resources, Inc.**
P.O. Box 998/Odessa, Florida 33556/ Toll-Free 1-800-331-TEST

Figure 7.6 Continued

directly his need for support and help. Instead, he maintains an independent, self-contained position and his distress finds expression in feelings of physical tiredness and weakness. Shawn's depression may have had some impact on his cognitive functioning, including attention and concentration, and his struggles with Spelling may be contributing to his feelings of insecurity. The test profiles suggest that, under these conditions, Shawn would have trouble developing effective solutions to his problems on his own. Results of testing, combined with historical information and observations, support the diagnoses of Dysthymic Disorder, Early Onset and Disorder of Written Expression. The prognosis for psychotherapy generally is not very favorable for adolescents with the type of profile produced by Shawn because of their denial of psychological problems and reluctance to obtain help from others. However, Shawn's functioning is currently not markedly disorganized, and he may respond to a treatment approach that emphasizes concrete, problem-solving methods.

Recommendations

Shawn is clearly in need of individual psychotherapy that should be directed toward reducing his depression and increasing feelings of self-efficacy. Although he may desire to solve his problems independently, he may be more amenable to therapy if the initial focus is on getting him to feel physically energized and developing problem-solving mechanisms, and if the therapist offers the frame that therapy would constitute a strong and independent step toward feeling better rather than dependency on others. Gradually, Shawn could be instructed in ways to communicate more effectively with his parents about his experiences of stress and pressure and his feelings of anger and frustration. Although Shawn appears to be capable of handling other academic tasks reasonably well, he would also benefit from continuation of an educational plan that provides individualized learning in Spelling.

Case Summary and Outcome

In therapy, Shawn conceded when pressed that he was depressed but generally tended to deny his experience of depression and to discount it. His therapist viewed him as chronically depressed but not actively suicidal, and noted that his academic underachievement was a means of acting out against his parents' academic achievements. Shawn's therapy attendance was sporadic and he attended a total of 10 individual psychotherapy sessions over a 4-month period. Some improvements in his functioning were, however, seen over the course of his treatment, including improved grades as a result of completion of homework assignments. He eventually dropped out of treatment after his grades began to improve, and when he felt he had the task of preparing for college application under control. He had entered his senior year of high school when he terminated treatment.

CASE REPORT 3

Name: Ruth S.
Age: 17
Sex: Female
Ethnicity: Caucasian
Grade: 12

Reason for Referral

Ruth's mother brought her to a psychologist working in an independent practice setting with the complaint that "Ruth is spinning out of control and is headed for disaster." Problems of heavy alcohol and drug use were described, and Ruth's conflicts with her parents had reportedly escalated in frequency and intensity. The assessment was conducted to facilitate diagnostic formulations and treatment planning.

Background Information

Ruth was the older of two children and had a 14-year-old brother. Her "workaholic" mother was employed as a physical therapist and her stepfather owned and operated a local restaurant. Ruth's biological father had been treated for Bipolar Disorder since his early adulthood and had been hospitalized twice in his twenties. He had been stabilized in recent years with Paxil, Wellbutrin, and Depakote, but died unexpectedly in a vehicular collision when his car was hit by a drunk driver. Ruth was 15 years old at the time of her father's death. Her mother remarried the following year.

This adolescent had normal prenatal development and birth, and her medical/developmental history between infancy and late childhood was unremarkable. However, she had a psychiatric history beginning in puberty. Her first experience of psychotherapy occurred at age 11 for treatment of depression and suicidal ideation. She continued to receive outpatient psychotherapy intermittently throughout her adolescent years, most recently after her father's death, which provoked a significant depressive episode. She had been previously treated briefly with Desipramine but was not taking any medications at the time of this referral. Ruth's reaction to her mother's remarriage consisted of intense anger, and this issue continued to play a central role in their battles. Her alcohol use, which had begun at age 15, increased to daily consumption. Ruth had also used marijuana daily since age 15 and had recently begun experimenting with Ecstasy, but denied intravenous drug use. She became sexually active at age 16 and acknowledged having had multiple sexual partners and unprotected sex on occasion.

In the clinical interview, Ruth voluntarily admitted to intermittent episodes of binge eating and purging during the preceding 6 months and stated that her mother was unaware of this problem. She also reported that she had been expelled from school due to marijuana possession, but had no other legal history. Prior to her expulsion, she had been obtaining below-average grades. Although Ruth described herself as a perennial "bad girl" and a "fat, ugly slob with no future," she was genuinely concerned about evolving a direction for career and identity development. It should be noted that Ruth's younger brother also had a history of psychological and behavioral problems, and had recently undergone psychiatric hospitalization for substance abuse, depression, and conduct-disordered behaviors.

Assessment Methods

Clinical Interview and Mental Status Examination
Minnesota Multiphasic Personality Inventory–Adolescent (MMPI-A)
Eating Disorder Inventory–2 (EDI-2)

Behavioral Observations and Mental Status Examination

Ruth presented as an attractive, normal-weight adolescent dressed in an avant-garde style consisting of loose cotton clothing and numerous strands of bead jewelry wrapped around her neck and wrists. Multiple piercings in her ears, nose, and eyebrows were also adorned with beads. Ruth was reasonably cooperative with interview questions and assessment procedures while presenting a demeanor suggesting that she had been through it all before and was exerting effort to be patient with redundant processes. A mental status examination revealed that her stream of thought was coherent and goal directed, and thought content was appropriate. Her affect was somewhat constricted and mood was judged to be mildly depressed. No usual psychomotor activity was observed, and her speech was fluent and normal in tone. Ruth displayed appropriate levels of attention and effort during testing.

Test Results and Interpretation

Ruth responded to all but two MMPI-A items, a level of item omission which clearly does not interfere with profile validity. The content of the omitted items did not appear significant to her history and presenting problems and were, most likely, an oversight. Response consistency indicators $VRIN$ and F_1/F_2 show no problems in terms of inconsistent responding, and the $TRIN$ score presents no evidence of a substantial response bias toward answering indiscriminately in either the *True* or *False* direction. The F-L-K configuration shows that Ruth was reasonably open to admitting difficulties and was not defensive or strongly motivated to present herself in an excessively positive light. Ruth's MMPI-A profiles are therefore valid for meaningful interpretation and are likely to represent an accurate picture of her current functioning.

The basic scale profile (see Figure 7.7), with elevations on scales *4, 2* and *0,* may be interpreted primarily as a *2-4* codetype, given that this two-point codetype is both well defined (i.e., 10 *T*-score points) and markedly elevated in relation to the remaining scales in the profile. Further support for the preference for codetype analysis over single-scale interpretation comes from the Profile Matches and Scores section of the MMPI-A interpretive report (presented later in Figure 7.11). The computer report indicates that the *2-4* codetype is selected as the preferred or "best-fit" codetype based on an analysis of all other two-point codetype profiles in the database, and the *2-4* codetype pattern in Ruth's profile matches well with the modal *2-4* codetype profile found in the database for the MMPI-A interpretive system. Specifically, this codetype analysis produces a coefficient-of-fit value of .93, indicating that Ruth's basic scale configuration pattern, involving the *2-4* codetype, is highly correlated with the

Figure 7.7 Profile for Basic Scales for Ruth S.

Minnesota Multiphasic Personality Inventory–Adolescent (MMPI-A). Copyright © the Regents of the University of Minnesota 1942, 1943 (renewed 1970), 1992. Reproduced by permission of the publisher: "Minnesota Multiphasic Personality Inventory–Adolescent" and "MMPI-A" are trademarks owned by the University of Minnesota.

basic clinical scale profile for the prototypic *2-4* mean profile employed in this interpretive system. Codetype descriptors are supplemented with individual scale correlates of scale *0*, which is elevated at a *T*-score level of 65. The description of Ruth's functioning is rounded out by the addition of correlates based on content scales *A-lse, A-sod, A-dep, A-las,* and *A-con,* which are elevated in either clinical or marginal ranges of elevation, characteristics measured by supplementary scales *R, PRO,* and *ACK,* and content areas revealed by subscales of scales *2, 4,* and *0* (see Figures 7.8 and 7.9).

A significant finding from Ruth's MMPI-A profiles concerns her behavioral disturbance marked by strong acting-out tendencies. Adolescents who obtain this profile are frequently impulsive and act without considering the consequences of their actions (*2-4* codetype, *A-con* scale). Their impulsivity may take several forms, including sexual promiscuity, school truancy, and elopement from home or from inpatient treatment sites. Externalization and acting out constitute the defense mechanisms they typically use to deal with their perceived difficulties (*2-4* codetype). Histories of poor school adjustment and school conduct problems are fairly commonplace for teenagers with this codetype, and their backgrounds often contain documentation of legal difficulties including arrests and convictions. In general, these adolescents tend to be indifferent to social norms and consequently have frequent clashes with authority figures. They have little tolerance for boredom and often turn to substance abuse and other risk-taking behaviors (*2-4* codetype and *A-con*) as a means of obtaining stimulation as well as for covering or self-medicating feelings of dysphoria and depression. In adulthood, these individuals are frequently identified as alcoholics. It should be noted that substance abuse problems are only minimally acknowledged by Ruth (marginal-range score on scale *ACK*) and the evidence for her potential for developing serious substance abuse difficulties is limited on the MMPI-A substance-related supplementary scales (i.e., marginal-range scale *PRO*; normal-range *MAC-R*). Her alcohol and drug abuse problems are therefore best reflected in her *2-4* codetype pattern. A more typical pattern for adolescent substance abusers may involve the presence of a *2-4* or *4-9* codetype on the basic scale profile, co-occurring with elevations on supplementary scales *MAC-R, ACK,* and *PRO.*

In the affective realm, Ruth's functioning is characterized by despondency (scales *2* and *A-dep*). She is likely to be apathetic and despairing, and her endorsement of one of three suicide-related items indicates that she had

Figure 7.8 Profile for Content and Supplementary Scales for Ruth S.

Minnesota Multiphasic Personality Inventory–Adolescent (MMPI-A). Copyright © the Regents of the University of Minnesota 1942, 1943 (renewed 1970), 1992. Reproduced by permission of the publisher. "Minnesota Multiphasic Personality Inventory–Adolescent" and "MMPI-A" are trademarks owned by the University of Minnesota.

Figure 7.9 Profile for Harris-Lingoes and Si Subscales for Ruth S.

Minnesota Multiphasic Personality Inventory–Adolescent (MMPI-A). Copyright © the Regents of the University of Minnesota 1942, 1943 (renewed 1970), 1992. Reproduced by permission of the publisher: "Minnesota Multiphasic Personality Inventory–Adolescent" and "MMPI-A" are trademarks owned by the University of Minnesota.

thoughts of killing herself. The Harris-Lingoes subscale results indicate that Ruth's depression appears to affect emotional, cognitive, and physical aspects of her functioning. She feels unhappy and unmotivated (D_1), reports low energy (D_2), has trouble concentrating (D_4), is brooding and ruminative (D_5), and experiences somatic complaints (D_3). Notably, anger is not a strong element in her test profiles (see $A\text{-}ang$ score), suggesting that it may be overshadowed by her dysphoria or dissipated by acting out. Ruth also shows tendencies to inhibit and repress her feelings (scale R), which may add to an internal state of discomfort.

Ruth's self-concept is marked by negative features. She is prone to experience substantial feelings of worthlessness, self-criticism, and guilt, and to feel generally inadequate, and her self-perception is likely to be one of a flawed, useless individual (scales 2 and $A\text{-}lse$). Associated with these feelings are tendencies to avoid developing goals for herself and giving up easily when challenges and obstacles to achievement arise ($A\text{-}las$). She is likely to view her life as uninteresting and unrewarding (Pd_5). Results from Ruth's EDI-2 profiles indicate marked feelings of body dissatisfaction and an overall sense of ineffectiveness which provide support for her judgment of herself as unworthy.

Interpersonally, Ruth may not overtly exhibit difficulties in getting acquainted with others and may even create a good first impression in social situations (scale 4). However, she is internally quite insecure and introverted, and may be acutely uncomfortable in social situations (scale 0). She is prone to dislike and avoid group activities ($A\text{-}sod$ and Si_2), perhaps because she believes that others see her in the likeness of her own "fat, ugly slob" self-image. Her relationships with peers are likely to remain superficial, and her relationships with adults, particularly parents and authority figures, chiefly conflictual (Pd_1, Pd_2).

The MMPI-A Structural Summary, shown in Figure 7.10, offers a useful perspective on the broad range of disturbances experienced by Ruth and highlights some important emphases. The most salient dimension is Familial Alienation, indicating that her poor relationship with her parents and frequent battles with them is a significant area of difficulty. The General Maladjustment dimension, within which 57% of the scales are elevated, indicates substantial emotional distress and maladjustment, including depression, fatigue, and suicidal thoughts, which may ordinarily be obscured by Ruth's behavioral acting

MMPI-A Structural Summary

Robert P. Archer and Radhika Krishnamurthy

Name: **RUTH S.**   Date: _____

Age: **17**   Grade: **12**

Gender: **FEMALE**   School: _____

Test-Taking Attitudes

1. Omissions (raw score total)

2 ? (Cannot Say scale)

2. Consistency (T-score values)

50 VRIN

59 F TRIN

56 F₁ vs. **57** F₂

3. Accuracy (check if condition present)

Overreport

_____ F scale T score ≥ 90

_____ All clinical scales except 5 and 0 ≥ 60

Underreport

_____ High L (T ≥ 65)

_____ High K (T ≥ 65)

_____ All clinical scales except 5 and 0 < 60

Factor Groupings
(enter T-score data)

1. General Maladjustment

_____ Welsh's A

_____ Scale 7

_____ Scale 8

✓ Scale 2

✓ Scale 4

✓ D₁ (Subjective Depression)

✓ D₄ (Mental Dullness)

✓ D₅ (Brooding)

✓ Hy₃ (Lassitude-Malaise)

✓ Sc₁ (Social Alienation)

_____ Sc₂ (Emotional Alienation)

✓ Sc₃ (Lack of Ego Mastery – Cognitive)

✓ Sc₄ (Lack of Ego Mastery – Conative)

✓ Si₃ (Alienation)

_____ Pd₄ (Social Alienation)

✓ Pd₅ (Self-Alienation)

_____ Pa₂ (Poignancy)

✓ A-dep

_____ A-anx

✓ A-lse

_____ A-aln

_____ A-obs

_____ A-trt

13 /23 Number of scales with T ≥ 60

2. Immaturity

_____ IMM

_____ Scale F

_____ Scale 8

_____ Scale 6

✓ ACK

_____ MAC-R

_____ Pa₁ (Persecutory Ideas)

_____ Sc₂ (Emotional Alienation)

_____ Sc₆ (Bizarre Sensory Experiences)

_____ A-sch

_____ A-biz

_____ A-aln

✓ A-con

_____ A-fam

_____ A-trt

2 /15 Number of scales with T ≥ 60

Figure 7.10 MMPI-A Structural Summary for Ruth S.

Reproduced by special permission of Psychological Assessment Resources, Inc., from the MMPI-A Structural Summary by Robert P. Archer, PhD, Copyright 1994. Further reproduction is prohibited without permission from PAR, Inc.

3. Disinhibition/Excitatory Potential

_____ Scale 9

_____ Ma_2 (Psychomotor Acceleration)

_____ Ma_4 (Ego Inflation)

_____ Sc_5 (Lack of Ego Mastery, Defective Inhibition)

_____ D_2 (Psychomotor Retardation) (low score)*

_____ Welsh's R (low score)*

_____ Scale K (low score)*

_____ Scale L (low score)*

_____ A-ang

_____ A-cyn

✓ A-con

_____ MAC-R

1 /12 Number of scales with $T \geq 60$ or ≤ 40 for scales with asterisk

4. Social Discomfort

✓ Scale 0

_____ Si_1 (Shyness/Self-Consciousness)

✓ Hy_1 (Denial of Social Anxiety) (low score)*

_____ Pd_3 (Social Imperturbability) (low score)*

_____ Ma_3 (Imperturbability) (low scores)*

✓ A-sod

✓ A-lse

_____ Scale 7

4 /8 Number of scales with $T \geq 60$ or $T \leq 40$ for scales with asterisk

5. Health Concerns

_____ Scale 1

_____ Scale 3

_____ A-hea

_____ Hy_4 (Somatic Complaints)

✓ Hy_3 (Lassitude-Malaise)

✓ D_3 (Physical Malfunctioning)

2 /6 Number of scales with $T \geq 60$

6. Naivete

_____ A-cyn (low score)*

_____ Pa_3 (Naivete)

_____ Hy_2 (Need for Affection)

_____ Si_3 (Alienation–Self and Others) (low score)*

_____ Scale K

0 /5 Number of scales with $T \geq 60$ or $T \leq 40$ for scales with asterisk

7. Familial Alienation

✓ Pd_1 (Familial Discord)

_____ A-fam

✓ Scale 4

✓ PRO

3 /4 Number of scales with $T \geq 60$

8. Psychoticism

_____ Pa_1 (Persecutory Ideas)

_____ Scale 6

_____ A-biz

_____ Sc_6 (Bizarre Sensory Experiences)

0 /4 Number of scales with $T \geq 60$

Note. The presentation of scales under each factor label is generally organized in a descending order from the best to the least effective marker. Within this overall approach, scales are grouped logically in terms of basic clinical scales, Harris-Lingoes and *Si* subscales, and content scales. The majority of scales included in this summary sheet were correlated $\geq .60$ or $\leq -.60$ with the relevant factor for the MMPI-A normative sample.

PAR **Psychological Assessment Resources, Inc.**
P.O. Box 998/Odessa, Florida 33556/Toll-Free 1-800-331-TEST

Figure 7.10 Continued

out. The Social Discomfort dimension is also noteworthy, with 50% of the scales in this dimension meeting critical levels, and serves to highlight Ruth's self-consciousness and social withdrawal. This MMPI-A Structural Summary is additionally remarkable for what is *not* prominent. Specifically, the Immaturity and Disinhibition/Excitatory Potential dimensions, reflecting antisocial inclinations, are not significant for Ruth. This finding suggests that her acting out is likely an ineffective and misdirected expression of her underlying depression and does not represent the presence of core antisocial or disinhibited components to her personality.

Summary and Diagnostic Impression

The test results, in conjunction with Ruth's history, point to substantial and wide-ranging disturbance in her functioning. The presence of Bipolar Disorder in her paternal history, and the fact that Ruth's brother is also experiencing a pattern of psychiatric problems similar to hers, indicates that her risk for affective disorder may be high. Although depression is the central affective disturbance seen in this evaluation, Ruth should be monitored for the development of Bipolar Disorder during this transitional age between adolescence and young adulthood. Ruth's substance abuse, eating disorder, family conflicts, and expulsion from school all contribute to the disarray in her life and are important treatment issues. As discussed in Chapter 6, substance abuse is an independent risk factor for delinquency that often accompanies other behavioral disturbances in adolescents, and eating disorders are associated with broad psychological disturbances and emotional distress not restricted to a specific MMPI-A configural pattern. These various problem areas reflect the considerable maladjustment seen in this adolescent. The following diagnoses were generated from the assessment:

Axis I: Major Depression, Recurrent, Moderate
          Eating Disorder, Not Otherwise Specified
          Alcohol Abuse
          Cannabis Abuse
Axis II: No diagnosis
Axis III: No diagnosis
Axis IV: Problems with primary support group: father's death,
          mother's remarriage
Axis V: Current GAF: 52; Highest GAF past year: 60

The prognosis for individuals with the type of profile produced by Ruth is guarded. They are likely to show recurrences of acting out despite sincere intentions to contain their actions, and a pattern of chronic difficulties is likely to unfold. Ruth's affective distress may, however, serve as a motivational element for becoming engaged in the therapy process and learning methods of coping with her distress.

Recommendations

Multiple interventions are warranted to address Ruth's difficulties promptly:

1. Outpatient psychotherapy should be provided as an initial step toward providing symptomatic relief and averting further behavioral escalation or affective deterioration to levels that may require psychiatric hospitalization. Ongoing suicide risk assessment should be incorporated into the therapy, and Ruth's eating disorder should also be addressed either within the context of the individual therapy or through a referral to a specialized outpatient eating disorders program for adolescents. Other issues that deserve attention include assisting Ruth to deal with her grief over her father's death, and development of objectives for her immediate future.

2. Ruth should be referred to a psychiatrist for evaluation regarding the usefulness of a trial of antidepressant medication.

3. Substance abuse treatment is a major priority. A trial of outpatient substance abuse treatment may be attempted concurrent with outpatient psychotherapy, but residential treatment should be considered if issues of noncompliance interfere with progress.

4. Family therapy is clearly indicated, given the central role of family conflict and discord in Ruth's history and in her MMPI-A self-report.

Case Summary and Outcome

Ruth was readmitted to school shortly after she began psychotherapy. She remained in therapy for 2 years during and after her senior year of high school, although she periodically "fired" her therapist as a means of establishing some sense of control over her life. She did not, however, follow through with a referral made to an eating disorder specialist. Ruth found employment after graduating from high school and worked in a minimum-wage job for a year. She subsequently moved away when she was admitted to a college in another state and felt a strong sense of joy and pride at her accomplishment. Her freshman year in college was, however, not without incident. She continued to abuse alcohol and marijuana, and she and a friend were charged with marijuana possession when stopped for a motor vehicle violation. Having been placed on academic and legal probation as a result, Ruth transferred to a college in her hometown, secured a part-time job in a pet store, moved into an apartment with a new boyfriend, and resumed therapy at her own initiation. She worked actively with her therapist to try to understand and contain her self-destructive tendencies that were heavily fueled by her underlying depression and poor self-esteem. She also refilled her prescription for Prozac, an intervention that had been provided at the referral of her psychologist. Her relationship with her mother and stepfather remained somewhat conflictual, but mitigated in intensity largely as a result of reduced contact.

COMPUTERIZED INTERPRETIVE REPORT

The output from the second version of the MMPI-A interpretive system presents several features, including information derived from the MMPI-A Structural Summary. The report also provides the ability to compare an individual adolescent's basic scale profile with modal or prototypic profiles, thereby providing an estimate of the degree to which an adolescent's specific profile matches the profile database and characteristics for that given codetype configuration. This interpretive system provides information concerning the validity scales and basic clinical scales, both individually and in configural patterns, as well as additional interpretive information for the content and supplementary scales and Harris-Lingoes subscales. The final stages of the report include the MMPI-A Structural Summary factor groupings and an interpretation of the Structural Summary pattern, as well as the MMPI-A profile for the validity and clinical scales, content and supplementary scales, and the Harris-Lingoes and *Si* subscales. The amount of information provided in the MMPI-A interpretive system is controlled by the selection of various output options and may be restricted to any configuration of output desired by the user. In Figure 7.11, all output, except the production of MMPI-A profiles, has been selected in order to exhibit the various options encompassed in the program.

MMPI-A INTERPRETIVE SYSTEM

developed by

Robert P. Archer, Ph.D.
and PAR Staff

Client Information

Client : Ruth S.
Sex : Female
Age : 17
Grade Level : 12
Prepared For : Dr. Robert P. Archer

The following MMPI-A interpretive information should be viewed as only one source of hypotheses about the adolescent being evaluated. No diagnostic or treatment decision should be based solely on these data. Instead, statements generated by this report should be integrated with other sources of information concerning this client, including additional psychometric test findings, mental status results, psychosocial history data, and individual and family interviews, to reach clinical decisions.

The information contained in this report represents combinations of actuarial data derived from major works in the MMPI and MMPI-A literatures. This report is confidential and intended for use by qualified professionals only. This report should not be released to the adolescent being evaluated or to her family members.

Figure 7.11 Computer Interpretive Report for Ruth S.

PROFILE MATCHES AND SCORES

Scale		Client Profile	Highest Scale Codetype	Best Fit Codetype
Codetype match:			2-4/4-2	2-4/4-2
Coefficient of Fit:			0.93	0.93
Scores:	F	57	56	56
	L	43	50	50
	K	49	51	51
	Hs (1)	53	52	52
	D (2)	75	69	69
	Hy (3)	49	55	55
	Pd (4)	79	69	69
	Mf (5)	43	46	46
	Pa (6)	56	55	55
	Pt (7)	56	54	54
	Sc (8)	53	55	55
	Ma (9)	48	46	46
	Si (0)	65	55	55
Codetype Definition in T-score Points:		10	14	14
Mean Clinical Scale Elevation:		58.6	57.0	57.0
Mean Excitatory Scale Elevation:		60.0	57.1	57.1
Mean age-females:			15.7	15.7
Mean age-males:			16.3	16.3
% of cases:			3.3	3.3

Configural clinical scale interpretation is provided in the report for the following codetype(s): 2-4/4-2

Unanswered (?) Items = 2   Welsh Code: 42'0+−6718/395: F/KL:

Figure 7.11 Continued

CONFIGURAL VALIDITY SCALE INTERPRETATION

This adolescent has produced a consistent MMPI-A response pattern as reflected in acceptable values on validity scales VRIN and TRIN.

This F-L-K validity scale configuration is indicative of an adolescent who responded to the MMPI-A in a valid, accurate, and cooperative manner. The validity scale features produced by this teenager are characteristic of normal adolescents, and are unusual for teenagers evaluated in psychiatric settings.

Both F1 and F2 are below T-score values of 90. T-score values of 90 or greater on either F1 or F2 are likely to indicate problems with profile validity.

VALIDITY SCALES

Raw (?) = 2

There were a few items omitted in completing this MMPI-A. These omissions may represent areas of limitation in the adolescent's life experience which rendered certain items unanswerable, or limitations in the adolescent's reading ability. There is little probability of profile distortion as a result of these few item omissions.

VRIN T = 50

VRIN scores in this range suggest that the adolescent responded to test items with an acceptable level of consistency.

TRIN T = 59F

TRIN scores in this range suggest that the adolescent responded to test items with an acceptable level of consistency.

F1 T = 56

Scores in this range suggest that the adolescent has responded in a valid manner to items which appear in the first stage of the MMPI-A test booklet.

F2 T = 57

Scores in this range suggest that the adolescent has responded in a valid manner to items which appear in the latter stage of the MMPI-A test booklet.

F T = 57

Scores in this range usually indicate that the respondent has answered the test items in a manner similar to most normal adolescents. While some clinical scale elevations

Figure 7.11 Continued

may occur, this teenager has not reported many symptoms of highly deviant/unusual psychopathology.

L T = 43

Scores in this range are typically obtained by confident and open adolescents who generally respond in a candid manner to test items. Low values on scale L are occasionally obtained by adolescents employing an "all true" or "fake bad" response set.

K T = 49

The majority of adolescents score in this range, which represents an appropriate balance between self-disclosure and guardedness. Prognosis for psychotherapy is often good in that such adolescents are open to discussion of life problems and symptoms.

CONFIGURAL CLINICAL SCALE INTERPRETATION

2-4/4-2 Codetype

This MMPI-A pattern is classified as a 2-4/4-2 codetype, which occurs commonly in adolescent and adult samples and is found for roughly 5% of adolescents in psychiatric settings. Adolescents who obtain this common profile type typically have difficulties with impulse control and act without sufficient deliberation. There is often a marked disregard for accepted social standards, and repeated difficulties with authority figures are common. There is usually a history of legal violations including arrests, legal convictions, and court actions. Additionally, substance and alcohol abuse are frequent. In general, the impulse control problems exhibited by adolescents with the 2-4/4-2 codetype take many forms, including hospital elopement risks, promiscuous sexual behavior, school truancy, and running away from home. These adolescents typically perceive their parents as unaffectionate and inconsistent and feel alienated and distant from their families.

Psychiatric diagnoses associated with this codetype include the Substance-Related Disorders (303.X0, 304.X0, and 305.X0), Oppositional Defiant Disorder (313.81), Conduct Disorder (312.8), Dysthymic Disorder (300.4), and Personality Disorders (301.XX) including Personality Disorder NOS (301.9). Primary defense mechanisms typically include acting-out, displacement, and externalization. Given the high rate of substance abuse and/or dependence associated with this profile for both adolescents and adults, careful evaluation should be given to the need for treatment efforts targeted to this area. Additionally, the typical picture of alienation and anger directed toward family members that is exhibited by these adolescents often supports the integration of family therapy into comprehensive treatment efforts.

Figure 7.11 Continued

CLINICAL SCALES

Hs (1) = 53

The obtained score is within normal or expected ranges. This adolescent has not expressed a pattern of unusual concerns or preoccupations regarding physical health or functioning.

D (2) = 75

Scores in this range are typically found for adolescents who are depressed, dissatisfied, hopeless, and self-depreciatory. They often experience apathy, loss of interest in daily activities, loss of self-confidence, and feelings of inadequacy and pessimism. Additionally, these adolescents often experience substantial feelings of guilt, worthlessness, and self-criticism, and may experience suicidal ideation. However, this degree of distress may serve as a positive motivator for psychotherapy efforts.

Hy (3) = 49

The obtained score is within normal or expected ranges and this adolescent probably has the capacity to acknowledge unpleasant issues or negative feelings.

Pd (4) = 79

Scale 4 high points are very common among adolescents, particularly in psychiatric or criminal justice settings. Scores in this range are typical for adolescents who are characterized as rebellious, hostile toward authority figures, and defiant. These adolescents often have histories of poor school adjustment and problems in school conduct. Higher scores on this scale present an increased probability of overtly delinquent behavior. These adolescents often show an inability to delay gratification and are described as being impulsive and having little tolerance for frustration and boredom. Primary defense mechanisms typically involve acting-out, and such behaviors may be unaccompanied by feelings of guilt or remorse. While these adolescents typically create a good first impression and maintain an extroverted and outgoing interpersonal style, their interpersonal relationships tend to be shallow and superficial. They are eventually viewed by others as selfish, self-centered, and egocentric.

Mf (5) = 43

The obtained score on Mf is within normal or expected ranges and indicates standard interest patterns in traditional feminine activities.

Pa (6) = 56

The obtained score is within normal or expected ranges and items related to paranoid ideation or excessive suspiciousness were not typically endorsed.

Figure 7.11 Continued

Pt (7) = 56

The obtained score is within normal or expected ranges and this adolescent appears to be capable of meeting current life experiences without excessive worry or apprehension.

Sc (8) = 53

The obtained score is within normal or expected ranges and suggests intact reality testing and coherent thought processes.

Ma (9) = 48

The obtained score is within normal or expected ranges and reflects a typical energy or activity level for normal adolescents.

Si (0) = 65

Adolescents who produce scores in this range are socially introverted, insecure, and uncomfortable in social situations. They tend to be shy, timid, submissive, and lacking in self-confidence. They are unlikely to engage in impulsive behaviors and are at low risk for acting-out or delinquency.

CONTENT AND SUPPLEMENTARY SCALES

Content Scales

Anxiety (A-anx) = 50

The obtained score on this content scale is within normal or expected ranges.

Obsessiveness (A-obs) = 51

The obtained score on this content scale is within normal or expected ranges.

Depression (A-dep) = 68

Scores in this range are often produced by adolescents who are depressed and despondent. These teenagers may be apathetic and easily fatigued. Their depression may include the occurrence of suicidal ideation and a sense of hopelessness or despair.

Health Concerns (A-hea) = 55

The obtained score on this content scale is within normal or expected ranges.

Alienation (A-aln) = 55

Figure 7.11 Continued

The obtained score on this content scale is within normal or expected ranges.

Bizarre Mentation (A-biz) = 48

The obtained score on this content scale is within normal or expected ranges.

Anger (A-ang) = 44

The obtained score on this content scale is within normal or expected ranges.

Cynicism (A-cyn) = 46

The obtained score on this content scale is within normal or expected ranges.

Conduct Problems (A-con) = 63

Scores in this range represent marginal elevations on the Conduct Problems Scale. This score may reflect an adolescent who has rebellious tendencies and problems with authority figures. These adolescents may display histories of disciplinary action in their school settings.

Low Self-Esteem (A-lse) = 73

Scores in this range may be produced by adolescents who feel inadequate, incompetent, or useless. They lack self-confidence and believe they have many faults and flaws. These teenagers may be interpersonally passive and socially uncomfortable.

Low Aspirations (A-las) = 66

Scores in this range are produced by adolescents who have few, or no, educational or life goals or objectives. These adolescents often have patterns of poor academic achievement. They tend to become frustrated quickly and give up, and do not apply themselves in challenging situations.

Social Discomfort (A-sod) = 72

Scores in this range are produced by adolescents who are uncomfortable in social situations and may be described as introverted and shy. They avoid social events and find it difficult to interact with others.

Family Problems (A-fam) = 58

The obtained score on this content scale is within normal or expected ranges.

School Problems (A-sch) = 59

The obtained score on this content scale is within normal or expected ranges.

Negative Treatment Indicators (A-trt) = 52

The obtained score on this content scale is within normal or expected ranges.

Figure 7.11 Continued

Supplementary Scales

MacAndrew Alcoholism (MAC-R) = 55

Adolescents who score in this range are not likely to abuse alcohol or drugs. The most notable exception to this conclusion would be adolescents who are primarily neurotic in terms of their personality configuration and who employ alcohol and drugs as a means of "self-medication."

Alcohol-Drug Problem Acknowledgment (ACK) = 60

Scores in this range are within acceptable or normal ranges on the ACK Scale. Since an adolescent may underreport drug or alcohol use related attitudes or symptoms, however, scores from the MAC-R and PRO Scales should also be carefully reviewed to assist in screening for alcohol and drug related problems.

Alcohol-Drug Problem Proneness (PRO) = 63

Scores in this range are within acceptable or normal ranges on the PRO Scale.

Immaturity (IMM) = 57

The obtained score on the IMM Scale is within normal or expected ranges.

Anxiety (A) = 54

The obtained score is within normal or expected ranges and indicates unremarkable levels of anxiety and discomfort.

Repression (R) = 63

Adolescents who score in this range are often unexcitable, inhibited, submissive, and conventional, and tend to show little feeling. Scores in this range are infrequently obtained by adolescents evaluated in psychiatric settings.

HARRIS-LINGOES AND SI SUBSCALES

The interpretation of Harris-Lingoes and Si Subscales is provided in this program because of the potential relevance of these data to adolescent profiles. The correlates of these research scales have not been examined in adolescent populations, however, and the user is cautioned that the following interpretive statements are based on findings in adult populations.

Figure 7.11 Continued

Subjective Depression (D1) = 72

High D1 scorers feel depressed, unhappy, and nervous. They lack energy and interest, and are not coping well with their problems. They show deficits in concentration and attention, lack self-confidence, and feel shy and uneasy in social situations.

Psychomotor Retardation (D2) = 67

High D2 scorers are characterized as immobilized. They lack energy to cope with everyday activities, withdraw from inter-personal relationships, and deny having hostile and aggressive impulses.

Physical Malfunctioning (D3) = 71

High D3 scorers are preoccupied with health and physical functioning, and they typically report a wide variety of specific somatic symptoms and complaints.

Mental Dullness (D4) = 73

High D4 scorers lack energy to cope with problems of everyday life. They report difficulties in concentrating and they complain of poor memory and judgment. They lack self-confidence, feel inferior to others, get little enjoyment out of life, and may feel that life is no longer worthwhile.

Brooding (D5) = 65

High D5 scorers lack energy and brood and ruminate excessively about life not being worthwhile. They feel inferior and are easily hurt by criticism. At times, they report feeling like they are losing control of their thought processes.

Denial of Social Anxiety (Hy1) = 37

Low Hy1 scorers tend to be socially introverted and bashful, and are greatly influenced by social standards and customs.

Need for Affection (Hy2) = 34

Low Hy2 scorers tend to be negative, critical, and suspicious in relationships with others. They see other people as selfish and unreasonable.

Lassitude-Malaise (Hy3) = 76

High Hy3 scorers generally feel unhappy, uncomfortable, and not in good health. They present vague somatic complaints, including weakness and fatigue, and complain about functioning below par both physically and mentally. They may have a poor appetite and report problems in sleeping.

Figure 7.11 Continued

Somatic Complaints (Hy4) = 53

The obtained score is within normal or expected ranges.

Inhibition of Aggression (Hy5) = 35

Low Hy5 scorers openly admit to experiencing hostile and aggressive impulses.

Familial Discord (Pd1) = 66

High Pd1 scorers view their home situations as unpleasant and lacking in love, support, and understanding. They describe their families as rejecting, critical, and controlling.

Authority Problems (Pd2) = 65

High Pd2 scorers resent authority and societal demands, and they often have histories of academic and legal difficulties. They have definite opinions about what is right and wrong, and they stand up for their beliefs.

Social Imperturbability (Pd3) = 43

The obtained score is within normal or expected ranges.

Social Alienation (Pd4) = 57

The obtained score is within normal or expected ranges.

Self-Alienation (Pd5) = 75

High Pd5 scorers describe themselves as feeling uncomfortable and unhappy. They have problems in concentration and attention, and they do not find their life to be especially interesting or rewarding. They verbalize guilt and regret and display negative emotions in an exhibitionistic manner. Excessive alcohol abuse may be a problem.

Persecutory Ideas (Pa1) = 57

The obtained score is within normal or expected ranges.

Poignancy (Pa2) = 51

The obtained score is within normal or expected ranges.

Naivete (Pa3) = 51

The obtained score is within normal or expected ranges.

Social Alienation (Sc1) = 61

The obtained score is within normal or expected ranges.

Figure 7.11 Continued

Emotional Alienation (Sc2) = 48

The obtained score is within normal or expected ranges.

Lack of Ego Mastery-Cognitive (Sc3) = 67

High Sc3 scorers admit to strange thought processes, feelings of unreality, and problems with concentration and attention. At times, they may feel that they are "losing their minds."

Lack of Ego Mastery-Conative (Sc4) = 60

The obtained score is within normal or expected ranges.

Lack of Ego Mastery-Defective Inhibition (Sc5) = 44

The obtained score is within normal or expected ranges.

Bizarre Sensory Experiences (Sc6) = 46

The obtained score is within normal or expected ranges.

Amorality (Ma1) = 55

The obtained score is within normal or expected ranges.

Psychomotor Acceleration (Ma2) = 49

The obtained score is within normal or expected ranges.

Imperturbability (Ma3) = 44

The obtained score is within normal or expected ranges.

Ego Inflation (Ma4) = 47

The obtained score is within normal or expected ranges.

Shyness/Self-Consciousness (Si1) = 55

The obtained score on the Si1 Subscale is within expected or normal ranges.

Social Avoidance (Si2) = 78

Adolescents who produce scores in this range dislike or avoid group activities, and may often seek to minimize social contacts or involvements.

Alienation-Self and Others (Si3) = 60

The obtained score on the Si3 Subscale is within expected or normal ranges.

Figure 7.11 Continued

MMPI-A Structural Summary

Factor Grouping

1. General Maladjustment
   - 54 Welsh's A
   - 56 Scale 7
   - 53 Scale 8
   - 75 Scale 2
   - 79 Scale 4
   - 72 D1 (Subjective Depression)
   - 73 D4 (Mental Dullness)
   - 65 D5 (Brooding)
   - 76 Hy3 (Lassitude-Malaise)
   - 61 Sc1 (Social Alienation)
   - 48 Sc2 (Emotional Alienation)
   - 67 Sc3 (Lack of Ego Mastery-Cognitive)
   - 60 Sc4 (Lack of Ego Mastery-Conative)
   - 60 Si3 (Alienation)
   - 57 Pd4 (Social Alienation)
   - 75 Pd5 (Self-Alienation)
   - 51 Pa2 (Poignancy)
   - 68 A-dep
   - 50 A-anx
   - 73 A-lse
   - 55 A-aln
   - 51 A-obs
   - 52 A-trt

13/23 Num. scales with T ≥ 60

62.2 Mean T-score elevation

3. Disinhibition/Excitatory Potential
   - 48 Scale 9
   - 49 Ma2 (Psychomotor Acceleration)
   - 47 Ma4 (Ego Inflation)
   - 44 Sc5 (Lack of Ego Mastery Defective Inhibition)
   - 67 D2 (Psychomotor Retardation)-low*
   - 63 Welsh's R-low*
   - 49 Scale K-low*
   - 43 Scale L-low*
   - 44 A-ang
   - 46 A-cyn
   - 63 A-con
   - 55 MAC-R

1/12 Num. scales with T ≥ 60 or T ≤ 40 for scales with '*'

49.5 Mean T score (high)

55.5 Mean T score (low)

2. Immaturity
   - 57 IMM
   - 57 Scale F
   - 53 Scale 8
   - 56 Scale 6
   - 60 ACK
   - 55 MAC-R
   - 57 Pa1 (Persecutory Ideas)
   - 48 Sc2 (Emotional Alienation)
   - 46 Sc6 (Bizarre Sensory Exper.)
   - 59 A-sch
   - 48 A-biz
   - 55 A-aln
   - 63 A-con
   - 58 A-fam
   - 52 A-trt

2/15 Num. scales with T ≥ 60

54.9 Mean T-score elevation

4. Social Discomfort
   - 65 Scale 0
   - 55 Si1 (Shyness/Self-Conscious)
   - 37 Hy1 (Denial Social Anx.)-low*
   - 43 Pd3 (Soc Imperturbability)-low*
   - 44 Ma3 (Imperturbability)-low*
   - 72 A-sod
   - 73 A-lse
   - 56 Scale 7

4/8 Num. scales w/T ≥ 60 or T ≤ 40 for scales with '*'

64.2 Mean T score (high)
41.3 Mean T score (low)

Figure 7.11 Continued

5. Health Concerns
   53 Scale 1
   49 Scale 3
   55 A-hea
   53 Hy4 (Somatic Complaints)
   76 Hy3 (Lassitude-Malaise)
   71 D3 (Physical Malfunctioning)
2/6 Num. scales with T ≥ 60
59.5 Mean T-scale elevation

6. Naivete
   46 A-cyn-low*
   51 Pa3 (Naivete)
   34 Hy2 (Need for Affection)
   60 Si3 (Alien. Self/Other)-low*
   49 Scale K

0/5 Num. scales w/T ≥ 60 or T ≤ 40
for scales with '*'
44.7 Mean T score (high)
53.0 Mean T score (low)

7. Familial Alienation
   66 Pd1 (Familial Discord)
   58 A-fam
   79 Scale 4
   63 PRO
3/4 Num. scales with T ≥ 60
66.5 Mean T-score elevation

8. Psychoticism
   57 Pa1 (Persecutory Ideas)
   56 Scale 6
   48 A-biz
   46 Sc6 (Bizarre Sensory Exper.)
0/4 Num. scales with T ≥ 60
51.8 Mean T-score elevation

STRUCTURAL SUMMARY INTERPRETATION

The following structural summary information provides an assessment of the adolescent's functioning along the eight basic factor dimensions found for the 69 scales and subscales of the MMPI-A. Information is provided for those factors which appear to be most salient in describing this adolescent psychopathology based on the criterion that a majority (greater than 50%) of the scales or subscales within a particular factor are critically elevated for each factor interpreted below. For factors meeting this criterion, interpretations are organized from the factor showing the highest percentage of significant scale and subscale scores to those factors showing the lowest percentage. This is based on the assumption that the higher the percentage of scales or subscales within a factor that produce critical values, the more likely it is that that factor or dimension provides a salient or important description of the adolescent. Further, examination of the specific pattern of scale elevations within a

Figure 7.11 Continued

dimension can provide the clinician with additional and useful information in refining the description of the adolescent for that factor.

This adolescent has produced significant elevations on 3 of the 4 scales and subscales associated with the Familial Alienation Dimension. Adolescents who produce significant elevations on this factor are more likely to experience significant family conflicts and to encounter disciplinary problems at school. They are frequently seen as hostile, delinquent or aggressive, and may be verbally abusive, threatening or disobedient at home.

This adolescent is reporting significant elevations on 13 of the 23 scales and subscales associated with the General Maladjustment Factor. Adolescents who score high on this dimension are likely to experience significant problems in adjustment and are self-conscious, socially withdrawn, timid, dependent, ruminative, and depressed. They are also more likely than other teenagers to report symptoms of tiredness and fatigue, sleep difficulties, and suicidal ideation.

****END OF REPORT****

Figure 7.11 Continued

CASE REPORT 4

Name: Tamara P.
Age: 16
Sex: Female
Ethnicity: African American
Grade: 10

Reason for Referral

Tamara's mother brought her for treatment to her local community mental center that had advertised a new outpatient group treatment program for sexually abused teenagers. Tamara had reportedly become quiet and withdrawn in recent months and had lost weight. Her mother attributed these changes to her past experience of sexual abuse, evoked by a class project involving developing a public service announcement for the community concerning child sexual abuse. The assessment was conducted as part of the intake assessment.

Background Information

Tamara lived with her biological parents and two sisters, aged 12 and 13 years. She had a good relationship with family members and was especially close to her mother. Her parents, who had a strong marital relationship, jointly owned and operated a successful hardware store that provided a comfortable standard of living for the family.

Tamara had an unremarkable developmental history and was described by her mother as an intelligent "bright-eyed child" from infancy. Her medical history generally consisted of no more than usual childhood illnesses, but she developed allergies to mold, grass, and pollen at age 13 and suffered seasonal sinus headaches. She took over-the-counter medications for her allergies and headaches. Tamara's educational history reflected consistent achievement of good grades. She was very conscientious about studying for tests and completing her homework, and had received all As and Bs since entering high school.

The normal course of development of this teenager was disrupted when a childhood friend of her father came to stay with the family when she was 11 years old. This 35-year-old single man had declared bankruptcy when a business venture failed, and was invited by Tamara's father to move in with them temporarily and assist in the operation of the store while he attempted a fresh start in a new city. The abuse reportedly began within a few weeks of his arrival and consisted of fondling her and coercing her to perform oral sex on him. There was reportedly no vaginal penetration. The abuse continued for approximately 6 months, ending only when Tamara disclosed her abuse experiences to her mother. Her mother was very supportive of her, promptly contacted child protective services, and proceeded to initiate legal charges against the perpetrator. Tamara's father, who was described as guilt-ridden, had never talked about the incident within the family. Tamara's abuser was convicted of the sexual offenses and served a prison term, but had been recently released. His whereabouts were unknown to Tamara and her family.

Tamara stated that she had become very cautious of adult men as well as teenaged boys since her abuse and had difficulty trusting people. She reported experiencing recurrent thoughts of the abuse which disrupted her sleep, and having to exert considerable effort to distract herself from these intrusive thoughts during waking hours. She also acknowledged increased irritability and impatience, particularly toward her sisters, which made her feel guilty and remorseful. She felt close to her small group of girlfriends but had begun avoiding social activities with them, feeling that they could not understand her current state of irritability and distress. She denied any romantic interests or sexual activity, and reported no experience with alcohol or drug use.

Assessment Methods

Clinical Interview and Mental Status Examination
Minnesota Multiphasic Personality Inventory–Adolescent (MMPI-A)
Child Behavior Checklist–Parent Report and Youth Self-Report versions
Children's Depression Inventory (CDI)
Trauma Symptom Checklist for Children (TSCC)
Rotter Incomplete Sentences Blank–High School Form

Behavioral Observations and Mental Status Examination

Tamara was dressed in a beige skirt and white blouse, with her hair tied back from her face, when she presented at the treatment facility. Her clothing style and subdued demeanor made her appear older than her chronological age. She had no remarkable physical characteristics or mannerisms. She cooperated fully with assessment procedures but did not smile or engage in small talk, and her responses to interview questions were serious and formal in tone. A mental status examination revealed no problems with thinking or speech, but her affect was observed to be constricted and her mood was depressed. Tamara denied suicidal ideation, stating that suicide was unthinkable because it would hurt her family and because she had plans for her life. During the testing sessions she was focused, task oriented, and showed no signs of fatigue or loss of interest.

Summary of Other Test Results

The parent-reported CBCL profile suggested that Tamara exhibited considerable emotional distress, reflected in elevations above the 98% percentile on the

Withdrawn, Somatic Complaints, and *Anxious/Depressed* internalizing scales. Tamara's self-report on the CBCL was congruent with her mother's CBCL report in terms of showing an internalizing pattern, but her scale elevations on the internalizing scales were lower, falling between the 84th and 93rd percentile ranks. No externalizing problems were identified in either report. Results from the CDI also indicated the presence of depressive symptomatology with characteristics of anhedonia and negative mood. The TSCC indicated generalized anxiety and worry, post-traumatic symptoms (including intrusive thoughts and memories), discomfort with sexual matters, and fear of men. Tamara's responses to the Incomplete Sentence Blank were candid and self revealing. She said, "I feel *guilty and confused*" and "Dating *makes me nervous.*" She also admitted that "I secretly *hide my feelings*" and her understanding of her struggles was evident in "I suffer *the most when I am alone.*" Tamara's concern for family members was also apparent; for example, "What pains me *is seeing mom worry about me.*"

MMPI-A Results and Interpretation

An examination of the validity section of Tamara's basic scale profile, shown in Figure 7.12, indicates that there are no problems with profile validity. There are no omitted items (*Cannot Say* raw score of 0), and measures of response consistency (*VRIN*, F_1 vs. F_2) and acquiescent and nay-saying response biases (*TRIN*) are clearly within acceptable limits. The accuracy of the profile is also deemed acceptable and the *F-L-K* configuration indicates the absence of overreporting or underreporting response sets. The MMPI-A profiles are therefore suitable for valid and meaningful interpretation.

Tamara's clinical scale profile is complex and contains multiple scale elevations. This basic scale profile produces a Welsh code of 210"73+−468/59: KF/L:, which reveals that scales *2, 1, 0, 7,* and *3,* respectively, are elevated in the clinical range. Further, it is useful to note that scale *2, 1,* and *0* are all substantially elevated at a *T*-score level ≥ 80, while scales *7* and *3* are only moderately ($T \geq 65$ to $T = 70$) elevated within the clinical range. A basic scale profile with multiple elevations could be approached from a number of useful interpretive directions involving various combinations of codetype and single-scale interpretive strategies. One of these useful approaches for deriving sets of two-point codetypes involves an A-B-C method developed by Alex Caldwell and described by Archer, Krishnamurthy, and Jacobson (1994). The method

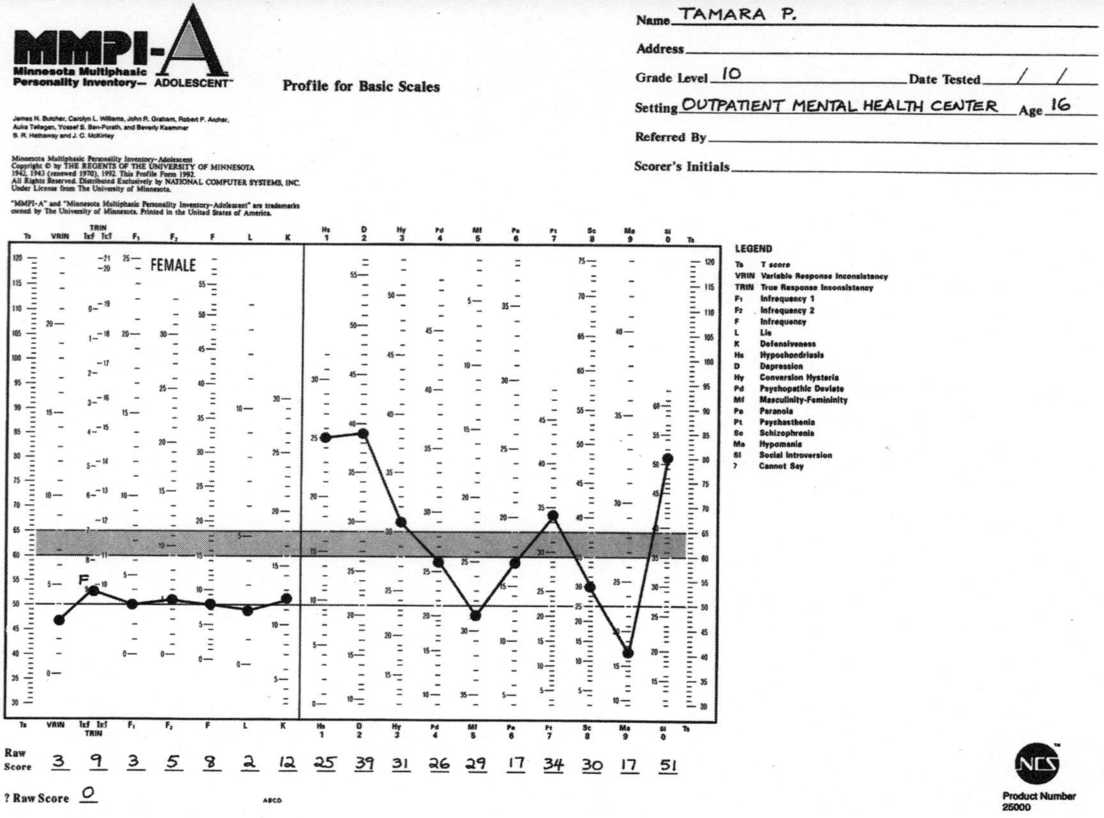

Figure 7.12 Profile for Basic Scales for Tamara P.

Minnesota Mutiphasic Personality Inventory–Adolescent (MMPI-A). Copyright © the Regents of the University of Minnesota 1942, 1943 (renewed 1970), 1992. Reproduced by permission of the publisher: "Minnesota Multiphasic Personality Inventory–Adolescent" and "MMPI-A" are trademarks owned by the University of Minnesota.

involves assigning the letter "A" to the highest scale in the profile, a "B" to the next highest scale, and a "C" to the third highest scale, and the process could potentially be extended to represent all clinically elevated scales in the clinical scale profile. In Tamara's profile, A = scale *2*, B = scale *1*, and C = scale *0*. Scales *7* and *0* may be best handled in her profile as individual scale additions to the codetype descriptors. The next step would involve obtaining all possible combinations of the three highest scales, i.e., A-B, A-C, and B-C, which is represented by the two-point codetypes of *2-1, 2-0,* and *1-0*. The *2-1* codetype receives the greater emphasis in the interpretive process because these scales are most elevated in the basic scale profile, and these data are supplemented with descriptors from the remaining two codetypes. Further, given the substantial difference in *T*-score elevation between scales *2, 1,* and *0,* in contrast to scales *3* and *7*, correlates from the former set of scales should receive more emphasis and interpretive weight than the latter scales. The test interpreter could then organize the codetype descriptors in the manner presented in Table 7.1 to obtain an overview of the codetype information concerning major areas of functioning.

Tamara's profile interpretation would continue with the addition of descriptors from content scales *A-sod, A-hea, A-trt, A-anx,* and *A-las,* which are in the clinical range of elevation, and from the marginally elevated *A-lse, A-obs, A-dep, A-aln* scales. Supplementary scales *A* and *R,* and subscales of scales *2, 3,* and *0* would further contribute to interpretive expansion and refinement. The interpretive process would end with a review of the MMPI-A Structural Summary dimensions.

The converging evidence from the numerous scale elevations on Tamara's MMPI-A profiles across basic scales, content scales, supplementary scales, and subscales (see Figures 7.13 and 7.14) indicate that her major symptomatic presentation is in terms of neurotic and internalizing symptoms (see *2-1, 2-0,* and *1-0* codetypes; scales *3* and *7*; subscales of scales *2* and *3*; all elevated content scales; *A* and *R*). She is apt to feel tired and run down (all A-B-C codetypes, *A-hea*, D_2, D_4, Hy_3) and her interests in previously enjoyed activities are diminished markedly to a level of sensation-avoidant behaviors (see low *MAC-R* score). She may also experience a variety of physical symptoms which, although possibly related in part to her allergies, are also likely to be secondary to her states of tension and dysphoria (*2-1* and *1-0* codetypes; scale *3*; D_3; Hy_4; *A-hea*). In fact, various physical complaints across gastrointestinal, neurologi-

Table 7.1 Summary of Major Findings from Two-Point Codetypes

Codetype	Symptoms/ Traits	Behaviors	Affect	Interpersonal Relationships	Diagnostic Considerations
2-1	Fatigue, physical dysfunction, rumination	Quiet, indecisive	Depressed, fearful	Withdrawn, dependent, hypersensitive	Somatic, anxiety, and depressive disorders
2-0	Introversion, tension, lethargy, inferiority	Conforming, unassertive	Anxious, depressed	Inept, passive, sensitive, lonely	Schizoid and obsessive-compulsive disorders
1-0	Physical symptoms	Ruminative, unassertive	Dysphoric, anxious	Shy, withdrawn	Avoidant and somatic disorders

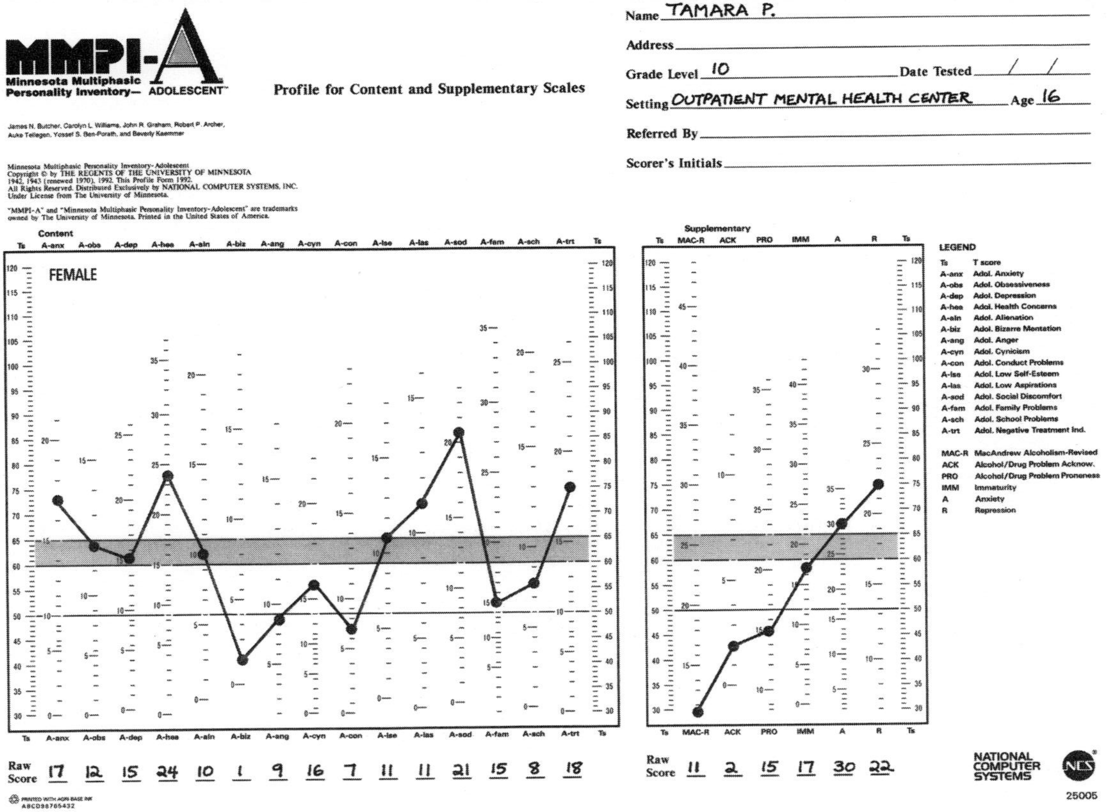

Figure 7.13 Profile for Content and Supplementary Scales for Tamara P.

Minnesota Multiphasic Personality Inventory–Adolescent (MMPI-A). Copyright © the Regents of the University of Minnesota 1942, 1943 (renewed 1970), 1992. Reproduced by permission of the publisher. "Minnesota Multiphasic Personality Inventory–Adolescent" and "MMPI-A" are trademarks owned by the University of Minnesota.

Figure 7.14 Profile for Harris-Lingoes and Si Subscales for Tamara P.

cal, sensory, and cardiovascular systems may be reported in addition to respiratory distress (*Hs* and *A-hea*).

Tamara's affective expressions are largely overcontrolled, but inner feelings of anxiety (scale *7, A, A-anx*), depression (*A-dep, D₁*), and fear (*2-1* codetype; *Si₃*) dominate her affective functioning. She appears quite insecure and self-doubting (*7, A-lse*) and may have strong feelings of guilt (see scale *A*) that perpetuate her physical and emotional distress. Suicidal ideation may be present that is concealed from others in her efforts to protect family members from worrying about her (*A-dep, A-lse*). Tamara's cognitive functioning is marked by rumination, intrusive and obsessive thoughts, and deficits in concentration (*7, A-anx, A-obs, D₅*) which would impair her ability to make decisions.

Behaviorally, Tamara is unlikely to engage in acting-out behaviors (scales *R* and *3*). Teenagers with her profile are prone to be quiet and socially conforming and, in fact, may be strongly motivated to be perceived as causing little trouble to others (*2-1* and *2-0* codetypes). An inhibited, unassertive presentation is likely to be characteristic of her (all codetypes). Self-critical and perfectionistic tendencies are apparent, and obsessive or compulsive actions may be used to defend against anxiety (scale *7, A-lse*). It appears, however, that Tamara's defenses are failing, and troubling thoughts and feelings are intruding into her consciousness (scales *A* and *R*). Her achievement motivation (scales *3* and *7*), currently expressed in good academic performance, may be increasingly challenged (*A-las*) if her emotional distress and physical inertia persist.

Tamara shows marked difficulties in the interpersonal domain. She displays characteristics of passivity and dependence (*2-1* and *2-0* codetypes; *A-lse*) and may rely heavily on getting approval from others but may find that that her need for acceptance is not satiated. She is likely to be fearful and hypersensitive in her interactions with others and feels inept and anxious in dealing with members of the other sex (*2-0, Si₁, Si₂, A-sod*). She is at risk for strong feelings of isolation resulting from a pattern of increasing social withdrawal and discomfort. Moderate feelings of alienation are also apparent (*A-aln, Si₃*), reflecting her feeling that others would not understand or sympathize with her plight, which may generate increased pessimism and further social isolation.

Tamara's MMPI-A Structural Summary, shown in Figure 7.15, identifies three major areas of difficulty. The most salient findings come from the Social Discomfort and the Health Concerns dimensions. Each of these factor dimensions have 100% of their relevant scales elevated at critical ranges indicat-

MMPI-A Structural Summary

Robert P. Archer and Radhika Krishnamurthy

Name: TAMARA P.   Date: _____

Age: 16   Grade: 10

Gender: FEMALE   School: _____

Test-Taking Attitudes

1. missions (raw score total)

____0____ ? (Cannot Say scale)

2. Consistency (T-score values)

__47__ VRIN

__53 F__ TRIN

__50__ F$_1$ vs. __51__ F$_2$

3. Accuracy (check if condition present)

Overreport

_____ F scale T score ≥ 90

_____ All clinical scales except 5 and 0 ≥ 60

Underreport

_____ High L (T ≥ 65)

_____ High K (T ≥ 65)

_____ All clinical scales except 5 and 0 < 60

Factor Groupings
(enter T-score data)

1. General Maladjustment

- ✓ Welsh's A
- ✓ Scale 7
- ____ Scale 8
- ✓ Scale 2
- ____ Scale 4
- ✓ D$_1$ (Subjective Depression)
- ✓ D$_4$ (Mental Dullness)
- ✓ D$_5$ (Brooding)
- ✓ Hy$_3$ (Lassitude-Malaise)
- ✓ Sc$_1$ (Social Alienation)
- ✓ Sc$_2$ (Emotional Alienation)
- ____ Sc$_3$ (Lack of Ego Mastery – Cognitive)
- ✓ Sc$_4$ (Lack of Ego Mastery – Conative)
- ✓ Si$_3$ (Alienation)
- ✓ Pd$_4$ (Social Alienation)
- ____ Pd$_5$ (Self-Alienation)
- ✓ Pa$_2$ (Poignancy)
- ✓ A-dep
- ✓ A-anx
- ✓ A-lse
- ✓ A-aln
- ✓ A-obs
- ✓ A-trt

__19__/23 Number of scales with T ≥ 60

2. Immaturity

- ____ IMM
- ____ Scale F
- ____ Scale 8
- ____ Scale 6
- ____ ACK
- ____ MAC-R
- ✓ Pa$_1$ (Persecutory Ideas)
- ✓ Sc$_2$ (Emotional Alienation)
- ____ Sc$_6$ (Bizarre Sensory Experiences)
- ____ A-sch
- ____ A-biz
- ✓ A-aln
- ____ A-con
- ____ A-fam
- ✓ A-trt

__4__/15 Number of scales with T ≥ 60

Figure 7.15 MMPI-A Structural Summary for Tamara P.

3. Disinhibition/Excitatory Potential

_____ Scale 9

_____ Ma$_2$ (Psychomotor Acceleration)

_____ Ma$_4$ (Ego Inflation)

_____ Sc$_5$ (Lack of Ego Mastery, Defective Inhibition)

_____ D$_2$ (Psychomotor Retardation) (low score)*

_____ Welsh's R (low score)*

_____ Scale K (low score)*

_____ Scale L (low score)*

_____ A-ang

_____ A-cyn

_____ A-con

_____ MAC-R

O /12 Number of scales with $T \geq 60$ or ≤ 40 for scales with asterisk

4. Social Discomfort

✓ Scale 0

✓ Si$_1$ (Shyness/Self-Consciousness)

✓ Hy$_1$ (Denial of Social Anxiety) (low score)*

✓ Pd$_3$ (Social Imperturbability) (low score)*

✓ Ma$_3$ (Imperturbability) (low scores)*

✓ A-sod

✓ A-lse

✓ Scale 7

8 /8 Number of scales with $T \geq 60$ or $T \leq 40$ for scales with asterisk

5. Health Concerns

✓ Scale 1

✓ Scale 3

✓ A-hea

✓ Hy$_4$ (Somatic Complaints)

✓ Hy$_3$ (Lassitude-Malaise)

✓ D$_3$ (Physical Malfunctioning)

6 /6 Number of scales with $T \geq 60$

6. Naivete

_____ A-cyn (low score)*

_____ Pa$_3$ (Naivete)

_____ Hy$_2$ (Need for Affection)

_____ Si$_3$ (Alienation–Self and Others) (low score)*

_____ Scale K

O /5 Number of scales with $T \geq 60$ or $T \leq 40$ for scales with asterisk

7. Familial Alienation

_____ Pd$_1$ (Familial Discord)

_____ A-fam

_____ Scale 4

_____ PRO

O /4 Number of scales with $T \geq 60$

8. Psychoticism

✓ Pa$_1$ (Persecutory Ideas)

_____ Scale 6

_____ A-biz

_____ Sc$_6$ (Bizarre Sensory Experiences)

1 /4 Number of scales with $T \geq 60$

Note. The presentation of scales under each factor label is generally organized in a descending order from the best to the least effective marker. Within this overall approach, scales are grouped logically in terms of basic clinical scales, Harris-Lingoes and Si subscales, and content scales. The majority of scales included in this summary sheet were correlated $\geq .60$ or $\leq -.60$ with the relevant factor for the MMPI-A normative sample.

PAR **Psychological Assessment Resources, Inc.**
P.O. Box 998/Odessa, Florida 33556/Toll-Free 1-800-331-TEST

Figure 7.15 Continued

ing that her interpersonal discomfort and high level of physical complaints and concerns are creating substantial problems for her and are central treatment issues. The General Maladjustment dimension is also significant in her profile; i.e., more than half the scales in this factor are in critical ranges, indicating that internal states of upheaval and turmoil have produced considerable disruption in her functioning, and a markedly high overall level of emotional distress.

Summary and Diagnostic Impression

The findings from this adolescent's MMPI-A, together with other test findings, observations, interview reports, and background information, indicate that Tamara is in substantial distress, manifested in internalizing symptoms and physical health concerns. She is displaying the sequelae often found in victims of sexual trauma, and there is no doubt that recent events have reactivated traumatic memories and provoked deterioration in her functioning. As noted in Chapter 6, there is no characteristic or typical MMPI-A profile for sexually abused teenagers; however, sexually abused adolescents often show multiple MMPI-A scale elevations that reflect affective distress, as Tamara does, and may also show disorganization in thinking and overall functioning.

The diagnosis of Post-Traumatic Stress Disorder (PTSD) is supported in this case by Tamara's symptoms and affective/cognitive experiences, although other anxiety-related disorders would also need to be considered in her diagnostic evaluation. Tamara would need swift interventions to prevent further disorganization in her functioning. Although her enervated state, self-doubt, and overall pessimism may render her treatment prognosis guarded, her openness in revealing her feelings in the testing is promising. The presence of a supportive family is also an asset that should serve to reinforce treatment efforts.

Recommendations

Referral to the sexual abuse treatment group should be carefully weighed in light of Tamara's interpersonal withdrawal and discomfort. Participating in a group with other teenage girls who have been victims of abuse offers a venue for her to feel understood and less alone. However, she would probably respond better, at least initially, to supportive psychotherapy offered in an individual therapy format. The concurrent provision of both forms of therapy may be considered in this case. Treatment approaches should also be directed toward desensitizing Tamara to interpersonal fears and developing social competence and assertiveness skills. Additionally, Tamara is advised to see her primary care physician for a physical examination, and a psychiatric referral should also be made to consider adjunctive pharmacological treatment if her intrusive thoughts and high level of affective distress do not abate.

🖋 TEST YOURSELF 🖋

1. **Which of the following types of information is not appropriate for the background section of a test report?**
   (a) mention of previous hospitalization
   (b) statements about family violence
   (c) information about test scores and results
   (d) facts concerning school failure

2. **The summary section of the report should**
   (a) highlight the central findings and conclusions.
   (b) present personal opinions.
   (c) furnish new information.
   (d) focus on observational findings.

3. **Discussion of the adolescent's interpersonal functioning could include findings about**
   (a) conflict with parents.
   (b) estrangement from peers.
   (c) defiance toward authority figures.
   (d) all of the above.

4. **Which of the following is best avoided in the interpretive section of the test report?**
   (a) discussion of examinee strengths
   (b) listing of raw scores
   (c) examiner's long-range predictions
   (d) (b) and (c)

5. **Rules of confidentiality dictate that the adolescent's parent / legal guardian should never be present for the test feedback.** True or False?

Answers: 1. c; 2. a; 3. d; 4. d; 5. False

Appendix A

Item Composition of MMPI-A Basic Scales, Harris-Lingoes Subscales, *Si* (*Social Introversion*) Subscales, Supplementary Scales, and Content Scales

Table A.1 *Basic Scales*

VRIN (*Variable Response Inconsistency;* 50 item-response pairs)

1. For each of the following response pairs *add* 1 point.

6 T – 86 F	69 T – 452 F	144 T – 247 F	253 T – 266 F
6 F – 86 F	70 T – 223 T	146 T – 167 T	286 F – 314 T
20 T – 211 F	71 F – 91 T	154 T – 178 F	292 F – 331 T
25 T – 106 F	77 T – 107 F	160 F – 227 T	304 F – 335 F
25 F – 106 T	77 F – 107 T	177 F – 283 T	309 T – 402 F
34 F – 81 T	78 F – 90 T	182 T – 258 F	318 F – 370 T
43 T – 248 F	79 T – 119 F	182 F – 258 T	332 T – 337 T
46 F – 475 F	80 T – 101 F	185 F – 383 T	355 T – 375 F
53 F – 62 T	94 F – 469 T	188 T – 403 F	463 T – 476 T
57 T – 191 F	95 F – 132 T	188 F – 403 T	477 T – 478 F
60 T – 121 T	99 T – 323 F	212 T – 298 F	477 F – 478 T
63 T – 120 T	124 F – 379 T	215 T – 405 F	
63 F – 120 F	128 F – 465 F	215 F – 405 T	

Males: Mean 4.64; SD 3.40. *Females:* Mean 3.86; SD 2.84.

Table A.I Continued

TRIN (*True Response Inconsistency;* 24 item-response pairs)

1. For each of the following response pairs *add* 1 point:

14 T – 424 T	63 T – 120 T	119 T – 184 T	304 T – 335 T
37 T – 168 T	70 T – 223 T	146 T – 167 T	355 T – 367 T
60 T – 121 T	71 T – 283 T	242 T – 260 T	463 T – 476 T
62 T – 360 T	95 T – 294 T	264 T – 331 T	

2. For each of the following response pairs *subtract* 1 point:

46 F – 475 F	71 F – 283 F	158 F – 288 F
53 F – 91 F	82 F – 316 F	245 F – 257 F
63 F – 120 F	128 F – 465 F	304 F – 335 F

3. Then add 9 points to the total raw score.

Males: Mean 9.21; SD 1.79. *Females:* Mean 9.40; SD 1.56.

F_1 (*Infrequency 1;* 33 items)

True

12	17	22	30	33	39	51	57	63	69	80	92	108
132	136	144	155	173	187	215	219	224	230	236		

False

6	74	86	98	104	120	182	193	198

Males: Mean 4.06; SD 3.95. *Females:* Mean 3.13; SD 3.07.

F_2 (*Infrequency 2;* 33 items)

True

242	250	264	273	283	297	303	309	315	321	328	332	337
342	350	358	366	384	392	399	405	415	422	428	433	439
458	463	470										

False

258	289	374	447

Males: Mean 5.09; SD 4.98. *Females:* Mean 4.57; SD 4.61.

(continued)

Table A.1 Continued

F (*Infrequency;* 66 items)

True

12	17	22	30	33	39	51	57	63	69	80	92	108
132	136	144	155	173	187	215	219	224	230	236	242	250
264	273	283	297	303	309	315	321	328	332	337	342	350
358	366	384	392	399	405	415	422	428	433	439	458	463
470												

False

6	74	86	98	104	120	182	193	198	258	289	374	447

Males: Mean 9.15; SD 8.44. *Females:* Mean 7.70; SD 7.22.

L (*Lie;* 14 items)

True

(None)

False

15	26	38	48	73	89	98	103	117	133	147	176	192
243												

Males: Mean 2.94; SD 2.34. *Females:* Mean 2.26; SD 1.92.

K (*Defensiveness;* 30 items)

True

79

False

26	34	55	72	107	111	116	121	124	130	142	150	151
160	164	185	201	227	265	271	289	298	317	318	320	325
327	333	341										

Males: Mean 12.70; SD 4.73. *Females:* Mean 11.54; SD 4.39.

Table A.1 Continued

Scale 1: Hs (*Hypochondriasis;* 32 items)

True

| 17 | 25 | 36 | 50 | 56 | 93 | 97 | 106 | 143 | 167 | 231 |

False

| 2 | 3 | 8 | 10 | 18 | 42 | 44 | 54 | 87 | 113 | 135 | 140 | 146 |
| 157 | 166 | 168 | 172 | 196 | 210 | 233 | 239 |

Males: Mean 7.68; SD 4.66. *Females:* Mean 9.28; SD 5.04.

Scale 2: D (*Depression;* 57 items)

True

| 5 | 14 | 17 | 28 | 35 | 36 | 43 | 53 | 70 | 88 | 113 | 121 | 124 |
| 139 | 141 | 163 | 167 | 174 | 203 | 218 |

False

2	4	9	10	18	26	34	40	42	46	52	65	71
72	91	105	112	128	134	135	138	140	142	158	171	179
180	200	208	209	212	222	229	232	243	289	298

Males: Mean 18.95; SD 5.51. *Females:* Mean 20.81; SD 5.45.

Scale 3: Hy (*Hysteria;* 60 items)

True

| 11 | 17 | 28 | 36 | 37 | 41 | 62 | 97 | 159 | 165 | 167 | 205 | 216 |

False

2	3	7	8	9	10	13	23	26	42	44	55	72
77	87	91	94	107	110	111	118	119	123	129	135	142
145	146	150	152	154	157	160	166	168	172	178	183	196
201	210	225	227	233	237	246	248

Males: Mean 20.94; SD 5.66. *Females:* Mean 22.85; SD 5.12.

(continued)

Table A.1 Continued

Scale 4: Pd (Psychopathic Deviate; 49 items)

True

16	19	20	28	29	32	39	49	51	53	68	78	85
90	95	101	109	184	191	206	211	247	269	286		

False

9	31	67	75	79	91	116	119	123	140	150	151	153
160	164	178	197	202	204	212	227	244	246	249	298	

Males: Mean 19.48; SD 5.28. *Females:* Mean 20.33; SD 5.50.

Scale 5: Mf-m (Masculinity-Femininity [Masculine]; 44 items)

True

59	61	64	76	114	116	122	131	159	169	185	194	197
206	235	240	251	253								

False

1	23	24	60	65	66	72	82	99	100	103	115	126
127	156	183	186	188	190	217	220	221	223	238	241	254

Males: Mean 21.28; SD 3.98.

Scale 5: Mf-f (Masculinity-Femininity [Feminine]; 44 items)

True

59	61	64	76	114	116	122	131	169	185	194	206	235
240	253											

False

1	23	24	60	65	66	72	82	99	100	103	115	126
127	156	159	183	186	188	190	197	217	220	221	223	238
241	251	254										

Females: Mean 28.24; SD 3.73.

Table A.I Continued

Scale 6: Pa (Paranoia; 40 items)

True

15	16	20	21	22	39	95	109	132	136	137	139	155
219	253	259	266	285	286	287	314	315	332	337	350	

False

77	91	94	96	100	107	228	239	249	263	265	267	277
294	295											

Males: Mean 12.60; SD 4.12. *Females:* Mean 12.99; SD 4.15.

Scale 7: Pt (Psychasthenia; 48 items)

True

11	15	21	28	35	53	62	70	78	85	90	124	141
163	167	185	205	226	255	257	259	266	270	281	282	284
288	290	293	296	297	300	305	306	307	308	309	310	311

False

3	4	9	105	134	158	170	274	301

Males: Mean 17.97; SD 7.60. *Females:* Mean 20.79; SD 8.07.

Scale 8: Sc (Schizophrenia; 77 items)

True

15	16	19	20	21	28	29	32	35	39	41	43	45
62	81	88	132	137	141	159	161	163	173	175	181	205
208	214	218	219	226	231	236	240	251	255	256	259	261
264	268	272	273	276	278	279	283	287	291	296	299	300
302	303	305	309	314	321	332						

False

6	9	31	86	87	102	158	169	172	182	198	239	258
260	262	271	275	322								

Males: Mean 21.98; SD 10.23. *Females:* Mean 23.26; SD 10.62.

(continued)

Table A.1 Continued

Scale 9: Ma (Hypomania; 46 items)

True

14	19	21	47	52	58	81	83	94	109	116	125	137
149	161	162	175	181	189	194	195	199	200	205	207	213
214	222	226	228	232	234	237	252	313				

False

84	89	96	102	103	130	148	151	160	227	246

Males: Mean 21.14; SD 5.01. *Females:* Mean 21.81; SD 4.81.

Scale 0: Si (Social Introversion; 62 items)

True

27	28	53	67	96	100	107	121	129	151	154	160	178
203	227	235	248	257	265	270	276	280	282	288	304	306
308	316	317	326	327	330	334	340					

False

29	46	75	82	102	125	174	180	197	217	221	239	245
262	292	298	301	312	319	323	324	329	331	335	336	338
339	343											

Males: Mean 25.99; SD 7.84. *Females:* Mean 26.97; SD 8.01.

Table A.2 Harris-Lingoes Subscales

D_1 (Subjective Depression; 32 items)

True

28	35	36	43	53	70	88	121	124	139	141	163	167
203	218											

False

2	9	40	46	71	91	105	112	134	142	171	179	180
209	243	289	298									

Males: Mean 8.58; SD 4.25. *Females:* Mean 9.87; SD 4.64.

Table A.2 Continued

D_2 (*Psychomotor Retardation;* 14 items)

True

| 35 | 43 | 163 | 218 |

False

| 9 | 26 | 34 | 46 | 52 | 72 | 128 | 179 | 180 | 200 |

Males: Mean 4.80; SD 2.01. *Females:* Mean 4.79; SD 1.84.

D_3 (*Physical Malfunctioning;* 11 items)

True

| 17 | 113 | 167 | 174 |

False

| 2 | 18 | 42 | 135 | 138 | 140 | 142 |

Males: Mean 3.26; SD 1.49. *Females:* Mean 3.70; SD 1.60.

D_4 (*Mental Dullness;* 15 items)

True

| 14 | 28 | 35 | 70 | 88 | 141 | 163 | 218 |

False

| 9 | 10 | 40 | 71 | 105 | 158 | 179 |

Males: Mean 3.62; SD 2.48. *Females:* Mean 3.90; SD 2.61.

D_5 (*Brooding;* 10 items)

True

| 35 | 53 | 88 | 121 | 124 | 139 | 163 | 203 |

False

| 71 | 91 |

Males: Mean 2.78; SD 2.04. *Females:* Mean 3.77; SD 2.15.

(continued)

Table A.2 Continued

Hy_1 (*Denial of Social Anxiety;* 6 items)

True

(None)

False

123   154   160   178   227   248

Males: Mean 3.13; SD 1.77. *Females:* Mean 3.31; SD 1.77.

Hy_2 (*Need for Affection;* 12 items)

True

216

False

23   55   72   77   94   107   118   145   201   225   246

Males: Mean 5.04; SD 2.33. *Females:* Mean 4.88; SD 2.40.

Hy_3 (*Lassitude-Malaise;* 15 items)

True

28   36   62   167   205

False

2   3   9   10   42   91   119   135   142   146

Males: Mean 4.00; SD 2.54. *Females:* Mean 4.74; SD 2.79.

Hy_4 (*Somatic Complaints;* 17 items)

True

11   17   37   41   97 . 165

False

8   44   87   152   157   166   168   172   196   210   233

Males: Mean 4.02; SD 2.85. *Females:* Mean 4.95; SD 3.07.

Table A.2 Continued

Hy₃ (Inhibition of Aggression; 7 items)

True

(None)

False

  7   13   26   110   111   129   150

Males: Mean 2.86; SD 1.33. *Females:* Mean 2.92; SD 1.30.

Pd₁ (Familial Discord; 9 items)

True

19   51   184   191   269

False

79   119   202   204

Males: Mean 3.41; SD 1.86. *Females:* Mean 3.87; SD 1.93.

Pd₂ (Authority Problems; 8 items)

True

32   101

False

31   67   123   153   246   249

Males: Mean 3.37; SD 1.58. *Females:* Mean 2.75; SD 1.47.

Pd₃ (Social Imperturbability; 6 items)

True

(None)

False

67   123   151   160   178   227

Males: Mean 3.33; SD 1.58. *Females:* Mean 3.20; SD 1.63.

(continued)

Table A.2 Continued

Pd_4 (*Social Alienation;* 12 items)

True

| 16 | 20 | 39 | 53 | 78 | 95 | 109 | 206 | 211 | 286 |

False

| 123 | 150 |

Males: Mean 4.83; SD 2.18. *Females:* Mean 5.36; SD 2.25.

Pd_5 (*Self-Alienation;* 12 items)

True

| 28 | 29 | 49 | 53 | 68 | 78 | 85 | 90 | 109 | 247 |

False

| 9 | 91 |

Males: Mean 4.29; SD 2.43. *Females:* Mean 4.74; SD 2.54.

Pa_1 (*Persecutory Ideas;* 17 items)

True

| 16 | 20 | 39 | 95 | 109 | 132 | 136 | 137 | 155 | 219 | 285 | 286 | 314 |
| 315 | 332 | 337 |

False

294

Males: Mean 4.10; SD 2.78. *Females:* Mean 4.09; SD 2.71.

Pa_2 (*Poignancy;* 9 items)

True

| 20 | 139 | 253 | 259 | 266 | 287 | 350 |

False

| 96 | 228 |

Males: Mean 3.22; SD 1.63. *Females:* Mean 3.74; SD 1.89.

Table A.2 Continued

Pa₃ (Naivete; 9 items)

True

15

False

77	94	100	107	263	265	267	295

Males: Mean 3.93; SD 1.89. *Females:* Mean 3.75; SD 1.97.

Sc₁ (Social Alienation; 21 items)

True

16	19	20	39	43	132	137	181	208	240	259	264	272
300	302	314										

False

86	258	260	262	322

Males: Mean 6.17; SD 3.29. *Females:* Mean 6.46; SD 3.24.

Sc₂ (Emotional Alienation; 11 items)

True

62	88	219	255	283	303	309	321

False

9	198	271

Males: Mean 2.29; SD 1.81. *Females:* Mean 2.29; SD 1.81.

Sc₃ (Lack of Ego Mastery, Cognitive; 10 items)

True

28	29	141	163	173	279	291	296	305

False

158

Males: Mean 2.94; SD 2.20. *Females:* Mean 3.10; SD 2.29.

(continued)

Table A.2 Continued

Sc₄ (Lack of Ego Mastery, Conative; **14 items)**

True

| 28 | 35 | 45 | 62 | 88 | 218 | 219 | 255 | 279 | 283 | 305 |

False

| 9 | 198 | 271 |

Males: Mean 4.10; SD 2.57. *Females:* Mean 4.35; SD 2.71.

Sc₅ (Lack of Ego Mastery, Defective Inhibition; **11 items)**

True

| 21 | 81 | 161 | 175 | 205 | 226 | 256 | 273 | 300 | 309 | 332 |

False

(None)

Males: Mean 3.47; SD 2.07. *Females:* Mean 4.20; SD 2.16.

Sc₆ (Bizarre Sensory Experiences; **20 items)**

True

| 21 | 29 | 41 | 161 | 175 | 214 | 231 | 236 | 276 | 278 | 287 | 291 | 299 |
332

False

| 87 | 102 | 169 | 172 | 239 | 275 |

Males: Mean 5.01; SD 3.33. *Females:* Mean 5.46; SD 3.45.

Ma₁ (Amorality; **6 items)**

True

125   213   232   234   252

False

246

Males: Mean 2.71; SD 1.40. *Females:* Mean 2.37; SD 1.30.

Table A.2 Continued

Ma_2 (*Psychomotor Acceleration;* 11 items)

True

| 14 | 81 | 83 | 116 | 162 | 195 | 205 | 226 | 228 |

False

| 96 | 102 |

Males: Mean 6.52; SD 2.13. *Females:* Mean 7.13; SD 1.97.

Ma_3 (*Imperturbability;* 8 items)

True

| 149 | 189 | 207 |

False

| 89 | 130 | 151 | 160 | 227 |

Males: Mean 3.16; SD 1.59. *Females:* Mean 2.94; SD 1.52.

Ma_4 (*Ego Inflation;* 9 items)

True

| 47 | 52 | 58 | 94 | 137 | 181 | 199 | 200 | 313 |

False

(None)

Males: Mean 4.45; SD 1.83. *Females:* Mean 4.61; SD 1.74.

Table A.3 *Si (Social Introversion)* Subscales

Si_1 (*Shyness/Self-Consciousness;* 14 items)

True

| 151 | 154 | 160 | 178 | 227 | 248 | 257 | 270 |

False

| 46 | 245 | 262 | 301 | 312 | 336 |

Males: Mean 6.21; SD 3.12. *Females:* Mean 6.23; SD 3.28.

(continued)

Table A.3 Continued

Si_2 (*Social Avoidance;* 8 items)

True

304   316

False

82   292   319   331   335   339

Males: Mean 2.52; SD 2.03. *Females:* Mean 1.90; SD 1.85.

Si_3 (*Alienation–Self and Others;* 17 items)

True

27	28	53	100	107	129	265	280	282	288	306	308	317
326	327	334	340									

False

(None)

Males: Mean 7.58; SD 3.43. *Females:* Mean 8.22; SD 3.68.

Table A.4 Supplementary Scales

MAC-R (*MacAndrew Alcoholism Scale–Revised;* 49 items)

True

7	22	46	49	66	78	80	99	101	109	110	122	161
165	177	191	202	210	214	222	241	250	262	269	312	323
342	348	376	380	382	386	392	393	395	407	429	470	

False

70   103   113   131   153   159   235   249   268   279   305

Males: Mean 21.07; SD 4.44. *Females:* Mean 19.73; SD 4.14.

Table A.4 Continued

ACK (*Alcohol/Drug Problem Acknowledgment;* 13 items)

True

| 81 | 144 | 161 | 247 | 269 | 338 | 342 | 429 | 458 | 467 | 474 |

False

| 249 | 431 |

Males: Mean 3.90; SD 2.45. *Females:* Mean 3.68; SD 2.38.

PRO (*Alcohol/Drug Problem Proneness;* 36 items)

True

| 32 | 38 | 57 | 82 | 101 | 117 | 191 | 336 | 345 | 376 | 381 | 389 | 435 |
| 438 | 440 | 452 | 455 | 462 | 476 |

False

| 40 | 142 | 143 | 153 | 188 | 272 | 304 | 403 | 410 | 418 | 424 | 436 | 451 |
| 457 | 459 | 460 | 463 |

Males: Mean 16.55; SD 4.42. *Females:* Mean 16.74; SD 4.17.

IMM (*Immaturity;* 43 items)

True

16	20	24	45	63	72	94	101	128	218	224	269	307
351	354	358	362	371	389	400	405	418	423	425	426	441
444	452	453	466

False

| 64 | 71 | 105 | 120 | 153 | 170 | 322 | 336 | 419 | 431 | 436 | 448 | 476 |

Males: Mean 13.47; SD 6.29. *Females:* Mean 11.75; SD 6.31.

(continued)

Table A.4 Continued

A (*Anxiety;* 35 items)

True

28	35	53	62	78	121	129	203	218	227	235	255	259
270	281	290	291	305	308	310	317	318	320	326	368	369
370	372	377	379	383	385	394	404					

False

360

Males: Mean 14.59; SD 7.17. *Females:* Mean 16.90; SD 7.67.

R (*Repression;* 33 items)

True

(None)

False

1	7	10	13	34	42	66	112	115	122	128	138	161
171	180	186	188	232	239	240	277	289	325	329	331	335
339	341	348	386	388	390	396						

Males: Mean 13.41; SD 4.37. *Females:* Mean 13.33; SD 3.50.

Table A.5 Content Scales

A-anx (*Adolescent–anxiety;* 21 items)

True

14	28	36	163	185	255	279	281	285	318	353	377	383
402	404	468										

False

134	196	209	375	424

Males: Mean 7.84; SD 4.09. *Females:* Mean 9.03; SD 4.40.

Table A.5 Continued

A-obs (Adolescent–obsessiveness; 15 items)

True

52	78	83	129	185	293	307	308	310	368	370	394	412
421	444											

False

(None)

Males: Mean 6.91; SD 3.32. *Females:* Mean 7.88; SD 3.23.

A-dep (Adolescent–depression; 26 items)

True

35	49	53	62	68	88	124	139	177	203	219	230	242
259	283	311	347	371	372	379	399					

False

3	9	71	91	360

Males: Mean 7.59; SD 4.57. *Females:* Mean 9.17; SD 5.08.

A-hea (Adolescent–health concerns; 37 items)

True

11	17	25	37	41	50	56	93	97	106	143	167	187
231	422	443	470									

False

18	42	44	54	87	112	113	135	138	152	157	168	172
174	193	210	233	239	275	374						

Males: Mean 7.88; SD 5.31. *Females:* Mean 9.03; SD 5.53.

A-aln (Adolescent–alienation; 20 items)

True

16	20	39	211	227	242	317	362	369	413	438	446	463
471	473											

False

74	104	260	448	450

Males: Mean 5.95; SD 3.36. *Females:* Mean 5.62; SD 3.49.

(continued)

Table A.5 Continued

A-biz (Adolescent–bizarre mentation; 19 items)

True

22	29	92	132	155	173	250	278	291	296	299	314	315
332	417	428	433	439								

False

387

Males: Mean 4.00; SD 3.13. *Females:* Mean 4.05; SD 3.09.

A-ang (Adolescent–anger; 17 items)

True

26	34	111	128	201	282	367	378	382	388	401	416	445
453	458	461										

False

355

Males: Mean 7.94; SD 3.23. *Females:* Mean 8.51; SD 3.09.

A-cyn (Adolescent–cynicism; 22 items)

True

47	55	72	77	100	107	118	211	213	225	238	263	265
267	295	325	330	334	371	373	395	406				

False

(None)

Males: Mean 12.36; SD 4.51. *Females:* Mean 12.34; SD 4.72.

A-con (Adolescent–conduct problems; 23 items)

True

32	99	117	224	232	234	252	345	354	356	361	391	442
445	455	456	462	469	477	478						

False

96	249	465

Males: Mean 9.62; SD 4.03. *Females:* Mean 8.15; SD 3.85.

Table A.5 Continued

A-lse (Adolescent–low self-esteem; 18 items)

True

67	70	124	280	306	358	379	384	385	400	415	430	432
441	468											

False

58   74   105

Males: Mean 5.00; SD 3.21. *Females:* Mean 5.83; SD 3.46.

A-las (Adolescent–low aspirations; 16 items)

True

27   39   218   340   351   430   464

False

170   188   324   397   403   409   411   436   447

Males: Mean 5.85; SD 2.63. *Females:* Mean 6.00; SD 2.72.

A-sod (Adolescent–social discomfort; 24 items)

True

43   151   160   178   248   264   290   304   316   328   408   410   475

False

46   82   245   262   292   319   331   335   336   339   450

Males: Mean 8.33; SD 4.36. *Females:* Mean 7.19; SD 4.31.

A-fam (Adolescent–family problems; 35 items)

True

19	57	137	181	184	191	194	215	240	269	277	302	303
344	352	359	363	366	381	396	405	438	440	454		

False

6   79   86   119   182   258   365   398   451   457   460

Males: Mean 11.37; SD 5.62. *Females:* Mean 12.53; SD 5.67.

(continued)

Table A.5 Continued

A-sch (*Adolescent–school problems;* 20 items)

True

12	33	69	80	101	220	257	338	364	380	389	425	435
443	452	464	466									

False

153   166   459

Males: Mean 6.32; SD 3.37. *Females:* Mean 5.83; SD 3.15.

A-trt (*Adolescent–negative treatment indicators;* 26 items)

True

20	27	88	242	256	340	356	357	358	369	371	414	418
420	421	423	426	427	432	434	444	449	472			

False

419   431   437

Males: Mean 9.11; SD 4.21. *Females:* Mean 9.30; SD 4.41.

Appendix B

T-score Conversions for MMPI-A Basic Validity and Clinical Scales, Content and Supplementary Scales, and the Harris-Lingoes and Si (Social Introversion) Subscales

Table B.1 Uniform and Linear T-Score Conversions for Validity and Clinical Scales

Basic Profile Scales

A. Boys

Raw	VRIN	TRIN	F_1	F_2	F	L	K	Hs	D	Hy	Pd	Mf	Pa	Pt	Sc	Ma	Si	Raw
0	36	101F	40	40	39	37	30	31	30	30	30	30	30	30	30	30	30	0
1	39	96F	42	42	40	42	30	35	30	30	30	30	30	30	30	30	30	1
2	42	90F	45	44	42	46	30	38	30	30	30	30	30	30	30	30	30	2
3	45	85F	47	46	43	50	30	41	30	30	30	30	30	32	31	30	30	3
4	48	79F	50	48	44	55	32	43	30	30	30	30	30	33	33	30	30	4
5	51	73F	52	50	45	59	34	45	30	30	30	30	32	35	34	30	30	5
6	54	68F	55	52	46	63	36	47	30	30	30	30	35	36	35	30	30	6
7	57	62F	57	54	47	67	38	49	30	30	30	30	38	37	36	30	30	7
8	60	57F	60	56	49	72	40	50	30	31	30	30	40	38	38	30	30	8
9	63	51F	63	58	50	76	42	52	32	32	31	30	42	39	39	30	30	9
10	66	54T	65	60	51	80	44	54	34	32	33	30	44	41	40	32	30	10
11	69	60T	68	62	52	84	46	55	36	34	35	30	46	42	41	34	31	11
12	72	66T	70	64	53	89	49	58	38	35	37	30	48	43	41	35	32	12
13	75	71T	73	66	55	93	51	60	40	36	39	30	50	44	42	37	33	13
14	78	77T	75	68	56	97	53	63	41	38	41	32	52	45	43	38	35	14
15	81	82T	78	70	57		55	65	43	39	42	34	54	46	44	39	36	15

(continued)

Table B.I Continued

Basic Profile Scales

A. Boys (continued)

Raw	VRIN	TRIN	F_1	F_2	F	L	K	Hs	D	Hy	Pd	Mf	Pa	Pt	Sc	Ma	Si	Raw
16	83	88T	80	72	58		57	68	45	41	44	37	57	47	45	41	37	16
17	86	93T	83	74	59		59	71	46	43	45	39	60	48	45	42	38	17
18	89	99T	85	76	60		61	74	48	45	47	42	63	49	46	43	40	18
19	92	105T	88	78	62		63	76	50	46	48	44	66	50	47	45	41	19
20	95	110T	90	80	63		65	79	51	48	50	47	69	51	47	46	42	20
21	98	116T	93	82	64		68	82	53	50	51	49	73	53	48	48	44	21
22	101	120T	95	84	65		70	84	55	52	53	52	76	54	49	50	45	22
23	104	120T	98	86	66		72	87	56	54	55	54	79	55	50	52	46	23
24	107	120T	101	88	68		74	90	58	56	57	57	82	57	50	54	47	24
25	110		103	90	69		76	92	60	58	60	59	85	58	51	56	49	25
26	113		106	92	70		78	95	62	59	62	62	88	60	52	59	50	26
27	116		108	94	71		80	98	65	61	65	64	92	62	53	62	51	27
28	119		111	96	72		82	100	67	63	67	67	95	64	54	65	53	28
29	120		113	98	74		84	103	69	64	70	69	98	65	55	68	54	29
30	120		116	100	75		87	106	71	66	72	72	101	67	56	72	55	30
31	120		118	102	76			108	73	68	75	74	104	69	57	75	56	31
32	120		120	104	77			111	75	69	78	77	107	71	59	78	58	32
33	120		120	106	78				77	71	80	79	111	72	60	81	59	33
34	120				79				79	72	83	82	114	74	61	84	60	34
35	120				81				81	74	85	84	117	76	63	87	62	35
36	120				82				83	76	88	87	120	78	64	90	63	36
37	120				83				85	77	90	89	120	79	66	93	64	37

Upper table:

38	65	96	67	81	120	92	93	79	88
39	67	100	68	83	120	95	95	81	90
40	68	103	70	85	120	97	98	82	92
41	69	106	71	86		100	101	84	94
42	70	109	73	88		102	103	86	96
43	72	112	74	90		105	106	87	98
44	73	115	75	92		107	108	89	100
45	74	118	77	94			111	90	102
46	76	120	78	95			113	92	104
47	77		80	97			116	94	106
48	78		81	99			118	95	108
49	79		82				120	97	111
50	81		84					99	113
51	82		85					100	115
52	83		87					102	117
53	85		88					104	119
54	86		89					105	120
55	87		91					107	120
56	88		92					108	120
57	90		94					110	120
58	91		95					112	
59	92		97					113	
60	94		98					115	
61	95		99						
62	96		101						
63			102						
64			104						
65			105						
66			106						

Lower table:

38	84	120
39	85	120
40	87	120
41	88	120
42	89	120
43	90	120
44	91	120
45	92	120
46	94	120
47	95	120
48	96	120
49	97	120
50	98	120
51	100	
52	101	
53	102	
54	103	
55	104	
56	106	
57	107	
58	108	
59	109	
60	110	
61	111	
62	113	
63	114	
64	115	
65	116	
66	117	

(continued)

Table B.1 Continued

Basic Profile Scales

Raw	VRIN	TRIN	F_1	F_2	F	L	K	Hs	D	Hy	Pd	Mf	Pa	Pt	Sc	Ma	Si	Raw
								A. Boys (*continued*)										
67															108			67
68															109			68
69															111			69
70															112			70
71															113			71
72															115			72
73															116			73
74															118			74
75															119			75
76															120			76
77															120			77
								B. Girls										
0	36	110F	40	40	39	38	30	30	30	30	30	120	30	30	30	30	30	0
1	40	104F	43	42	41	43	30	32	30	30	30	120	30	30	30	30	30	1
2	43	97F	46	44	42	49	30	35	30	30	30	120	30	30	30	30	30	2
3	47	91F	50	47	43	54	31	38	30	30	30	118	30	31	30	30	30	3
4	50	85F	53	49	45	59	33	40	30	30	30	115	30	31	32	30	30	4
5	54	78F	56	51	46	64	35	42	30	30	30	112	32	33	33	30	30	5
6	58	72F	59	53	48	70	37	44	30	30	30	110	34	34	35	30	30	6
7	61	65F	63	55	49	75	40	46	30	30	30	107	37	35	36	30	30	7

8	30	30	37	36	39	104	30	30	30	48	42	80	50	57	66	59F	65	8
9	30	30	38	37	41	102	30	30	30	49	44	85	52	60	69	53F	68	9
10	30	31	39	38	43	99	32	30	31	51	46	90	53	62	72	54T	72	10
11	30	33	40	39	45	96	34	30	33	53	49	96	55	64	76	60T	75	11
12	31	34	41	40	47	94	36	32	34	54	51	101	56	66	79	67T	79	12
13	33	36	42	41	49	91	38	33	36	56	53	106	57	68	82	73T	82	13
14	34	37	43	42	52	88	40	35	38	58	56	111	59	70	85	79T	86	14
15	35	38	43	43	54	86	41	36	40	61	58		60	73	89	86T	89	15
16	36	39	44	44	56	83	43	38	41	63	60		61	75	92	92T	93	16
17	38	41	45	45	59	80	44	39	43	65	62		63	77	95	99T	96	17
18	39	42	45	46	62	77	46	41	45	68	65		64	79	98	105T	100	18
19	40	43	46	47	65	75	47	42	46	70	67		66	81	102	111T	103	19
20	41	45	47	48	68	72	48	44	48	72	69		67	83	105	118T	107	20
21	43	46	47	49	71	69	50	46	50	75	72		68	86	108	120T	110	21
22	44	48	48	50	73	67	51	48	52	77	74		70	88	112	120T	114	22
23	45	50	48	51	76	64	53	49	53	79	76		71	90	115	120T	117	23
24	46	52	49	52	79	61	55	51	55	82	78		73	92	118	120T	120	24
25	48	55	50	53	82	59	57	53	57	84	81		74	94	120		120	25
26	49	58	51	55	85	56	59	55	59	86	83		75	96	120		120	26
27	50	61	51	56	88	53	62	58	61	89	85		77	99	120		120	27
28	51	64	52	58	91	51	64	60	63	91	88		78	101	120		120	28
29	53	68	53	59	93	48	67	62	65	93	90		79	103	120		120	29
30	54	71	54	61	96	45	69	65	67	96	92		81	105	120		120	30
31	55	75	55	63	99	43	72	67	69	98			82	107	120		120	31
32	56	78	56	65	102	40	74	70	71	101			84	109	120		120	32
33	58	82	58	67	105	37	77	72	73				85	112	120		120	33
34	59	85	59	68	108	35	79	74	75				86		120		120	34
35	60	89	60	70	111	32	82	77	77				88		120		120	35
36	61	92	62	72	113	30	84	79	79				89		120		120	36
37	63	96	63	74	116	30	86	82	81				91		120		120	37

(continued)

Table B.1 Continued

Basic Profile Scales

B. Girls (continued)

Raw	VRIN	TRIN	F_1	F_2	F	L	K	Hs	D	Hy	Pd	Mf	Pa	Pt	Sc	Ma	Si	Raw
38	120				92				83	84	89	30	119	76	65	99	64	38
39	120				93				85	86	91	30	120	78	66	103	65	39
40	120				95				87	89	94	30	120	79	68	106	66	40
41	120				96				89	91	96	30		81	69	109	68	41
42	120				97				91	94	99	30		83	71	113	69	42
43	120				99				93	96	101	30		85	72	116	70	43
44	120				100				95	98	104	30		87	74	120	71	44
45	120				102				97	101	106			88	75	120	73	45
46	120				103				99	103	109			90	77	120	74	46
47	120				104				101	106	111			92	78		75	47
48	120				106				103	108	114			94	80		76	48
49	120				107				105	111	116				81		78	49
50	120				109				107	113					83		79	50
51					110				109	115					84		80	51
52					111				111	118					86		81	52
53					113				113	120					87		82	53

54	114	120	115	89	84	54
55	115	120	117	90	85	55
56	117	120	119	92	86	56
57	118	120	120	93	87	57
58	120	120		95	89	58
59	120	120		96	90	59
60	120	120		98	91	60
61	120			99	92	61
62	120			101	94	62
63	120			102		63
64	120			104		64
65	120			105		65
66	120			107		66
67				108		67
68				110		68
69				111		69
70				113		70
71				114		71
72				116		72
73				117		73
74				119		74
75				120		75
76				120		76
77				120		77

Table B.2 Uniform T-Score Conversions for Content Scales

Content Scales

A. Boys

Raw	A-anx	A-obs	A-dep	A-bea	A-aln	A-biz	A-ang	A-cyn	A-con	A-lse	A-las	A-sod	A-fam	A-sch	A-trt	Raw
0	32	32	32	31	33	36	30	30	30	34	30	32	30	31	30	0
1	35	35	35	35	36	41	32	30	31	39	34	35	32	36	32	1
2	37	38	38	39	40	45	35	33	34	42	38	37	35	39	35	2
3	39	40	41	42	42	48	38	35	36	45	41	39	37	42	38	3
4	41	42	43	44	45	50	40	36	38	47	43	41	39	44	40	4
5	43	44	45	46	47	53	42	38	40	49	46	43	40	46	42	5
6	45	46	47	48	49	55	44	39	42	52	49	45	42	48	43	6
7	47	48	49	49	52	58	46	40	43	54	52	47	43	50	45	7
8	49	51	51	50	54	62	48	41	45	58	56	49	44	53	46	8
9	52	54	52	52	58	66	51	42	47	62	62	51	46	56	48	9
10	54	58	54	53	62	70	54	43	49	66	69	53	47	60	50	10
11	57	63	57	54	66	74	58	45	52	71	75	55	48	65	52	11
12	59	67	59	55	70	77	64	46	54	75	81	58	50	69	55	12
13	63	72	61	57	74	81	69	48	57	79	88	60	51	74	58	13
14	66	77	64	59	78	85	74	50	61	84	94	63	53	78	61	14
15	69	82	66	62	82	89	79	53	64	88	100	66	54	82	65	15
16	72		69	64	87	93	85	57	68	92	106	69	57	87	69	16
17	75		71	67	91	97	90	60	72	97		72	59	91	73	17
18	79		74	69	95	101		65	75	101		75	62	96	77	18
19	82		77	72	99	105		69	79			78	64	100	81	19
20	85		79	74	103			74	83			81	67	105	85	20
21	88		82	77				78	86			83	70		88	21
22			84	80				82	90			86	72		92	22
23			87	82					94			89	75		96	23

(continued)

Table A (continued), rows 24–37:

	C1	C2	C3	C4	C5	C6	C7	C8	C9	C10	C11	C12	C13	C14	C15	
24		85				89			92		78			100		24
25		87				92					81			104		25
26		90				94					83			108		26
27		92									86					27
28		95									89					28
29		97									91					29
30		100									94					30
31		102									97					31
32		105									100					32
33		108									102					33
34		110									105					34
35		113									108					35
36		115														36
37		118														37

B. Girls

	C1	C2	C3	C4	C5	C6	C7	C8	C9	C10	C11	C12	C13	C14	C15	
0	30	30	31	30	33	36	30	30	30	33	31	32	30	31	30	0
1	33	33	34	34	37	41	30	31	32	37	35	36	30	35	33	1
2	36	36	36	37	41	45	33	33	35	40	38	39	33	39	36	2
3	39	38	39	39	43	48	36	35	38	43	40	41	35	42	38	3
4	41	40	41	42	46	50	38	37	40	45	43	43	37	45	40	4
5	43	42	43	44	48	53	40	38	43	47	45	45	39	47	42	5
6	44	43	44	45	50	55	42	40	45	50	48	47	40	50	43	6
7	45	45	46	47	53	58	44	41	47	52	52	49	42	53	45	7
8	47	48	48	49	55	62	46	42	49	55	56	51	43	56	46	8
9	48	51	49	50	59	65	49	43	51	58	61	53	44	59	48	9
10	50	54	51	52	62	69	52	44	53	62	66	55	45	63	50	10
11	52	59	52	53	66	73	57	45	56	65	72	58	46	67	52	11
12	54	64	54	55	69	76	62	46	59	69	77	60	48	71	54	12
13	57	70	56	56	73	80	67	48	63	73	82	63	49	75	57	13

(continued)

Table B.2 Continued

Content Scales

B. Girls (continued)

Raw	A-anx	A-obs	A-dep	A-bea	A-aln	A-biz	A-ang	A-cyn	A-con	A-lse	A-las	A-sod	A-fam	A-scb	A-trt	Raw
14	61	75	58	58	77	84	72	50	66	77	87	66	50	79	60	14
15	65	81	61	60	80	87	77	53	70	81	93	69	52	83	64	15
16	69		63	62	84	91	83	56	74	84	98	72	54	87	67	16
17	73		66	64	87	95	88	60	77	88		75	56	90	71	17
18	77		68	66	91	98		64	81	92		78	58	94	75	18
19	81		71	68	94	102		68	85			81	61	98	78	19
20	85		73	70	98			72	88			84	64	102	82	20
21	89		76	72				77	92			86	67		85	21
22			78	74				81	96			89	70		89	22
23			81	76					99			92	73		93	23
24			83	78								95	75		96	24
25			86	80									78		100	25
26			88	82									81		104	26
27				84									84			27
28				86									87			28
29				88									90			29
30				90									92			30
31				92									95			31
32				95									98			32
33				97									101			33
34				99									104			34
35				101									107			35
36				103												36
37				105												37

Table B.3 Linear T-Score Conversions for Supplementary Scales (boys and girls)

Supplementary Scales

	Boys						Raw	Girls						
Raw	MAC-R	ACK	PRO	IMM	A	R		MAC-R	ACK	PRO	IMM	A	R	Raw
0	30	34	30	30	30	30	0	30	35	30	31	30	30	0
1	30	38	30	30	31	30	1	30	39	30	33	30	30	1
2	30	42	30	32	32	30	2	30	43	30	35	31	30	2
3	30	46	30	33	34	30	3	30	47	30	36	32	30	3
4	30	50	30	35	35	30	4	30	51	30	38	33	30	4
5	30	54	30	37	37	31	5	30	56	30	39	34	30	5
6	30	59	30	38	38	33	6	30	60	30	41	36	30	6
7	30	63	30	40	39	35	7	30	64	30	42	37	32	7
8	30	67	31	41	41	38	8	30	68	30	44	38	35	8
9	30	71	33	43	42	40	9	30	72	31	46	40	38	9
10	30	75	35	44	44	42	10	30	77	34	47	41	40	10
11	30	79	37	46	45	44	11	30	81	36	49	42	43	11
12	30	83	40	48	46	47	12	31	85	39	50	44	46	12
13	32	87	42	49	48	49	13	34	89	41	52	45	49	13
14	34		44	51	49	51	14	36		43	54	46	52	14
15	36		46	52	51	54	15	39		46	55	48	55	15
16	39		49	54	52	56	16	41		48	57	49	58	16
17	41		51	56	53	58	17	43		51	58	50	60	17
18	43		53	57	55	60	18	46		53	60	51	63	18
19	45		56	59	56	63	19	48		55	61	53	66	19
20	48		58	60	58	65	20	51		58	63	54	69	20
21	50		60	62	59	67	21	53		60	65	55	72	21
22	52		62	64	60	70	22	55		63	66	57	75	22
23	54		65	65	62	72	23	58		65	68	58	78	23

(continued)

Table B.3 Continued

Supplementary Scales

	Boys							Girls						
Raw	MAC-R	ACK	PRO	IMM	A	R	Raw	MAC-R	ACK	PRO	IMM	A	R	Raw
24	57		67	67	63	74	24	60		67	69	59	80	24
25	59		69	68	65	76	25	63		70	71	61	83	25
26	61		71	70	66	79	26	65		72	73	62	86	26
27	63		74	72	67	81	27	68		75	74	63	89	27
28	66		76	73	69	83	28	70		77	76	64	92	28
29	68		78	75	70	86	29	72		79	77	66	95	29
30	70		80	76	71	88	30	75		82	79	67	98	30
31	72		83	78	73	90	31	77		84	81	68	100	31
32	75		85	79	74	92	32	80		87	82	70	103	32
33	77		87	81	76	95	33	82		89	84	71	106	33
34	79		89	83	77		34	84		91	85	72		34
35	81		92	84	78		35	87		94	87	74		35
36	84		94	86			36	89		96	88			36
37	86			87			37	92			90			37
38	88			89			38	94			92			38
39	90			91			39	97			93			39
40	93			92			40	99			95			40
41	95			94			41	101			96			41
42	97			95			42	104			98			42
43	99			97			43	106			100			43
44	102						44	109						44
45	104						45	111						45
46	106						46	113						46
47	108						47	116						47
48	111						48	118						48
49	113						49	120						49

Table B.4 Linear T-Score Conversions for Harris-Lingoes and Si (Social Introversion) Subscales

Subscales D, Hy, and Pd

A. Boys

Raw	D_1	D_2	D_3	D_4	D_5	Hy_1	Hy_2	Hy_3	Hy_4	Hy_5	Pd_1	Pd_2	Pd_3	Pd_4	Pd_5	Raw
0	30	30	30	35	36	32	30	34	36	30	32	30	30	30	32	0
1	32	31	35	39	41	38	33	38	39	36	37	35	35	32	36	1
2	35	36	42	43	46	44	37	42	43	44	42	41	42	37	41	2
3	37	41	48	47	51	49	41	46	46	51	48	48	48	42	45	3
4	39	46	55	52	56	55	46	50	50	59	53	54	54	46	49	4
5	42	51	62	56	61	61	50	54	53	66	59	60	61	51	53	5
6	44	56	68	60	66	66	54	58	57	74	64	67	67	55	57	6
7	46	61	75	64	71		58	62	60	81	69	73		60	61	7
8	49	66	82	68	76		63	66	64		75	79		65	65	8
9	51	71	89	72	81		67	70	67		80			69	69	9
10	53	76	95	76	85		71	74	71					74	73	10
11	56	81	102	80			76	77	74					78	78	11
12	58	86		84			80	81	78					83	82	12
13	60	91		88				85	82							13
14	63	96		92				89	85							14
15	65			96				93	89							15
16	67								92							16
17	70								96							17
18	72															18
19	75															19

Table B.4 Continued

Subscales D, Hy, and Pd

A. Boys (continued)

Raw	D_1	D_2	D_3	D_4	D_5	Hy_1	Hy_2	Hy_3	Hy_4	Hy_5	Pd_1	Pd_2	Pd_3	Pd_4	Pd_5	Raw
20	77															20
21	79															21
22	82															22
23	84															23
24	86															24
25	89															25
26	91															26
27	93															27
28	96															28
29	98															29
30	100															30
31	103															31
32	105															32

B. Girls

Raw	D_1	D_2	D_3	D_4	D_5	Hy_1	Hy_2	Hy_3	Hy_4	Hy_5	Pd_1	Pd_2	Pd_3	Pd_4	Pd_5	Raw
0	30	30	30	35	33	31	30	33	34	30	30	31	30	30	31	0
1	31	30	33	39	37	37	34	37	37	35	35	38	36	31	35	1
2	33	35	39	43	42	43	38	40	40	43	40	45	43	35	39	2
3	35	40	46	47	46	48	42	44	44	51	45	52	49	39	43	3
4	37	46	52	50	51	54	46	47	47	58	51	59	55	44	47	4
5	40	51	58	54	56	60	50	51	50	66	56	65	61	48	51	5

Index	A	B	C	D	E	F	G	H	I	J	K	L	M	N	O
6	42	57	64	58	60	65	55	55	53	74	61	72	67	53	55
7	44	62	71	62	65		59	58	57	81	66	79		57	59
8	46	67	77	66	70		63	62	60		71	86		62	63
9	48	73	83	70	74		67	65	63		77			66	67
10	50	78	89	73	79		71	69	66					71	71
11	52	84	96	77			75	72	70					75	75
12	55	89		81			80	76	73					80	79
13	57	95		85				80	76						
14	59	100		89				83	79						
15	61			92				87	83						
16	63								86						
17	65								89						
18	68														
19	70														
20	72														
21	74														
22	76														
23	78														
24	80														
25	83														
26	85														
27	87														
28	89														
29	91														
30	93														
31	96														
32	98														

(continued)

Table B.4 Continued

Subscales Pa, Sc, Ma, and Si

C. Boys

Raw	Pa_1	Pa_2	Pa_3	Sc_1	Sc_2	Sc_3	Sc_4	Sc_5	Sc_6	Ma_1	Ma_2	Ma_3	Ma_4	Si_1	Si_2	Si_3	Raw
0	35	30	30	31	37	37	34	33	35	31	30	30	30	30	38	30	0
1	39	36	34	34	43	41	38	38	38	38	30	36	31	33	43	31	1
2	42	42	40	37	48	46	42	43	41	45	30	43	37	36	47	34	2
3	46	49	45	40	54	50	46	48	44	52	33	49	42	40	52	37	3
4	50	55	50	43	59	55	50	53	47	59	38	55	48	43	57	40	4
5	53	61	56	46	65	59	53	57	50	66	43	62	53	46	62	42	5
6	57	67	61	49	71	64	57	62	53	73	48	68	58	49	67	45	6
7	60	73	66	53	76	68	61	67	56		52	74	64	53	72	48	7
8	64	79	72	56	82	73	65	72	59		57	81	69	56	77	51	8
9	68	85	77	59	87	77	69	77	62		62		75	59		54	9
10	71			62	93	82	73	82	65		66			62		57	10
11	75			65	98		77	86	68		71			65		60	11
12	78			68			81		71					69		63	12
13	82			71			85		74					72		66	13
14	86			74			88		77					75		69	14
15	89			77					80							72	15
16	93			80					83							75	16
17	96			83					86							77	17
18				86					89								18
19				89					92								19
20				92					95								20
21				95													21

D. Girls

Raw																	Raw
0	35	30	31	30	37	36	34	31	34	32	30	31	30	31	40	30	0
1	39	36	36	33	43	41	38	35	37	39	30	37	30	34	45	30	1
2	42	41	41	36	48	45	41	40	40	47	30	44	35	37	51	33	2
3	46	46	46	39	54	50	45	44	43	55	30	50	41	40	56	36	3
4	50	51	51	42	59	54	49	49	46	63	34	57	47	43	61	39	4
5	53	57	56	46	65	58	52	54	49	70	39	64	52	46	67	41	5
6	57	62	61	49	70	63	56	58	52	78	44	70	58	49	72	44	6
7	61	67	66	52	76	67	60	63	54		49	77	64	52	78	47	7
8	64	73	72	55	81	71	63	68	57		54	83	70	55	83	49	8
9	68	78	77	58	87	76	67	72	60		59		75	58		52	9
10	72			61	93	80	71	77	63		65			62		55	10
11	76			64	98		75	82	66		70			65		58	11
12	79			67			78		69					68		60	12
13	83			70			82		72					71		63	13
14	87			73			86		75					74		66	14
15	90			76					78							68	15
16	94			79					81							71	16
17	98			83					83							74	17
18				86					86								18
19				89					89								19
20				92					92								20
21				95													21

References

Achenbach, T. M., & Edelbrock, C. (1983). *Manual for the Child Behavior Checklist and Revised Child Behavior Profile*. Burlington, VT: University of Vermont.

Alperin, J. J., Archer, R. P., & Coates, G. D. (1996). Development and effects of an MMPI-A K-correction procedure. *Journal of Personality Assessment, 67,* 155–168.

American Psychological Association (1986). Committee on psychological tests and assessment (CPTA). *Guidelines for computer-based tests and interpretation*. Washington, DC: Author.

Andrucci, G. L., Archer, R. P., Pancoast, D. L., & Gordon, R. A. (1989). The relationship of MMPI and sensation seeking scales to adolescent drug use. *Journal of Personality Assessment, 53,* 253–266.

Arbisi, P. A., & Ben-Porath, Y. S. (1995). An MMPI-2 infrequent response scale for use with psychopathological populations: The Infrequency-Psychopathology scale, F(p). *Psychological Assessment, 7,* 424–431.

Archer, R. P. (1984). Use of the MMPI with adolescents: A review of salient issues. *Clinical Psychology Review, 4,* 241–251.

Archer, R. P. (1987). *Using the MMPI with adolescents*. Hillsdale, NJ: Lawrence Erlbaum Associates.

Archer, R. P. (1992). *MMPI-A: Assessing adolescent psychopathology*. Hillsdale, NJ: Lawrence Erlbaum Associates.

Archer, R. P. (1997). *MMPI-A: Assessing adolescent psychopathology* (2nd ed.). Mahwah, NJ: Lawrence Erlbaum Associates.

Archer, R. P., Belevich, J. K. S., & Elkins, D. E. (1994). Item-level and scale-level factor structures of the MMPI-A. *Journal of Personality Assessment, 62,* 332–345.

Archer, R. P., & Elkins, D. E. (1999). Identification of random responding on the MMPI-A. *Journal of Personality Assessment, 73,* 407–421.

Archer, R. P., & Gordon, R. A. (1991 August). Use of content scales with adolescents: Past and future practices. In R. C. Colligan (Chair), *MMPI and MMPI-2 supplementary scales and profile interpretation–content scales revisited*. Symposium conducted at the annual convention of the American Psychological Association, San Francisco, CA.

Archer, R. P., & Gordon, R. A. (1994). Psychometric stability of MMPI-A item modifications. *Journal of Personality Assessment, 62,* 416–426.

Archer, R. P., Gordon, R. A., Anderson, G. L., & Giannetti, R. (1989). MMPI special scale clinical correlates for adolescent inpatients. *Journal of Personality Assessment, 53,* 654–664.

Archer, R. P., Gordon, R. A., Giannetti, R., & Singles, J. (1988). MMPI scale clinical correlates for adolescent inpatients. *Journal of Personality Assessment, 52,* 707–721.

Archer, R. P., & Klinefelter, D. (1992). Relationships between MMPI codetypes and MAC scale elevations in adolescent psychiatric samples. *Journal of Personality Assessment, 58,* 149–159.

Archer, R. P., & Krishnamurthy, R. (1993). Combining the Rorschach and MMPI in the assessment of adolescents. *Journal of Personality Assessment, 60,* 132–140.

Archer, R. P., & Krishnamurthy, R. (1994). A structural summary approach for the MMPI-A: Development and empirical correlates. *Journal of Personality Assessment, 63,* 554–573.

Archer, R. P., & Krishnamurthy, R. (1996). The Minnesota Multiphasic Personality Inventory–Adolescent (MMPI-A). In C. S. Newmark (Ed.), *Major psychological assessment instruments* (2nd ed., pp. 59–107). Boston: Allyn & Bacon.

Archer, R. P., & Krishnamurthy, R. (1997a). MMPI-A and Rorschach indices related to depression and conduct disorder: An evaluation of the incremental validity hypothesis. *Journal of Personality Assessment, 69,* 517–533.

Archer, R. P., & Krishnamurthy, R. (1997b). MMPI-A scale-level factor structure: Replication in a clinical sample. *Assessment, 4,* 337–349.

Archer, R. P., Krishnamurthy, R., & Jacobson, J. M. (1994). *MMPI-A casebook.* Tampa, FL: Psychological Assessment Resources.

Archer, R. P., Maruish, M., Imhof, E. A., & Piotrowski, C. (1991). Psychological test usage with adolescent clients: 1990 survey findings. *Professional Psychology: Research and Practice, 22,* 247–252.

Archer, R. P., & Newsom, C. R. (2000). Psychological test usage with adolescent clients: Survey update. *Assessment, 7,* 227–235.

Archer, R. P., & Slesinger, D. (1999). MMPI-A patterns related to the endorsement of suicidal ideation. *Assessment, 6,* 51–59.

Archer, R. P., Tirrell, C. A., & Elkins, D. E. (2001). An evaluation of an MMPI-A short form: Implications for adaptive testing. *Journal of Personality Assessment, 76,* 76–89.

Archer, R. P., White, J. L., & Orvin, G. H. (1979). MMPI characteristics and correlates among adolescent psychiatric inpatients. *Journal of Clinical Psychology, 35,* 498–504.

Arita, A. A., & Baer, R. A. (1998). Validity of selected MMPI-A content scales. *Psychological Assessment, 10,* 59–63.

Baer, R. A., Ballenger, J., Berry, D. T. R., & Wetter, M. W. (1997). Detection of random responding on the MMPI-A. *Journal of Personality Assessment, 68,* 139–151.

Baer, R. A., Ballenger, J., & Kroll, L. S. (1998). Detection of underreporting on the MMPI-A in clinical and community samples. *Journal of Personality Assessment, 71,* 98–113.

Baer, R. A., Kroll, L. S., Rinaldo, J., & Ballenger, J. (1999). Detecting and discriminating between random responding and overreporting on the MMPI-A. *Journal of Personality Assessment, 72,* 308–320.

Bagby, R. M., Nicholson, R. A., Buis, T., Radovanovic, H., & Fidler, B. J. (1999). Defensive responding on the MMPI-2 in family custody and access evaluations. *Psychological Assessment, 11,* 24–28.

Ball, J. C. (1960). Comparison of MMPI profile differences among Negro-white adolescents. *Journal of Clinical Psychology, 16,* 304–307.

Belkin, D. S., Greene, A. F., Rodrigue, J. R., & Boggs, S. R. (1994). Psychopathology and history of sexual abuse. *Journal of Interpersonal Violence, 9,* 535–547.

Ben-Porath, Y. S., Graham, J. R., Hall, G. C. N., Hirschman, R. D., & Zaragoza, M. S. (Eds.). (1995). *Forensic applications of the MMPI-2.* Thousand Oaks, CA: Sage Publications.

Ben-Porath, Y. S., Hostetler, K., Butcher, J. N., & Graham, J. R. (1989). New subscales for the MMPI-2 Social Introversion (Si) scale. *Psychological Assessment: A Journal of Consulting and Clinical Psychology, 1,* 169–174.

Butcher, J. N. (Ed.). (1987). *Computerized psychological assessment: A practitioner's guide.* New York: Basic Books.

Butcher, J. N. (Ed.). (1996). *International adaptations of the MMPI-2: A handbook of research and clinical applications.* Minneapolis: University of Minnesota Press.

Butcher, J. N., Dahlstrom, W. G., Graham, J. R., Tellegen, A., & Kaemmer, B. (1989). *Minnesota Multiphasic Personality Inventory–2 (MMPI-2): Manual for administration and scoring.* Minneapolis: University of Minnesota Press.

Butcher, J. N., & Owen, P. L. (1978). Objective personality inventories: Recent research and some contemporary issues. In B. B. Wolman (Ed.), *Clinical diagnosis of mental disorders: A handbook* (pp. 475–545). New York: Plenum.

Butcher, J. N., & Williams, C. L. (2000). *Essentials of the MMPI-2 and MMPI-A interpretation* (2nd edition). Minneapolis: University of Minnesota Press.

Butcher, J. N., Williams, C. L., Graham, J. R., Archer, R. P., Tellegen, A., Ben-Porath, Y. S., & Kaemmer, B. (1992). *MMPI-A (Minnesota Multiphasic Personality Inventory–Adolescent): Manual for administration, scoring, and interpretation.* Minneapolis: University of Minnesota Press.

Capwell, D. F. (1945). Personality patterns of adolescent girls: II. Delinquents and nondelinquents. *Journal of Applied Psychology, 29,* 284–297.

Claiborn, C. H. (1995). Review of the Minnesota Multiphasic Personality Inventory–Adolescent. In J. C. Conoley & J. C. Impara (Eds.), *The twelfth mental measurement yearbook* (pp. 626–628). Lincoln, NE: Buros Institute of Mental Measurements.

Cronbach, L. (1951). Coefficient alpha and the internal structure of tests. *Psychometrika, 16,* 297–334.

Cumella, E. J., Wall, A. D., & Kerr-Almeida, N. (1999). MMPI-A in the inpatient assessment of adolescents with eating disorders. *Journal of Personality Assessment, 73,* 31–44.

Cumella, E. J., Wall, A. D., & Kerr-Almeida, N. (2000). MMPI-2 in the inpatient assessment of women with eating disorders. *Journal of Personality Assessment, 75,* 387–403.

Dacey, C. M., Nelson, W. M., & Aikman, K. G. (1990). Prevalency rate and personality comparisons of bulimic and normal adolescents. *Child Psychiatry and Human Development, 20,* 243–251.

Dahlstrom, W. G., Archer, R. P., Hopkins, D. G., Jackson, E., & Dahlstrom, L. E. (1994). *Assessing the readability of the Minnesota Multiphasic Personality Inventory Instruments: The MMPI, MMPI-2, MMPI-A* (MMPI-2/MMPI-A Test Rep. No. 2). Minneapolis: University of Minnesota Press.

Dahlstrom, W. G., Lachar, D., & Dahlstrom, L. E. (1986). *MMPI patterns of American minorities.* Minneapolis: University of Minnesota Press.

Dancyger, I. F., Sunday, S. R., Eckert, E. D., & Halmi, K. A. (1997). A comparative analysis of Minnesota Multiphasic Personality Inventory profiles of anorexia nervosa at hospital admission, discharge, and 10-year follow up. *Comprehensive Psychiatry, 38,* 185–191.

Drake, L. E. (1946). A social I-E scale for the MMPI. *Journal of Applied Psychology, 30,* 51–54.

Ehrenworth, N. V., & Archer, R. P. (1985). A comparison of clinical accuracy ratings of interpretive approaches for adolescent MMPI responses. *Journal of Personality Assessment, 49,* 413–421.

Elhai, J. D., Frueh, B. C., Gold, P. B., Gold, S. N., & Hamner, M. B. (2000). Clinical presentations of posttraumatic stress disorder across trauma populations: A comparison of MMPI-2 profiles of combat veterans and adult survivors of child sexual abuse. *Journal of Nervous and Mental Disease, 188,* 708–713.

Engels, M. L., Moisan, D., & Harris, R. (1994). MMPI indices of childhood trauma among 110 female outpatients. *Journal of Personality Assessment, 63,* 135–147.

Finn, S. E. (1996). *Manual for using the MMPI-2 as a therapeutic intervention.* Minneapolis: University of Minnesota Press.

Follette, W. C., Naugle, A. E., & Follette, V. M. (1997). MMPI-2 profiles of adult women with child sexual abuse histories: Cluster-analytic findings. *Journal of Consulting and Clinical Psychology, 65,* 858–866.

Fontaine, J. L., Archer, R. P., Elkins, D. E., & Johansen, J. (2001). The effects of MMPI-A T-score elevation on classification accuracy for normal and adolescent samples. *Journal of Personality Assessment, 76,* 264–281.

Forbey, J. D., & Ben-Porath, Y. S. (2000). A comparison of sexually abused and non-sexually abused adolescents in a clinical treatment facility using the MMPI-A. *Child Abuse & Neglect, 24,* 557–568.

Gallucci, N. T. (1997a). Correlates of MMPI-A substance abuse scales. *Assessment, 4,* 87–94.

Gallucci, N. T. (1997b). On the identification of patterns of substance abuse with the MMPI-A. *Psychological Assessment, 3,* 224–232.

Gantner, A., Graham, J., & Archer, R. P. (1992). Usefulness of the MAC scale in differentiating adolescents in normal, psychiatric, and substance abuse settings. *Psychological Assessment, 4,* 133–137.

Gilberstadt, H., & Duker, J. (1965). *A handbook for clinical and actuarial MMPI interpretation.* Philadelphia: W. B. Saunders.

Gomez, F. C., Jr., Johnson, R., Davis, Q., & Velasquez, R. J. (2000). MMPI-A performance of African- and Mexican-American adolescent first-time offenders. *Psychological Reports, 87,* 309–314.

Gottesman, I. I., & Hanson, D. R. (1990, August). Can the MMPI at age 15 predict schizophrenics-to-be? In R. C. Colligan (Chair), *The MMPI and adolescents: Historical perspective, current research, future developments.* Symposium conducted at the annual convention of the American Psychological Association, Boston, MA.

Gottesman, I. I., & Prescott, C. A. (1989). Abuses of the MacAndrew Alcoholism scale: A critical review. *Clinical Psychology Review, 9,* 223–242.

Graham, J. R. (2000). *MMPI-2: Assessing personality and psychopathology* (3rd ed.). New York: Oxford University Press.

Greene, R. L. (2000). *The MMPI-2: An interpretive manual* (2nd ed.). Boston: Allyn & Bacon.

Griffith, P. L., Myers, R. W., Cusick, G. M., & Tankersley, M. J. (1997). MMPI-2 profiles of women differing in sexual abuse history and sexual orientation. *Journal of Clinical Psychology, 53,* 791–800.

Griffith, P. L., Myers, R. W., & Tankersley, M. J. (1996). MMPI-2 items which correctly identified women with histories of childhood sexual abuse. *Psychological Reports, 78,* 717–722.

Gumbiner, J. (1998). MMPI-A profiles of Hispanic adolescents. *Psychological Reports, 82,* 659–672.

Gynther, M. D. (1972). White norms and black MMPIs: A prescription for discrimination? *Psychological Bulletin, 78,* 386–402.

Hanson, D. R., Gottesman, I. I., & Heston, L. L. (1990). Long-range schizophrenia forecasting: Many a slip twixt cup and lip. In J. E. Rolf, A. Masten, D. Cicchetti, K. Neuchterlein, & S. Weintraub (Eds.), *Risk and protective factors in the development of psychopathology* (pp. 424–444). New York: Cambridge University Press.

Harris, R. E., & Lingoes, J. C. (1955). *Subscales for the MMPI: An aid to profile interpretation.* Department of Psychiatry, University of California School of Medicine and the Langley Porter Clinic. Mimeographed materials.

Hathaway, S. R. (1947). A coding system for MMPI profiles. *Journal of Consulting Psychology, 11,* 334–337.

Hathaway, S. R. (1965). Personality inventories. In B. B. Wolman (Ed.), *Handbook of clinical psychology* (pp. 451–476). New York: McGraw-Hill.

Hathaway, S. R., & McKinley, J. C. (1943). *The Minnesota Multiphasic Personality Inventory* (rev. ed.). Minneapolis: University of Minnesota Press.

Hathaway, S. R., & Monachesi, E. D. (1952). The Minnesota Multiphasic Personality Inventory in the study of juvenile delinquents. *American Sociological Review, 17,* 704–710.

Hathaway, S. R., & Monachesi, E. D. (1953). *Analyzing and predicting juvenile delinquency with the MMPI.* Minneapolis: University of Minnesota Press.

Hathaway, S. R., & Monachesi, E. D. (1957). The personalities of predelinquent boys. *Journal of Criminal Law and Criminology, 48,* 149–163.

Hathaway, S. R., & Monachesi, E. D. (1963). *Adolescent personality and behavior: MMPI patterns of normal, delinquent, dropout, and other outcomes.* Minneapolis: University of Minnesota Press.

Hicks, M. M., Rogers, R., & Cashel, M. (2000). Predictions of violent and total infractions among institutionalized male juvenile offenders. *The Journal of the American Academy of Psychiatry and the Law, 28,* 183–190.

Hillary, B. E., & Schare, M. L. (1993). Sexually and physically abused adolescents: An empirical search for PTSD. *Journal of Clinical Psychology, 49,* 161–165.

Janus, M-D., Tolbert, H., Calestro, K., & Toepfer, S. (1996). Clinical accuracy ratings of MMPI approaches for adolescents: Adding ten years and the MMPI-A. *Journal of Personality Assessment, 67,* 364–383.

Knisely, J. S., Barker, S. B., Ingersoll, K. S., & Dawson, K. S. (2000). Psychopathology in substance abusing women reporting childhood sexual abuse. *Journal of Addictive Diseases, 19,* 31–44.

Komro, K. A., Williams, C. L., Forster, J. L., Perry, C. L., Farbakhsh, K., & Stigler, M. H. (1999). The relationship between adolescent alcohol use and delinquent and violent behaviors. *Journal of Child and Adolescent Substance Abuse, 9,* 13–28.

Korbanka, J. E. (1997). An MMPI-2 scale to identify history of sexual abuse. *Psychological Reports, 81,* 979–990.

Krishnamurthy, R., & Archer, R. P. (1999). A comparison of two interpretive approaches for the MMPI-A structural summary. *Journal of Personality Assessment, 73,* 245–259.

Krishnamurthy, R., Archer, R. P., & House, J. J. (1996). The MMPI-A and Rorschach: A failure to establish convergent validity. *Assessment, 3,* 179–191.

Lachar, D., & Gruber, C. P. (1995). *Personality Inventory for Youth (PIY) manual: Administration and interpretation guide.* Los Angeles: Western Psychological Services.

Lanyon, R. I. (1995). Review of the Minnesota Multiphasic Personality Inventory–Adolescent. In J. C. Conoley & J. C. Impara (Eds.), *The twelfth mental measurement yearbook* (pp. 628–629). Lincoln, NE: Buros Institute of Mental Measurements.

Lees-Haley, P. (1991). MMPI-2 F and F-K scores of personal injury malingerers in vocational neuropsychological and emotional distress claims. *American Journal of Forensic Psychology, 9,* 5–14.

Loevinger, J. (1976). *Ego development: Conceptions and theories.* San Francisco: Jossey-Bass.

Losada-Paisey, G. (1998). Use of the MMPI-A to assess personality of juvenile male delinquents who are sex offenders and nonsex offenders. *Psychological Reports, 83,* 115–122.

MacAndrew, C. (1965). The differentiation of male alcoholic out-patients from nonalcoholic psychiatric patients by means of the MMPI. *Quarterly Journal of Studies on Alcohol, 26,* 238–246.

Marks, P. A., & Briggs, P. F. (1972). Adolescent norm tables for the MMPI. In W. G. Dahlstrom, G. S. Welsh, & L. E. Dahlstrom, *An MMPI handbook: Vol. 1. Clinical interpretation* (rev. ed., pp. 388–399). Minneapolis: University of Minnesota Press.

Marks, P. A., Seeman, W., & Haller, D. L. (1974). *The actuarial use of the MMPI with adolescents and adults.* Baltimore: Williams & Wilkins.

Massey, R. F., Walfish, S., & Krone, A. (1992). Cluster analysis of MMPI profiles of adolescents in treatment for substance abuse. *Journal of Adolescent Chemical Dependency, 2,* 23–33.

McCarthy, L., & Archer, R. P. (1998). Factor structure of the MMPI-A content scales: Item-level and scale-level findings. *Journal of Personality Assessment, 71,* 84–97.

McGrath, R. E., Pogge, D. L., Stein, L. A. R., Graham, J. R., Zaccario, M., & Piacentini, T. (2000). Development of an Infrequency-Psychopathology scale for the MMPI-A: The Fp-A scale. *Journal of Personality Assessment, 74,* 282–295.

Millon, T. (1993). *Millon Adolescent Clinical Inventory manual.* Minneapolis: National Computer Systems.

Moore, J. M., Thompson-Pope, S. K., & Whited, R. M. (1996). MMPI-A profiles of adolescent boys with a history of firesetting. *Journal of Personality Assessment, 67,* 116–126.

Morey, L. C. (2000, March). *PAI-Adolescent Version: Overview of progress to date.* Unpublished report.

Nichols, D. S. (2001). *Essentials of MMPI-2 assessment.* New York: Wiley.

Pena, L. M., Megargee, E. I., & Brody, E. (1996). MMPI-A patterns of male juvenile delinquents. *Psychological Assessment, 8,* 388–397.

Pryor, T., & Wiederman, M. W. (1996). Use of the MMPI-2 in the outpatient assessment of women with anorexia nervosa or bulimia nervosa. *Journal of Personality Assessment, 66,* 363–373.

Reynolds, W. M. (1998). *Adolescent Psychopathology Scale: Administration and interpretation manual.* Odessa, FL: Psychological Assessment Resources.

Roland, B. C., Zelhart, P. F., Cochran, S. W., & Funderburk, V. W. (1985). MMPI correlates of clinical women who report early sexual abuse. *Journal of Clinical Psychology, 41,* 763–766.

Schinka, J. A., Elkins, D. E., & Archer, R. P. (1998). Effects of psychopathology and demographic characteristics on MMPI-A scale scores. *Journal of Personality Assessment, 71,* 295–305.

Schork, E. J., Eckert, E. D., & Halmi, K. A. (1994). The relationship between psychopathology, eating disorder diagnosis, and clinical outcome at 10-year follow-up in anorexia nervosa. *Comprehensive Psychiatry, 35,* 113–123.

Scott, R., & Stone, D. (1986). MMPI measures of psychological disturbance in adolescent and adult victims of father-daughter incest. *Journal of Clinical Psychology, 42,* 251–259.

Shaevel, B., & Archer, R. P. (1996). Effects of MMPI-2 and MMPI-A norms on T-score elevations for 18-year-olds. *Journal of Personality Assessment, 67,* 72–78.

Sherwood, N. E., Ben-Porath, Y. S., & Williams, C. L. (1997). *The MMPI-A content component scales: Development, psychometric characteristics, and clinical application.* Minneapolis: University of Minnesota Press.

Stein, L. A., McClinton, B. K., & Graham, J. R. (1998). Long-term stability of MMPI-A scales. *Journal of Personality Assessment, 70,* 103–108.

Sunday, S. R., Reeman, I. M., Eckert, E., & Halmi, K. A. (1996). Ten-year outcome in adolescent onset anorexia nervosa. *Journal of Youth and Adolescence, 25,* 533–544.

Timbrook, R. E., & Graham, J. R. (1994). Ethnic differences on the MMPI-2? *Psychological Assessment, 6,* 212–217.

Toyer, E. A., & Weed, N. C. (1998). Concurrent validity of the MMPI-A in a counseling program for juvenile offenders. *Journal of Clinical Psychology, 54,* 395–399.

U.S. Bureau of the Census. (1983). *Characteristics of the population: Number of inhabitants, United States summary. 1980 census of population.* Washington, DC: U.S. Government Printing Office.

Walfish, S., Massey, R., & Krone, A. (1990). MMPI profiles of adolescent substance abusers in treatment. *Adolescence, 25,* 567–572.

Weed, N. C., Butcher, J. N., & Williams, C. L. (1994). Development of the MMPI-A alcohol/drug problem scales. *Journal of Studies on Alcohol, 55,* 296–302.

Welsh, G. S. (1948). An extension of Hathaway's MMPI profile coding system. *Journal of Consulting Psychology, 12,* 343–344.

Welsh, G. S. (1956). Factor dimensions A and R. In G. S. Welsh & W. G. Dahlstrom (Eds.), *Basic reading on the MMPI in psychology and medicine* (pp. 264–281). Minneapolis: University of Minnesota Press.

Williams, C. L., & Butcher, J. N. (1989a). An MMPI study of adolescents: I. Empirical validity of standard scales. *Psychological Assessment: A Journal of Consulting and Clinical Psychology, 1,* 251–259.

Williams, C. L., & Butcher, J. N. (1989b). An MMPI study of adolescents: II. Verification and limitations of code type classifications. *Psychological Assessment: A Journal of Consulting and Clinical Psychology, 1,* 260–265.

Williams, C. L., Butcher, J. N., Ben-Porath, Y. S., & Graham, J. R. (1992). *MMPI-A content scales: Assessing psychopathology in adolescents.* Minneapolis: University of Minnesota Press.

Wrobel, N. H., & Lachar, D. (1995). Racial differences in adolescent self-report: A comparative validity study using homogeneous MMPI content measures. *Psychological Assessment, 7,* 140–147.

Annotated Bibliography

HISTORICAL SOURCES

Archer, R. P. (1987). *Using the MMPI with adolescents.* Hillsdale, NJ: Lawrence Erlbaum Associates.

This was the first textbook entirely devoted to an overview of the use of the MMPI with adolescent respondents. This text provided a comprehensive review of the literature through the mid-1980s, recommendations regarding the use of the original MMPI with adolescents, and several adolescent norm sets for the original form of the MMPI, including those of Marks and Briggs, Gottesman and his colleagues, and Colligan and his associates at the Mayo Clinic.

Hathaway, S. R., & Monachesi, E. D. (1963). *Adolescent personality and behavior: MMPI patterns of normal, delinquent, dropout, and other outcomes.* Minneapolis: University of Minnesota Press.

During the late 1940s and the 1950s Hathaway and Monachesi administered the MMPI to approximately 15,000 Minnesota ninth-graders, and readministered the test to nearly 4,000 of these adolescents during their senior year in high school. The massive data set proved valuable in establishing that the MMPI could predict delinquency, and also provided a body of crucial information concerning test-retest characteristics of the item pool, gender differences, and correlates of high and low scores for each of the 10 basic clinical scales.

Marks, P. A., Seeman, W., & Haller, D. L. (1974). *The actuarial use of the MMPI with adolescents and adults.* Baltimore: Williams & Wilkins.

This text contains actuarially based personality descriptors for a series of 29 MMPI high-point codetypes derived for adolescents in treatment settings. The Marks et al. clinical correlate study was crucial in providing clinicians with the first comprehensive correlate information necessary to interpret adolescent's codetype patterns, and has remained the definitive source for this material for the past quarter century.

Pancoast, D. L., & Archer, R. P. (1988). MMPI adolescent norms: Patterns and trends across four decades. *Journal of Personality Assessment, 52,* 691–706.

This study focused on the relative accuracy of the widely used adolescent norm set by Marks and Briggs in describing eight samples of normal adolescents collected from 1949 to 1964 (N = 17,286), and four studies (N = 1,758) of normal adolescents gathered between 1975 and 1987. The authors noted that normative changes appear to have occurred at some point in the late 1960s or early 1970s, underscoring the need for the collection of a contemporary adolescent normative sample.

PRIMARY SOURCES ON THE MMPI-A

Archer, R. P. (1997). *MMPI-A: Assessing adolescent psychopathology* (2nd ed.). Mahwah, NJ: Lawrence Erlbaum Associates.

This book focuses on giving clinicians practical information regarding the use of the MMPI-A, while also providing a comprehensive and contemporary review of the research literature on this instrument. The text includes a summary of the MMPI-A Structural Summary and illustrates interpretation principles through several clinical case examples.

Butcher, J. N., & Williams, C. L. (2000). *Essentials of MMPI-2 and MMPI-A interpretation* (2nd ed.). Minneapolis: University of Minnesota Press.

This text provides extensive information on interpretive strategies for both the MMPI-A and MMPI-2, including details on the rationale for the development of both instruments.

Butcher, J. N., Williams, C. L., Graham, J. R., Archer, R. P., Tellegen, A., Ben-Porath, Y. S., & Kaemmer, B. (1992). *MMPI-A (Minnesota Multiphasic Personality Inventory–Adolescent): Manual for administration, scoring, and interpretation.* Minneapolis: University of Minnesota Press.

This test manual should be in the library of all psychologists who use the MMPI-A. It provides extensive information on the reliability and validity of the MMPI-A and concise recommendations for the clinical use of this instrument. Appendices provide comprehensive scale membership and normative information, and correlates are provided for MMPI-A basic scales based on normative and clinical adolescent samples.

Dahlstrom, W. G., Archer, R. P., Hopkins, D. G., Jackson, E., & Dahlstrom, L. E. (1994). *Assessing the readability of the Minnesota Multiphasic Personality Inventory Instruments–the MMPI, MMPI-2, MMPI-A.* Minneapolis: University of Minnesota Press.

This monograph presents comprehensive information on the reading requirements of all MMPI forms and reports that the average difficulty level across forms was approximately the sixth grade. The authors noted that the most difficult items appeared on scale 9, and that approximately 6% of the MMPI-A items required at least a 10th-grade reading level.

Williams, C. L., Butcher, J. N., Ben-Porath, Y. S., & Graham, J. R. (1992). *MMPI-A content scales: Assessing psychopathology in adolescents.* Minneapolis: University of Minnesota Press.

This text is a comprehensive review of the development and use of the MMPI-A content scales by the individuals identified with the creation of this set of scales.

RESOURCES ON THE MMPI-A STRUCTURAL SUMMARY

Archer, R. P., Belevich, J. K. S., & Elkins, D. E. (1994). Item-level and scale-level factor structures of the MMPI-A. *Journal of Personality Assessment, 62,* 332–345.

This article presents information on the eight scale-level factors found for the MMPI-A in the norma-tive sample of 1,620 adolescents, and provides the basic foundation for the subsequent development of the MMPI-A Structural Summary.

Archer, R. P., & Krishnamurthy, R. (1994). A structural summary approach for the MMPI-A: Development and empirical correlates. *Journal of Personality Assessment, 63,* 554–573.

This article provides a description of each of the eight dimensions in the MMPI-A Structural Sum-mary and describes correlates related to each dimension in normal and clinical samples.

Archer, R. P., & Krishnamurthy, R. (1997). MMPI-A scale-level factor structure: Replica-tion in a clinical sample. *Assessment, 4,* 337–349.

The MMPI-A Structural Summary was based on a factor structure identified in an investigation of the MMPI-A normative sample. This study establishes the generalizability of the factor structure to a sample of 358 adolescents in clinical treatment settings.

Archer, R. P., Krishnamurthy, R., & Jacobson, J. M. (1994). *MMPI-A Casebook.* Tampa, FL: Psychological Assessment Resources.

This book provides a brief overview of the development of the MMPI-A and a series of 16 clinical case examples illustrating various principles of MMPI-A interpretation. Each of the clinical case ex-amples also includes an illustration of the MMPI-A Structural Summary approach, and Appendix C provides a comprehensive listing of the clinical correlates of each of the factor dimensions in the MMPI-A normative sample and for a sample of adolescents in a clinical treatment setting.

Krishnamurthy, R., & Archer, R. P. (1999). Empirically based interpretative approaches for the MMPI-A structural summary. *Journal of Personality Assessment, 73,* 245–259.

This study explored two methods of interpreting data on the MMPI-A Structural Summary. These methods were tallying a simple majority of scales and subscales within a specific factor with T-score el-evations at a critical level versus calculating the mean T scores generated by all the scales and sub-scales for each factor. This study established the comparability of these two approaches, permitting re-liance on the easier-to-use method of simply tallying the total number of scales and subscales to reach critical value. This study also provides information on two-factor co-elevation patterns as found in this clinical sample of adolescents.

CURRENT AND FUTURE DIRECTIONS

Archer, R. P. (1997). Future directions for the MMPI-A: Research and clinical issues. *Jour-nal of Personality Assessment, 68,* 95–109.

This article offers six suggestions concerning areas of productive research with the MMPI-A. These areas include studies of the utility of codetype interpretation, issues related to profile elevation, and the identification of criteria for evaluating the usefulness of traditional and new MMPI-A scales. Further, the remaining research areas involve establishing the optimal age ranges for use of the MMPI-A, detecting the effects of the revised instrument on clinician's test-use patterns with adolescents, and evaluating the optimal methods of using the MMPI-A Structural Summary approach.

Archer, R. P., Handel, R. W., & Lynch, K. D. (in press). The effectiveness of MMPI-A items in discriminating between normative and clinical samples. *Journal of Personality Assessment.*

This manuscript examines one of the major causes of the relatively low T-score values often found for adolescents in clinical samples. Specifically, this article presents data showing that many MMPI-A items do not show significant item-endorsement differences for adolescents in normative versus clinical settings. The article offers a provocative suggestion that the MMPI-A might be significantly shortened by eliminating these ineffective items.

Archer, R. P., & Newsom, C. R. (2000). Psychological test usage with adolescent clients: Survey update. *Assessment, 7,* 227–236.

This study updates an earlier survey done in 1991, which established that the MMPI was the objective personality assessment instrument most widely used with adolescents. The results of this updated survey indicated that the MMPI-A had maintained this dominance among objective personality assessment instruments. The most frequently cited advantages or strengths associated with the MMPI-A were the comprehensive clinical picture generated by this instrument, the availability of contemporary adolescent norms, its ease of administration, and the psychometric soundness and research base of the instrument. Most of the frequently cited disadvantages concerned the length of the instrument, required testing time, and reading level requirements.

Forbey, J. D., & Ben-Porath, Y. S. (1998). *A critical item set for the MMPI-A.* Minneapolis: University of Minnesota Press.

This monograph describes an effort to develop a set of critical items for the MMPI-A standard responses based on item-level responses of the MMPI-A normative sample and a group of 419 adolescents in a residential treatment facility in the Midwest. A final set of 82 items, identified based on a comparison of item endorsement frequencies, was placed into item groupings based on such content areas as aggression, conduct problems, and depression/suicidal ideation.

McCarthy, L., & Archer, R. P. (1998). Factor structure of the MMPI-A content scales: Item-level and scale-level findings. *Journal of Personality Assessment, 71,* 84–97.

This factor study of the MMPI-A content scales shows the strong relationships and overlap among these scales in MMPI-A normative and clinical samples. Results demonstrate that two factors, labeled General Maladjustment and Externalizing Tendencies, account for the majority of variance among the 15 content scales. Item-level factor analyses of individual content scales generally produced single-factor solutions.

Sherwood, N. E., Ben-Porath, Y. S., & Williams, C. L. (1997). *The MMPI-A Content Component Scales.* Minneapolis: University of Minnesota Press.

This monograph describes the rationale and development of a set of component scales for the 15 MMPI-A content scales. These scales are designed to augment the interpretation of the content scales in the same manner in which the Harris and Lingoes subscales are used to refine interpretation of basic clinical scales. Reliability and initial validity data are presented in conjunction with suggestions for clinical and research directions.

Index

About the Authors

Robert P. Archer, PhD, ABPP, is a Frank Harrell Redwood Distinguished Professor and vice chair of the Department of Psychiatry and Behavioral Sciences, at the Eastern Virginia Medical School, Norfolk, Virginia. Dr. Archer is the author of more than 100 articles and book chapters related to psychological assessment. He is also author of the texts *Using the MMPI with Adolescents* (1987) and *MMPI-A: Assessing Adolescent Psychopathology* (2nd ed.; 1997) and coauthor of the *MMPI-A Casebook* (1994). Dr. Archer served on the advisory committee to the University of Minnesota Press for the development of the MMPI-A and is a coauthor of the MMPI-A manual. He is currently working on a series of research projects related to the MMPI-2 and the MMPI-A. Dr. Archer is the editor of *Assessment,* a quarterly journal in publication since March 1994, and an associate editor for the *Journal of Personality Assessment.* He is an executive board member and diplomate of the American Board of Assessment Psychology.

Radhika Krishnamurthy, PsyD, is associate professor of psychology at Florida Institute of Technology in Melbourne, Florida, where she teaches assessment courses in the Doctor of Psychology program and serves as clinical practicum supervisor. She is coauthor, with Robert P. Archer, of the *MMPI-A Casebook* (1994), several published articles on the MMPI-A and Rorschach, book chapters on the MMPI-A (1996) and Rorschach (in press), and papers presented at the Society for Personality Assessment midwinter meetings and International Congress of Rorschach and Projective Methods. She serves as associate editor of *Assessment,* consulting editor for the *Journal of Personality Assessment,* and associate editor of the *SPA Exchange.* She is a fellow of the Society of Personality Assessment and past recipient of the Samuel J. and Anne G. Beck Award for outstanding early career research in personality assessment.